"Wait! Before you get serious about starting off on your own next odyssey, read David Hiscoe's coming-of-age quest as he searches for meaning in a world splintered senseless by the Vietnam War and racial inequality. David assuages his discontent by taking a long walk, sometimes painful, at times euphoric, in equal measure lonely, pointless, and hilarious, yet always (except in Pennsylvania!) awash in beauty. Hiscoe leads us into an Alice-in-Wonderland world where the pilgrim learns on the job that what might appear strange and contrary can be transformed into lessons to live by long after he emerges from the woods. An inspiring read for all walkers on the path to anywhere."

— Laura Waterman, author of *Losing the Garden: The Story of a Marriage* and many other books on mountain climbing and conservation.

"Emerging from a burgeoning pile of mediocre Appalachian Trail memoirs, Hiscoe's remembrance of his 1973 Maine-to-Georgia trek is finally that 'something different' readers long for. It contains soaring prose detailing the triumphs and ordeals of a young man reconciling his anger with the turbulent era in which he resides while thrilling to the literal ups and downs of trail life. It's a book for serious hikers as well as a cross section of a man's soul to be savored by anyone who craves great writing. Gritty, hilarious, poignant, and authentic. Don't pass this up."

— Richard Judy, author of *Thru: An Appalachian Trail Love Story*

Take the Path of Most Resistance

How the Appalachian Trail Saved Me from the Sixties
and Taught Me Everything You Need to Know

David Hiscoe

Andrew Benzie Books
Walnut Creek, California

Published by Andrew Benzie Books
www.andrewbenziebooks.com

Printed in the United States of America

First Edition: September 2018

10 9 8 7 6 5 4 3 2 1

ISBN 978-1-941713-71-6

www.takepathofmostresistance.com

Cover photograph by Barry Arney, by permission of Lisa Arney
Back cover photograph by Kathleen Mullan Harris
Chapter art by Greta Beekhuis
Cover and book design by Andrew Benzie

For Kathleen

and

to all of us who think that doing difficult things,
especially when we are young and unwise,
is worth celebrating and encouraging.

Though I have sometimes changed names and identifying details to protect the privacy of individuals, the people and events in this account reflect what actually happened to me on my walk from Maine to Georgia. The conversations recounted here all happened too. But I was often tired, sleepy, hungry, or in some degree of terror when I first heard them. And over the past forty-five years, I've replayed them over and over in my head, often late at night. I would be surprised if some of the dialogue hadn't become more literary in the retelling.

All in all though, I am reasonably sure if Huckleberry Finn read the book, he would decide that it "told the truth, mainly. There was things which he stretched, but mainly he told the truth."

TABLE OF CONTENTS

The mass of men lead lives of quiet desperation… There is no play in them, for this comes after work. But it is a characteristic of wisdom not to do desperate things.

Henry David Thoreau
Walden; or, Life in the Woods

What is this Titan that has possession of me? Think of our life… daily to be shown matter, to come in contact with it… the *solid* earth! the *actual* world! the *common* sense*! Contact! Contact! Who* are we? *Where* are we?

Henry David Thoreau
The Maine Woods

PROLOGUE

It was a long time ago. 1973.

Experts, everyone of them, now assure us that human sexual activity had been discovered only ten years earlier, that it was still practiced awkwardly, inexpertly, clumsily, usually in the dark. But we had no time for it anyway. When the nights came, we were too busy struggling in quiet panic to hang our food high enough in some mocking tree. For along the ancient and rugged ridges of the Appalachian Mountains, the dinosaurs were rumored to have long and agile necks, strong and bouncy legs. And the grasping, industrious mice in the trail shelters strung along the Appalachian Trail were different then too—fearsome, as large as Mercedes convertibles, as greedy as insurance lobbyists prowling bars packed with state legislators.

Richard Nixon was as yet president, scurrying around to complete the American retreat from Vietnam and rallying his lawyers to keep Watergate evidence out of Congressional hands. All four Beatles were still alive and still producing interesting music. For most of us, the Internet was over two decades away, and Al Gore had yet to direct his talents to transforming backwoods travel with the miracle of Gore-Tex® fabric. When it rained, as it always did, we walked the long miles sweating torrents of salty mess into heavy rubberized ponchos. We were grateful to have them.

Despite the persistence of long circulated rumors, back then we did actually wear manufactured footwear, even this early in the histories of epic walks. But since Nike wasn't really doing it yet, we trudged along in stiff leather alpine boots the approximate size and weight of farm tractors, just the kind that other adventurers always ended up eating as they slowly starved their way back from the polar regions.

In the geography of that ancient time, the trail itself always labored steeply uphill, both north and south invariably up; and we ascended doggedly through snow, always, even in summer. Worse yet, no one knew we were out there; we were alone and abandoned to our own devices. Cherubs by thousands may have thrived in the distant heavens above us, but not a single trail angel descended to meet us as we crossed an occasional road, never once bringing the Mountain Dew and brownie that might have encouraged our labors. The towns we passed through opened no hostels to cheaply bed us down. Indeed, their inhabitants often looked upon us as hardly better than beatniks. No helpful strangers offered to slack our packs, neither for love nor money; no civic-minded groups smiled upon us in the church basement, offering blueberry pancakes, orange juice, and kindness. Down in Georgia or up in Maine, at the height of the season in spring or an early summer weekend, you might, if you stayed all day, see two, maybe three, of us signing the trail register at the start of our walk. And at the first and the last registers of our journey, we signed as our mothers and fathers had called us from birth, for in those days few knew that one could acquire a fashionable new name for the trail.

Back in the misty, unmarked paths of time, back in 1973, I found myself among what was then one of the tiniest and least examined subcultures of American achievement. On June 6, when I hauled myself hand over scraped and bleeding fist to the top of Katahdin, crawled past the famous sign that marks the Maine terminus of the trail, and wobbled the first steps against the wind south towards Georgia, less than fifty backpackers had yet thru-hiked the entire Appalachian Trail since it was completed 36 years earlier.

We were few. Some say we then strode the earth like giants.

Others, more wise, know we had no clue what we were doing.

But we did it long enough ago that we can now claim the mantle of time-proven wisdom. We have a solemn duty to offer that hoary knowledge to the huge numbers of those ready to walk behind us.

In the many years since I hiked the trail, the AT pilgrimage down the spine of America has somehow become one of our nation's most iconic rites of passage, probably the premier one that doesn't require hoisting an assault weapon, getting naked for money, or birthing a scheme for internet profit. This book is dedicated to passing on my generation's age-earned sagacity, both to the eager tribes who are now lining up in Maine or Georgia to set out on their own quirky pilgrimages—and to all of us who still think that doing difficult things, especially when we are young and unwise, is worth celebrating and encouraging.

An introduction to boot learning

For over four decades now, a line in the "Education" section of my job résumé has proudly read, "Hiked 2,100 miles from Maine to Georgia on the Appalachian Trail." I could have, of course, put this item up instead under "Experience" along with "spent way too much time out in the sun tarring roofs in North Carolina summers," or "headed the new media team for a disintegrating $300 billion company whose shaky credibility rested on its online prowess," or "tried to teach first-year college writing to many a restless youth." These too were hard, grinding endurance trials that taught me a thing or two.

But as I enter retirement many years later, I don't spend much quality time dwelling on these other experiences. I did them, I'm proud of doing them, and they, of course, kept me adequately fed and comfortably clothed while I planned more important adventures. But I hardly ever drift off into sleep thinking about them.

Six or so out of every seven nights though, I do spend the last ten minutes of waking time still mulling over that hour in July of 1973 when I found my young, foolish self on Mount Washington in a freezing 97 mile-per-hour wind. That, or some other equally educational moment from my early walkabout. During five months in my early twenties, the AT became my version of what Herman Melville, after his brutal lessons on a whaling ship, would call "my Yale College and my Harvard."

This is the story of that education.

Throw in the weight of a backpack and the strains of the terrain—and then average fifteen miles of walking a day—and an AT thru-hiker completes the physical equivalent of slogging back-to-back marathons for something like 150 days in a row.

So when I finished the hike I had learned, first of all, that I was nothing less than your most epic of superheroes—archetypal in courage, resourcefulness, and endurance; capable of doing anything, anytime, anywhere.

Of course, like every other twenty-four year old, I suspected all this to be true a good, long time before I ever first put on the pack.

But when I put it down after 2,100 miles, I now had the muscle and the calluses—and a fully loaded reservoir of accumulated happiness—to cushion my next steps forward. When I later picked up the loads that really count—the weight of a spouse with cancer, ushering a parent through a final illness, or twelve hour work days when I'd rather be at home with a new-born son—I knew I could handle them with some semblance of grace. I think I can fully assure you right here and now that you won't, you can't, develop these sinews in an cubicle someplace programming a new shopping app or climbing the ladder at the law firm. So here's the main argument of this book, a spoiler right at the beginning:

Just getting out of school? Facing a screeching mid-life crisis? Laid off? Finally rewarded with retirement, and the lack of direction is a bit scary? Lost a bit, body, soul, or both?

Well, don't spoil the opportunity by getting a job. Don't snatch up the unnecessary loads that everyone seems so eager to put on your back, not yet anyhow. Don't waste time with preaching or brain shrinking either. And for God's sake, don't take some sordid position over at Google, even if they're calling twice a day and begging. Go do something hard. Better yet, go wrestle down something impossible. Even if your parents, fiancée, professors, or some other social network of demanding milkypants can't or won't understand. Harness into the heavy stuff later.

And here's why.

There are entire months of my adult life from which I cannot, no matter how much I concentrate, remember a single thing, a single good or bad meal, a single sunrise, a single kiss (or lack thereof), a single argument or embarrassment, a single glory. Not that my life hasn't been a full and satisfying one so far. I'm sure that most of those minutes in most of those months were alive and vibrant while I lived them. But they, like most of our memories from most of our days, have dulled into wisps of comfortable oblivion.

The memories from my Appalachian Trail walk have not faded. For a good fifteen years after I took off the Kelty pack on Georgia's Springer Mountain, I could tell you every place I slept for each of the twelve dozen nights I was on the trail, every place I ate my honey and cheese at every lunch, every fork in the woods where I lost the trail due to a poor marking, the ravages of last winter's storm, or the chainsaw of a careless logging operation.

I can't quite do the full listing anymore. But I can still come amazingly close. And I still have absolutely no problem at all remembering almost every person I met along the way. The views from certain mountain tops, the smells from certain fir thickets, the feel of the air outside on a 15 degree, sleety night—they are still as perfectly present as they were when I was a very young man slogging my way down the mountains of the east coast of the United States.

These memories continue to haunt me almost every night, when I look forward to reliving them as I nod off under my down comforter. Friendly ghosts all, they are both an incredible hoard of pleasure and an effective sleep aid as I drift away counting bear incursions instead of lines of sheep.

But these spots of time have even more insistently shined my way through my daylight hours. It is these daylight hauntings that this book is about.

Those of us without expert map and navigation skills—which is most of us—have a shot at walking the Appalachian Trail without becoming lost and starved because all 2,100 miles of it are lovingly marked with distinctive, easily visible white blazes painted every dozen yards along the footway. It is still possible to get disoriented while you're trekking along watching them unroll the correct route out in front of you. But it's really hard.

So, here's the metaphor that I'm working towards.

As I rambled through my own life after the trail, wobbly but mostly upright, I found that my AT memories kept tirelessly inserting themselves along the path, like those blazes pointing the way on rocks and trees from Maine to Georgia.

I've been a lot of things since I was a thru-hiker: a shamefully unskilled carpenter, a harried college professor, a busy business person, a father, husband, and grandfather, a collector of ragged cats and vintage guitars, a voter and taxpayer, and a friend, just to catalogue the most obvious. It used to surprise me when I'd change a career or move on to some new stage in my life and still keep finding the Appalachian Trail stepping in and handing me key parts of the script for the next role that I'd chosen.

It doesn't surprise me anymore. I'm reconciled to the haunting of these ghostly archetypes. In situation after situation, in crisis after crisis, in a minute of satisfaction after some victory, I now fully expect that the first thing that will project up on the screen of my brain will be something that happened to me years before at a river crossing in Pennsylvania, a campsite in New Hampshire, a fresh-water spring in the Smokies, or the sparsely stocked aisles of some rural grocery in Tennessee. For almost five months over forty-five years ago, I took an actual walk around real rocks, across real rivers, and over real mountains. But my AT thru-hike has long ago settled out into something less physical but more potent, a series of parables that inform how I continue to make sense of huge chunks of what happens around me.

Like anyone burdened with a cock-eyed philosophy that explains the world, I have long felt compelled to proclaim my wisdom to all those on the road beside me. My friends and family, every one of them, have all heard these stories many times. They urge me to find new audiences. So, it's your turn now.

The first question presented by every new audience always starts with "why." "Why didn't you just get a job?" "Why give up five months of your life to be cold, hungry, tired, and dirty?" "Why didn't you carry a water filter?" "Why don't you have good sense?"

I have two distinct layers of answers for these core questions, one I can explain very clearly, the other a bit more ethereal, but real and solid nonetheless. The first is very much tied to the type of person I was as a kid and to the times during which I came of age. The second is timeless.

To make sense of the first, I will have to dip for a few pages into the ugly politics of the time. This may initially seem like a strange detour into ancient history to you, but if you have waded through the toxic sludge of recent elections in the United States, I think, sadly enough, you'll recognize the essential landmarks in the terrain.

When I graduated from college in 1971, I was way too angry to be of much use to anyone. That anger didn't come naturally to me; it was a new role, not a part that I was used to playing. I'd been fine, dumb, and happy through a great childhood, right up until a strong-dose of inconvenient education kicked in during my teens. I had, in fact, grown up as one of the sweetest boys ever to inhabit the suburbs of middle class America, the boy who cried for weeks when his dog died, the boy who, to the spit-surprise awe of his high-school coach, stepped out on the mat for each wrestling match aspiring for, above all, only a tie. My goal wasn't to win (though I never tried to lose); it was to avoid hurting the feelings of my opponent by humiliating him in public. Really. That was me, bedrock deep.

But if I were sweet by nature, I was also totally baked up and stewed in the less than sweet mythologies of the time, in the white, conservative world of my upbringing in the 1950s and in the backs-to-the-wall Cold War struggle with global communism that was the movie score in the background of every event in my life.

It seemed perfectly normal to me that a middle-aged black woman came in to take care of my sisters and me every school day afternoon after my own mother died when I was 12. Black women were cooks and maids, and surrogate mothers, if necessary. Always had been as far as I knew. It also seemed totally normal when my father, a veteran of the world war and a Goldwater man, bought me my first rifle before I was a teen. By the time I had my first driver's license, you could usually find three or four firearms in my bedroom—on the wall, in desk drawers, in my closet, stacked in a corner. My friends and I played with them the way today's teens divert themselves with skateboards. I wasn't a hunter though. That's not what the guns were for. I was encouraged to live in intimate contact with instruments of lethal power because my protective and loving family assumed that part of my future, the burden I would bear, the price I would pay, would involve using more powerful versions of these weapons against men and boys from the Soviet Union or its proxies. The rifles and pistols were my training tools, my competitive advantage, the sort of insurance policy that today's parents might think they are giving their children when they sign them up for SAT tutoring. When I earned congressional appointments to West Point and the Air Force Academy during my senior year in 1966, it just seemed the natural next step.

In a bizarre turn of events though, high-school wrestling kept me out of the military and far away from Vietnam.

There are, of course, details that are particular to me about how all of my childhood certainties unraveled. But in the main I turned out to be a cliché of the 1960s.

During one of the last days of summer vacation in 1963, I was at a friend's house playing cards when his mother turned on the television behind us to watch Dr. King deliver his "I have a dream" speech at the March on Washington. As I turned my attention from Texas Hold'em to the black and white TV over my shoulder, I had no expectations other than to indulge in a little sarcastic fun-making at this earnest radical. But within minutes I found myself totally flabbergasted, totally hooked; the story he told was not one I had ever heard before, not even small parts of it. And though his dreams seemed so completely alien to everything my parents and teachers had taught me about the lives of the black people I'd grown up with, those dreams—even at first hearing—were totally, obviously, and completely just and decent, so disarmingly logical. How could anyone hear his plea for fairness and not reexamine his or her part in the obvious injustice?

A few years later two veterans did their part to further the education Dr. King had begun for me. A young Marine corporal and an angry Navy corpsman, both of them just mustered out of the military and both just back from sustained combat in Asia, gave the first hard whacks to my assumptions about world politics, pulled the first string that began disintegrating my certainties about the dangers that I and my fellow citizens faced from the hoards of communists that I'd always assumed were practically right outside my door in North Carolina.

I was a small, skinny kid in high school, too short to make the basketball team (though God knows I tried), too light for football, and too averse to sustained pain to be a competitive runner. But if I wanted an appointment to a military academy I needed to be an athlete. It was an absolute necessity. So I decided to make myself into a wrestler. The most immediate problem? My school was one of the few in the state to take the sport seriously. Two of my best friends and I each started the season at around 120 pounds. The problem? Both of my buddies had both already won state championships before I even joined the team as a senior. If I wanted to compete for the elite program at Cary High School, I either had to beat these guys out in the weight slots they already owned or get serious about losing weight and dropping down into less competitive positions on the squad. And I was nothing if not serious. That's how I ended up being the only kid asked one late Friday afternoon in early 1967 to stay over an extra day at Fort Bragg during my physical exams for entrance to West Point.

"Mr. Hiscoe," began the colonel who waited to interview me that Saturday morning, "It has been my experience that United States Army combat teams are currently not led by second lieutenants who weigh only 107 pounds." He was, I now realize, tossing me a big, juicy softball, an invitation to tear into his throat with a mighty comeback, a response that would show my aggressive tiger nature, the nature that should undergird any leader in the work for which I was trying to apply.

I was a polite kid though.

"Yes, sir," I responded. "I can understand that. Being big enough does seem important."

There were an hour or so of more questions, most of which I think I dealt with to his satisfaction. But the die was already cast by my first kitty-cat response and by my emaciated (if muscular, I must add) frame.

"Mr. Hiscoe."

"Yes, sir?"

"Here's what I want you to do."

"Yes, sir."

"Have you been accepted to other schools?"

"Yes, sir, several sir!"

"Well, young man, I want you to enroll in one of them this fall. The best one in the group, an engineering school if possible. And I want you to excel in your studies. But most of all, I want you to eat like a bear coming out of his hole in spring."

"But sir, I have six more wrestling matches left this year. I can't gain weight."

He was a cool character. His eyes, I'm pretty sure, did not roll.

"Not now, not today, Mr. Hiscoe. After the season is over, young man. Start eating after your last match. In the spring. Like the bear. I want you to bulk up. I want you to keep up the weight lifting, keep up the training, stay Army tough. But start making some strong tactical use of your knife and fork."

"Yes, sir."

"Get bigger, Mr. Hiscoe. Put your mind and soul to it. I want to see you back here next December weighing at least 135 pounds. We'll talk about your future leading men in the US Army then, when you've made yourself look ready for the part."

And that's how I ended up that September on a bench outside a lecture hall at North Carolina State University, waiting for my first freshman course to begin, eyeing the two tough-looking guys across from me, both with the beginnings of thick, manly beards and both wearing worn military utility jackets.

"You guys veterans?"

They looked at each other. The guy with the Navy pea coat was flashing eyes between my natty crocodile belt and my penny loafers.

"Yes," from the one in a pair of Marine dress trousers, cut off at the knees.

"Vietnam?"

They looked at each other.

"That's where they're fighting." Again the Marine.

I walked over and shook their hands.

They looked at each other.

"I can't tell you how much I admire you guys."

They looked at each other.

"Thanks. It was nothing."

This from the Marine too, a twenty something with dark plowed and splotched skin under his eyes, the beginnings of a distinctively non-military haircut, and a corporal's badge sewn carefully on his jacket.

The silence was painful, so I filled it by laying out my plan:

spend a year at NC State, gain weight, go to the Military Academy, lead men into battle to preserve Vietnamese freedom from invading communists.

They looked at each other.

"You ever been to Vietnam?"

"Wrong question, Paul. Ask him if he's ever been out of North Carolina."

I looked at them.

"You know even the tiniest little turd shit about Vietnam? Anything at all?"

I thought I did, but suspected that saying so might be the wrong answer.

"Seen too many movies." This from the guy with the pea jacket. Later I learned he'd served the last seven months of 1966 as medic for Marines operating to protect the American base at Da Nang. He'd once stuffed the cellophane from a cigarette package over a hole in a man's chest in an attempt to close off the wound that was sucking the air out him. It worked for a while, but not long enough to keep the Marine breathing until a helicopter could move him to a field hospital.

He warmed to his topic.

"You ever heard about Dien Ben Phu?"

I looked at him.

"You know anything at all about the French history in Indochina? You know that Uncle Ho begged for U.S. help to keep the French from taking over his country again after World War II, after the Viet Minh fought the Japanese with the Allies? Instead, we let the French go back to stealing the country blind like they'd done for a century. U.S. taxpayers paid the salaries of the French soldiers who held the bayonets during the robbery. You know that the Chinese hate the Russians, the Vietnamese have hated the Chinese for centuries?"

I had not even the slightest beginning of an idea what he was talking about, but it was clear he was planning to go on for a bit. "You know how to play dominoes?" he concluded with a spit-mouth, smart-aleck grimace. I didn't get the reference until years later.

The Marine tapped him on the arm.

"I don't think this is getting anybody anywhere, Paul. He's clueless. Poor education. Endemic in the state. Same one we had. Not his fault." He looked at me. "Here's the deal," he said, standing up. He was shorter than me by at least five inches. I wondered how he had passed the physical exam for the Marines, but decided not to ask.

"We're going to do you a favor.

You find your way over to the library and you check out these books." In a careful craft-like handwriting, he wrote a short list on a page of his spiral-bound composition book. The notebook had "English 101" in precise, block letters on the cover. He neatly tore the page out and handed it to me. Though he was short, he was intense. Six inches from my face, he looked like NBA material.

"You go read these. You go educate yourself. You come back and talk to us when you're done. Then you can join whatever you like, save the whole friggin' planet if you want." He stepped back. I thought he was finished, but he stepped forward into my face again. "It would be a good thing if you could somehow learn not to be a dumbass."

"Yeah," said the medic. He reached across my body and tapped me just above the left nipple. "If you enlist before you've done your book report, just know that I plan to send a friend over to rip out your internal organs and deliver 'em to me in a fried chicken box." A pause for effect. "I've got a pet raccoon that gets off on boy kidneys."

The Marine looked at Paul and did a tiny, respectful giggle. He again stepped back an inch or so out of my face. "Just be smart. That's all. Just have some clue what you're talking about."

It was, looking back on it now, probably the best introduction to the purposes of university life ever offered at any institution of higher learning.

I did my reading as suggested.

It didn't take long—a couple of days during the first week of classes before the schoolwork heated up. And it pulled the foundations from underneath my way of looking at where I stood in the world. Not so much because I immediately bought into the careful and considered arguments of the scholars and journalists I had been sent to study. More because it was immediately clear that I'd never even heard most of these arguments, never even knew they existed—and they were quite literally about life and death matters. Several of my classmates from high school were by now in boot camp being readied for combat. Several would reach Vietnam just in time for the Tet Offensive that spring. It seemed unbelievable to me that I could have been so sure of myself about things that were so important without having even marginally defensible reasons for my certainty.

Fifty years later it's clear to me that the books I read back then didn't get everything right. Nobody, for instance, saw the massacres in Cambodia coming. But my assigned readings were close enough with most of the other big stuff. "World communism" didn't need me to defeat it; the Soviet Union and China were already busy enough tearing each other apart. When South Vietnam fell just after I finished the Appalachian Trail, horrible things did indeed happen, especially to the Vietnamese who had thrown in their lot with us. But no Marxist hoards lined up to take over Thailand, Indonesia, and Malaysia on their way to destroy Japan and Australia and the rest of the civilized world, as the all the men who shared drinks with my father at the country club were so sure that they would. Just after the end of my AT hike, we finally gave up the cause, burned most of our secret documents, helicoptered into the sky from our embassy rooftop and came home. But never—not once in all the years since— has even one surfing competition ever been interrupted by Viet Cong troops invading a single California beach, a certainty according to the congressman who awarded my appointments to the military academies.

I was sobered by what I read in the NC State University library. I felt foolish and used. But I wasn't particularly angry. That came later, building up slowly over the next four or five years, oceans of bile behind a shoddily built earthen dam.

I was never a campus radical, never much a vocal frequenter of public demonstrations, never a chanter or much of a marcher. But for years I did make a first-class nuisance out of myself by constantly trying to get conversations started with relatives, friends, people at work, or, say, random strangers at the grocery store about the stink of the racial climate in my country and the deadly lack of wisdom in some of our commitments overseas.

Here's why I became increasingly exasperated. Mostly no one wanted to talk, though I did run into an endless line of bigmouths who seemed always ready to puff out their wheezy chests, thrust out their beer bellies and shout slogans. When I would bring up things I was learning in college about the appalling history of slavery and Jim Crow in North America or the legacy of the French empire in Vietnam, it would often be clear that the people I wanted to mull these over with could just care less. They had their opinions, and attempts to disturb these certainties were way too often treated as some sort of sneaky plot to confuse their determined hold on truth and virtue. This drove me nuts, a good boy who was inspired by high-school civics class to believe we were supposed to be informed citizens.

Years and years went by. The war was still there each morning when I woke up, and the George Wallace sticker on my father's car was replaced every so often, long after the twisted Alabama racist had lost his bid to be our president.

By 1968, five hundred Americans a week, many of them exactly my age and some of them boys I'd known in high school, were being killed in Vietnam. Martin Luther King, Jr. was shot to death at the end of my sophomore year. And still, the daily discussions I had with people at work, at home, and at school were not, it seemed to me, usually animated by a determined and energetic need to understand what was happening to all of us. In place of Jeffersonian debate, most of what I heard was a proud and defiant cry to remain militantly uninformed. Fueled by the increasing smugness and juvenile acting out of the anti-war folks and the arrogant know-nothingness encouraged in President Nixon's supporters, the conversations just got more and more nasty as I moved toward graduation.

One afternoon in 1970, I jumpstarted my ancient student car, drove a few miles out to the neighborhood I grew up in, and walked around my old block soliciting support for a budget provision that a bipartisan group of US senators was using to try to force the war to a close. At a house several doors up from my parents', a middle-aged college professor who had known me since I was nine welcomed my knock on his door with a vigorous threat to, as he put it, "beat my ass down to the consistency of a McDonald's milkshake." When I got back to my car a couple of hours later, all four tires were flat, one sliced beyond repair.

If you weren't alive then, it might be a little hard to resurrect the sense of just how ugly daily life was in the United States. But it's not that hard to get just a little of that nasty taste in your mouth, a little of the venomous bile soaking our civic life in 1971, when I was given my diploma. Just Google yourself over to any social media site that features current opinion on gun law, terrorism, or immigration. Here's the difference. These days, a thousand Americans aren't being slain every two weeks; our political leaders aren't being regularly assassinated at the moment; ill-treated minorities are only very occasionally burning large sections of their neighborhoods in our greatest cities. So you won't find spew of exactly the same strength and stink as it reached near the end of my college days. But today's conversations are flavored with the some of the same tastes of noxious, ignorant, know-it-all spite.

By the time I graduated from college, I was sick to death of that willful ignorance. I dreaded talking with my neighbors. I couldn't turn on TV and listen to the commentators without feeling myself begin to abscess and rupture.

I wanted, above all, to turn off the noise. I wanted to go and do something that shut out the ugliness for a bit, something totally engrossing, something hard that I could do totally by myself.

I had hiked on the Appalachian Trail many times before, and it seemed both solitary and difficult enough to do the trick, a likely place to step out of the damp, drizzly November in my soul and walk off my now constant desire, shared with Ishmael at the beginning of *Moby Dick*, to step into the streets and methodically knock the hats off random people. Ishmael went to sea to chase his white whale; my impulse was to go to the mountains and follow the white blazes.

If you—a stranger to me—had asked in 1973 why I was out trying to thru-hike the trail, I probably wouldn't have been rude enough to spout out this tsunami of anger and disappointment. But this was the story I was telling myself to explain why I'd rather sign up for five months of pointless and difficult excruciation than head off to grad school or knot a tie around my neck and start pulling myself up some ladder of profit.

It was only part of the full story though. There was also something else going on, something far less driven by the times, something that I think is always at play when we pick up a pack and go off into the woods, something that is at the core of the otherwise absurd sport of lugging large weights on our backs for long and painful distances.

I'm now just seconds away from bellying up to the infamous old bar where they, with great gusto and pomp, serve potent drafts of profundity and philosophy. It's going to get deep for the next ten paragraphs or so. Perhaps you're not the philosophical type. Or maybe you are one of those poor, thin souls who proudly display an "I'm so glad I'm not camping" magnet on your refrigerator. Maybe in your youth you were forced to sleep on the ground too long under dangerous or tiresome circumstances not of your own control, and you've sworn never to spend a night outside again. If so, you may just want to skip ahead and avoid the next few pages. You won't agree with me. And it's stressful, even painful, to wildly roll your eyes while following lines of words across a page.

But if you've walked yourself this far into the book already, you're probably someone, like the forty million or so Americans who have taken a substantial hike at least once in the last six months, who regularly gets a primal jolt of pleasure from walks down your own paths, both pleasant and difficult. So here it comes.

I am absolutely sure that the surge of pleasure that we get when we start out on a trail, pack on back, straps pulled down tightly, is primordial, a celebration of something so deep in our history as humans that it's probably nailed firmly on one of the double strands in our nuclear helix, something as cabled into our well-being as eating all the starches we can hunt and gather, locking eyes with our dogs, avoiding the claws of angry cats, or dropping into a coo voice when we talk to our gooey newborns.

The equipment we choose to carry tells the story.

All of us who love hiking love, of course, our backpacking gadgets and high-tech stuff. You marketers out there know you have me every time you bring out a new boot with a fabric that keeps me drier or weighs in at a half-ounce lighter. I couldn't be happier with the tiny holiday lights that REI sold me last week, the ones that integrate directly into the fabric of my tent and mean my headlamp will never again accidentally blind a companion when I'm looking for that missing sock that migrated south earlier in the night.

But the new gadgets aren't the sport's essence.

Older gear is a much better pointer to why backpacking has such a profound, even mystical, pull on so many of us. It's not an accident that we so much enjoy tying on the ritualistic headbands, eagerly gnawing into that primeval beef jerky and warming ourselves in clothes stuffed with the feathers of the birds of the sky. When we pack on these venerable necessities of the long walk, we tingle with that undeniable feeling that we are somehow assuming some deeper character and some more ancient strength. Each time we hoist on the pack, we all suspect, at least unconsciously, that we are somehow honoring, re-creating, and participating in something of the vast trips that our ancestors endured throughout our collective history. To be a human has, from the beginning, meant starting on foot across that dim, long-lost land bridge from Asia, making the hard trip to safety up the Inca Trail, moving toward a new future over the ruts to Oregon. Perhaps the brutal forced marches are even more deeply embedded, those evil journeys trudging—chains around the ankles and across to the legs of a dozen strangers—down through the Carolinas toward the deadly cane and cotton labor camps of Louisiana or moving at gunpoint from the ancestral home toward the Oklahoma territories.

At its very core, backpacking is mythic, even sacramental. Like pilgrims who honor their gods by suffering through impossible journeys along time-honored, sacred routes, we swing out of our cars, pull on the ritual gear, and begin something that is so completely satisfying because we are doing what our ancestors did in the most fabled journeys that, for good and for bad, have defined our lives on the planet.

At the very least, walking down the trail satisfies some soul-deep need that keeps us from stumbling out into the streets en masse and flogging ourselves with penitence chains—or acting out some other demented, destructive practice out of the need to connect to something that seems more real and permanent than our time-bound desk work.

Who hasn't, at the start of every trip, felt a little like he was heading out for Normandy, or hoisting on the axe, musket, and surveying tools to accompany Boone on a scouting trip for Newfound Gap, or setting out with fellow pilgrims to save our souls at Canterbury? When we step onto the trail, we inevitably stride out to the oldest rhythms held in our deep-brain histories.

And the longer and more epic the trip, the more it seems to align with our fundamental sense that we're doing what humans should be doing, that we're on main-travelled paths to basic lessons about the fundamental nature of our humanity. The very names of our trails and the most enticing destinations to which they lead say it all. Consider the Long Trail, the first American long distance recreational path, conceived almost two decades before the AT to provide a continuous route through the mountains of Vermont from the Massachusetts border up to Canada. On some elemental level, the Green Mountain Club members who named it in 1910 employed consummate marketing savvy, choosing a name that connects with the basic human need for the legendary journey, the closer to Homeric the better. It's the *Long* Trail, after all. It's that simple, that mythic. Our hearts seem to resonate to names that suggest an archetypal quest: the *Grand* Canyon, the *Great* Lakes, the *Long* March, the *Grand* Tetons, the *Great* Plains. The very names of these national treasures trigger memories of pilgrimages that stir something foundational in just about all of us. What self-respecting young person—even if her biggest dream is to grow up to spend her days trading in underpriced stocks—could resist a journey on something called the *Long* Trail?

When we swing on the pack and set foot to solid ground, we're stepping out on a long and noble trail indeed.

I first stepped out of everyday reality and into full-blown, rock-deep sacramental legend in 1967, rounding a bend on a side trail in the Smokies and dead-ending into the Appalachian Trail thirty years after it was first completed. Like most Americans at the time, I had never heard of it, had no idea that it existed. A weather-abused wood sign pointed one arrow to the right: Georgia, 200 miles. To the left—Maine, 1,850 miles.

From where I stood, gasping from the climb up to the ridge, I could see the two-inch by six-inch white blazes reeling off indefinitely through the woods in both directions, over, around, and through a landscape that seemed as old as hell and heaven. Aggressive winks from all the homecoming queens in North Carolina could not have more fervidly sparked my aroused imagination. In the late twentieth century, it was still possible to walk two thousand miles up the ribs of the North American continent; it was still possible to step out of the frivolities of my culture's summers of love and winters of televised discontent to live out a journey that could approximate the timeless walks of the past. As I stood on that side trail on that early afternoon, the hook went in too deep to be dislodged.

I had spent my late teens and early adult years living through the most plagued period of American domestic history since the Great Depression, maybe since the Civil War. And I had thrown myself into that history deeply while it was in the making. But by the end of my college years I felt more than a little disillusioned. In the face of the events that were trying our souls, my community seemed determined to act with hot-headed pettiness. Without much thought or much well considered strategy, I just wanted to walk away. But I also wanted to walk toward something that seemed more solid, something as timeless as the rock foundations I could see standing firm in the Smokies that day, something that would allow me to rope into all those who had walked through those thousands of impossible journeys that provided the firm substratum of the long history of the globe. I found it hard to imagine being petty and trifling while attempting something as all-consuming and elemental as a long walk through an ancient stretch of the oldest mountain range in the world. I felt unmoored, and the Appalachian Trail seemed to promise a more solid route across something that was sturdy and lasting.

Back at home, I started researching the walk—and quickly discovered that there wasn't much to be found. In 1970 only sixty-five people had hiked the whole trail, only a portion of them in one trip. And they hadn't left many footprints, at least not ones you could find in actual print. There was a rosy-hued *National Geographic* article from the year I was born. A lyrical 1967 book by a couple who had done some sections of the trail. Deep in the library basement, a few microfiche "aren't these weird people doing weird things" newspaper articles about early thru-hikers. And the ten volumes of trail guides published by the trail clubs that made up the Appalachian Trail Conference, all nobly earnest and detailed yard-by-yard, but offering little depth about what it was actually like to walk the trail itself.

It got a little better in the next few years: a short 1971 book by an early thru-hiker, a *National Geographic* photo collection, and what quickly became the holy text for AT hikes: Edward Garvey's *Appalachian Hiker: Adventure of a Lifetime.* But I suspected that even Garvey's warm description of his 1970 walk was more distraction than help, at least for me. Sixty-years old, a well-connected federal administrator, and friend, it seemed, to every newspaper editor and influential environmental player on the East Coast, Garvey spent his hiking days being met by trail officials, being picked up and driven to the homes of the glamorous, and keeping up with his voluminous correspondence, often with officials from the National Park Service. It was hardly the trail experience I could hope to expect.

So, I stoked myself to a fiery boil reading Eric Ryback's feverish, teen-aged descriptions of his pioneering thru-hikes of the just-opened Pacific Crest Trail and the embryonic Continental Divide Trail. Finishing up his accounts of constant battles with vicious wolves and other non-stop brushes with near-death experiences, I was sure I was now emotionally forewarned against whatever strange and malignant menaces I would meet on the path. Had hoards of flesh-eaters, pots at the ready, water aboil, awaited me on the high tablelands of Katahdin, I was prepared, even eager.

I didn't know it as I climbed over Katahdin's peak on June 6, 1973, but I was pulling myself atop the swelling crest of a huge wave of hikers that would totally transform the history of the Appalachian Trail and of long distance hiking as sport and spiritual quest. When the last straggling trekker signed his or her last register in the fall, eighty of us had made the trip. More people had completed the trail in this one year than had hiked it in total from 1937 to 1971. And that wave would continue to swell exponentially. The number of thru-hikes has roughly doubled every decade since. Guided by a wealth of good books and inspired videos, over 18,000 people have now done an end-to-end walk of the AT. In 2016 alone, over 1,100 people finished the entire walk, more than thru-hiked the Appalachian Trail in its entire first forty-five years of existence.

In 1973 we stumbled out onto the trail largely alone and supremely ignorant, as much befogged as helped by the few resources available for us. But we didn't know it at the time. We thought we knew what we were about. And—at least in my case—it helped that I was rebelliously hardheaded and stubborn, a Scotch-Irish, Southern member of both the ACLU and the NAACP. Without a whole lot of more thought, I just decided to go, bought a ticket to Bangor, Maine (my first-ever airplane ride), and jumped in with both boots—brand new ones, not a scuff on them.

As it turned out, stubbornness would prove to be a distinct advantage on the AT. And at least some of the dumb was soon to be scraped away, tender skin against rough leather.

MAINE

Learning to live head between legs, facing backwards

Seize the strangeness, even when it bites with its nose

"I might die in the trying," I thought as the pain pushed me to the edge. "But I'll go glory bound. If human courage and heroic devotion can make it so, I plan to safely bring this potato into the world."

Appalachian Trail stories almost always begin the same—with that first day of "what have I gotten myself into," the cruel moment in time when you learn that no amount of preparation, expensive gear, training, hard work, smart living, or good karma could have gotten you ready for this physical exhaustion. For most of us, "agony" was just the word across the dictionary page from "agranulocyte" until we faced the first uphill with a heavy pack and a stomach more likely filled with large, bickering crows than fluttering butterflies. And with lungs and knees screaming and exploding with the intensity of a derailed train car filled with Bakken crude, grinding and sparking on its side into the center of a sleepy little town in the middle of the night.

My trip, of course, had that beginning too. Three weeks before I flew to Maine, I had major surgery. A week before I carried the pack out on the tarmac to fly up to Katahdin, I still could not straggle more than 100 yards without a good rest, maybe a nap. A thoughtful person, being kind to himself, would have made the first few days on the trail as easy as possible as he healed and gained strength. I was not thoughtful. Ambushed by a lifetime of diligently following the rules, it never occurred to me that I could have hitched in to the first road the trail crosses five miles from its beginning, left the pack at the campground at the southern foot of the trail's first mountain, found my way merrily up to the top with no load, and then retraced my steps back down for a good night's sleep.

That's the way most people do it. But I didn't know that. Instead, I dragged sixty pounds of food and gear five miles over to the north side of Katahdin, up the infamously brutal Cathedral Trail, past the famous sign that marks the official beginning of the AT atop Baxter

Peak, and then five miles down to Katahdin Springs campground on the mountain's south side.

The Cathedral Trail pushes 2200 feet up Katahdin's Great Basin in little over a mile. So it absolutely deals out the required train wreck of prostration that plows into everyone that first day on the AT.

But that's not how I want to begin these stories.

I want to start instead with some advice from Ralph Waldo Emerson. In one of his all-too-few playful passages, he once suggested a handy technique for staying off the path of quiet desperation to which his friend Henry Thoreau claimed most of us are doomed. I'll pass it along, with the prudent suggestion that you may want to choose carefully where you practice his advice, lest you end up in some database of potential risks to society.

Every once in a while—Emerson said—you should stop a second, bend over, and stick your head down between your legs, eyes now upside down and facing backwards. With your comfortable ways of seeing then "unfixed" by this ungainly contortion, you will— he insists—look at a world made newly strange and wonderful from this fresh angle of vision.

That's the real story of my first week on the AT. Shakespeare has his magic islands and enchanted forests where characters go to winnow away the chaff and see reality more clearly; children in fairy tales blunder through portals into parallel lands that open up their eyes and hearts—that let them more deeply experience and understand their own worlds when they return. I had a week on Katahdin and in the 100 Mile Wilderness for my own mythical step into the realms of creative weirdness.

Act I

On my first day, the Appalachian Trail didn't, in fact, just unfix my vision. It quite literally took it away. The afternoon before reaching the official start of the path at the top of Baxter Peak, I had sat at my Chimney Pond campsite on Katahdin's north side and looked up through a cloud-free sky for hours at the Cathedral route up the mountain. It appeared, I couldn't help but nervously notice, to climb straight up the most dramatic and scary cirque on the East

Coast—a huge horseshoe clawed into the mountain rock by the bestial power of ancient glaciers. It would be the last clear view of this trail that I had.

Within fifteen minutes of setting out the next sunny morning, I was fully, completely, and totally stuffed inside a cloud sock. And not just your ordinary sock resting in your clean, orderly drawer in your clean, orderly house. More like that soggy and impossibly bunched one your dog has energetically dragged out of the dirty clothes and is mauling through the house with the joyful, unthinking violence of an untamed puppy beast. The wind shot bullets of mist and fog the density of concrete, and visibility careened down to somewhere around sixty inches. At times, I couldn't see my own feet below me as they stabbed around to find the footpath.

But oddly enough, the overall effect was to wrap me in quiet and stillness. My hiking partner—a friend from college out to keep me safe for the first week or so—and I were fully and completely wooled up in a very small world, with only wind, rain, granite, gravity, and the sounds of our own breathing for company. I haven't been back on the Cathedral Trail since that day, so I have no idea what it really looks like. I wouldn't doubt at all, given how scared I was on the way up it, that I'm getting ready to exaggerate its difficulty. But the socket-sized views of it I earned on June 6, 1973, were of a sustained rock climb—low-grade rock climbing, to be sure, maybe Class 3—but rock climbing without the reassurance of the customary harness and rope. Much of it involved careful hauls up over extended slabs of stone, sometimes using each other's knees or backs as steps to the next hand placement. All of it seemed vertical. All of it was terrifying. Our palms turned bloody from the constant stabs at handholds, wet fingers rasping across rocks that had once survived thousands of feet and hundreds of years of grounding glaciers with a solidity that had no trouble shredding the fragile skin of human hands.

During the three seconds when the wind opened up a tiny window to the ground below us, I caught the quickest, most desperate glimpse of where we started that morning, two thousand feet below at Chimney Pond. I was looking down with the same angle of vision I might have gotten sitting on an airplane wing thirty seconds or so after takeoff. Then the merciful clouds regrouped around us, shutting out the sense of just how exposed we were, and we started back grappling our way further up the mountain, sealed again in our envelope of concentration.

When we crawled out on the Katahdin Tableland in forty mile-an-hour winds, well over four hours into the day, I was never more scared, never more focused, and never more aware of just how massively violent and curious the physical world in which I walked could be.

After a brief pause bundled in the chaos of storm gear and packs, we regrouped and crabbed our way the last several hundred yards to the top of Baxter Peak and the beginning of the AT. I have no photos of the summit—the foggish haze on our lens ruined the two or three that we took through the bedlam of flapping straps and wind-flayed ponchos. But any image that any mechanical device could have pinholed onto paper would be a corruption of the experience of huddling unprotected up close to Maine rock for those two hundred seconds or so, assaulted by a universe gone all strange and titanic.

Like everyone around me, like everyone around you and like everyone we both know, I would many times in the future eat my peck of Thoreauvian desperation. But nothing—no matter how routine or normal or familiar—would ever again seem comfortably fixed or fully quiet to me. On my first day on Appalachian Trail, I had seen, felt, and heard the uncontrolled collisions, the epic searchings and matings, the wrenchings and grindings, the forces of the universe elemental, that are always just below every surface, just around every rock or cloud, however much our daily lives conspire to hide them. If you haven't felt what I'm talking about yet, just wait until the first time that someone you love dies suddenly, unexpectedly. Or pay careful attention when you next kiss someone for the first time. Once acknowledged, these forces are impossible to forget; you'll see them everywhere.

Thirty minutes down the trail the clouds disintegrated, the sun made the world normal again, and my hiking partner and I whistled our way off the mountain.

Act II

Two days later, the Trail again unfixed my vision with the force of a car door snatching a finger. "Lots of bugs in Maine in June" everyone from Henry Thoreau to my next-door neighbor in Raleigh had warned me. And there were indeed plenty of flying pests in the first thirty miles past Katahdin. Enough for me to think that, "yes this is bad alright. But I can handle it." The incredible lakes, trout streams, and acres of firs pumping out Christmas-tree perfumes were well worth the dozen or so mosquitos and black flies that were interminably tracking around me, waiting for quick pinch and a snack. Maine was, indeed, buggy, I decided. But no worse than, say, Yellowstone in July or my own backyard after a week of summer rain.

The bugs were definitely there on the third night out, as we deposited ourselves in the shelter facing beautiful Wadleigh Pond, too many and too bold to give a rat's bottom about our bug repellant. But bearable. And much less a nuisance, in fact, than the older guy who welcomed us to the campsite, eagerly shook our hands, and without any prompting on our part proudly let us know right off the bat that he was in charge of the National Guard troops who pulled the triggers on the students killed and wounded at Kent State a few years earlier. That was the warmup. Next came a long, full evening featuring his sorry trove of ethnic slurs, each hateful *bon mot* punctuated in the telling with wild, juggling stabs at the air with an old, but carefully sharpened Marine K-bar bayonet. But all in all, the black flies and our addled host were no real competition for the loons on the lake and the lake itself, hundreds of acres of beauty right out of Sierra Club calendar only 40 feet in front of the trail shelter. So all was well, even when an early evening hailstorm interrupted our swimming and sent us back into the lean-to to endure the violent racket of an inch of ice as it shelled the metal roof.

I can't prove it, but I think the hail did it.

Maybe it was the rapid change in temperature. Maybe the noise just woke up the beasts the way some trivial thing might rouse the monsters in a sci-fi disaster movie. The next morning, though, we headed out on the sunniest, most pleasant of days into the ravenous jaws of an entomological reckoning of biblical scale.

It started as just a mid-morning break for chocolate, nuts, and cheese on a pleasant abandoned tote road. Then the bugs flipped the switch. Not flipping the switch the way your computer gradually lightens as it begins to boot up. The change was instantaneous. One minute I was shooing off a small squad of mosquitoes dive-bombing my arms out of a pleasant blue Maine sky. The next the sun was dead to me, all light sucked into a solid Red Sea wall of pain chomped out by a million tiny proboscises.

In the half second before the hoards had fully gathered to all their numbers, I briefly, mouth slack open, watched my partner's face and exposed arms sprout what looked like an instant case of crimson measles. He later told me he was equally fascinated to watch bloody buds begin to blossom across every millimeter of my exposed skin. Within seconds though, the combo of swollen eyelids and the Viking hoards of malignant buzzers blotted out such happy views. At twenty feet, both of us were lost to each other in a dark blanket of insects.

The earth itself, it seemed, had opened up its ground; the world was unfixed.

The cheese, crackers, peanuts, raisins, and chocolate were abandoned on the ground in pre-attack picnic configuration (no small sacrifice for starving long distance hikers). We panicked on our packs and ran, not stopping until we plunged six miles down the trail into the middle of a smoky pine-bough fire built by two other tormented hikers on the sand beach at Lower Jo-Mary Lake.

The next morning we continued our merry way south, with yet another Emersonian adjustment to our vision. I saw the last fifty gloriously beautiful miles of the 100 Mile Wilderness exclusively through the tiny squares of wire screen we stripped from the windows of the 1920s-era cabins at Jo-Mary Lake, now abandoned by the wealthy wilderness tourists who once relished nights of bug-free comfort behind them. Wrapped around our heads to create something akin to a deep-sea diver's helmet, this small wiry part of Maine's outback history made its last trip back to civilization at a walker's pace. Unfortunately, the purloined wire also reacted poorly with human sweat and civilized skin, leaving me a perfectly square matrix of eruptions all over my face and neck, complementing nicely the healthy colony of festering bug bites.

As we exited the 100 Mile Wilderness three days later and I briefly stopped to clean up in the dimly lit bathroom of a gas station on the outskirts of Monson, I had my vision yet again unfixed. Looking into the mirror, I saw, instead of the old me, a scarlet-eyed, balloon-faced stranger gawking back. If the trail wasn't making me into a new person, it for sure was making me look like one.

Act III

If all AT stories begin with tales of exhaustion, they soon lockstep into a militant obsession with food. This obsession led to the third unfixing of my eyes in my first week on the trail, another uncomfortable parody of Emerson's advice that we must occasionally thrust our head down between our knees.

Under pack and hard terrain, the body requires somewhere around 6,000 calories a day; that's, say, the amount of oomph in ten of your average Big Macs. The math simply cannot be made to square up. The back and legs whine mightily at slogging the weight to supply that much energy, even if you could find a way to stuff all that bulk into a pack. The result of this chasm between need and practicality? The mind is soon consumed twenty hours a day feverishly trying to balance the two sides of the inexorable algebra. The stomach contributes to this cruel division of labor by complaining as ceaselessly as a newborn at midnight.

I tried to right the balance during the 100 Mile Wilderness by supplying myself with commercial, freeze-dried hiker food, expensive stuff that I carefully measured out to just enough to get to the trail's first resupply point in Monson. Being a follower of rules, I had, of course, taken as gospel the calm insistence on each package that it contained two adult servings. Just perfect for me and Mike, my partner for the first leg of the hike. Except that the small print (which I didn't read) revealed that each serving parsed out at about 300 calories, delivered in a stingy mass the size (and usually the consistency) of a baseball.

On night six, beside the bucolic, burbling chutes of Cooper

Brook, I decided to tip the equation more satisfactorily in my stomach's favor. Digging into the bottom of the pack, I pulled out our emergency hoard: three mega-bags of cheap instant mashed potatoes.

All would have been fine, I suspect, if I hadn't gotten bored in the interminable five minutes while the first package boiled up from a couple of ounces of dry flakes into two quarts of chunky mush. While the initial clump of flakes sucked in warm water and began plumping up to a satisfying bulk, I decided to make hilarious for my equally bored companion. Kicking back in an imaginary Barcalounger and turning on a phantom TV, I crammed fistful after fistful from the second bag of flakes—imaginatively transformed by my dapper humor into calorie-oiled potato chips—into my blubbering mouth. Mike rolled his eyes and went back to waxing his boots. Apparently the routine was unlikely to land me on *The Tonight Show*.

We divvied up the huge pot of reconstituted potatoes, did the requisite man burps, and settled into sleeping bags for some relaxed appreciation of the cool night and the exquisite miniature waterfalls up and down the stream beside us.

It was mildly humorous when we first noticed my stomach beginning to inflate, steadily and inexorably. At five minutes it would have done proud an aging fraternity boy's brew belly. We laughed.

At ten minutes, I was noticeably into the beginnings of a second trimester. I rolled on top of the bag, moaned pitifully, and Mike started up his finest rap on the travails of wilderness deliveries: "Boil me some water, no time to send for the Doc, we're gonna have to do this ourselves, Little Joe."

"Ye gentlemen in England now a-bed," I shot back, "shall think yourselves cursed that you had not the courage to share my honorable estate, here with me on your backs in this honorable dirt, knees contorted over head, bearing down hard, bringing forth this kingly spud, this budding and noble tuber."

By fifteen minutes, my skin was whitening to the shade of dehydrated potato flakes, my mouth was drying down to Saharan sand, and the belly was approaching the right size for a quick game of backwoods basketball. The pain had begun in earnest. I labored to keep calm.

A physics major in college, Mike later told me that as the catastrophe began to move toward its climax, he couldn't help but begin running the calculations. The problem, he told me, thoughtfully rubbing his new chin hairs and taking a long draw on his pipe, was that he didn't have all the data he needed. What is the maximum capacity of the human stomach, he wondered? What's the tensile stretch of tummy tissue before it begins to tear? How much bodily fluid can the mortal body redirect to the belly to water up a sizable mass of potato products? How pathetic would it be to hemorrhage out on Maine dirt—and to list cause of death as ill-advised Hungry Jack humor? How much does David Hiscoe have to hiccup out screams and roll panicked eyes like a horse in trapped in a fiery barn before he feels that his companion must find the control to stop giggling?

Seventeen minutes in and all smiles were gone, my face adopting the expressions of the movie character who watches the readout on the clock wind down toward zero as he lies roped up to the villain's stolen atomic bomb.

By twenty minutes, the potatoes had gestated to their full four-quart capacity. The stomach held. By morning, I was back to normal, by all outward appearances at least. Long-term psychic damages are difficult to measure.

Epilogue

Once off the AT and back into the desperate world of higher and higher education and then lucrative employment, my career path was no stranger than most. First, I blundered into a cutthroat graduate program in medieval studies where my fellow students had been studying Latin since they were babies, church patristics since first grade, and medieval philosophy since middle school. Not cause for panic though, not nearly as bloody as an afternoon with a herd of Maine's most energetic black flies.

Doctoral degree in hand and soon starved out of teaching medieval literature in universities that, abandoned by state legislatures eager to cut taxes, were no longer offering a decent wage, I skidded into a series of increasingly high-profile marketing jobs, armed without even a threadbare stitch of business education or experience. A bit risky, I thought. But, it probably won't burst my intestines.

Then another bend on the job trail and I found myself routinely given a day or so to write a speech for a governor or a university chancellor or a corporate CEO, always on a subject that was new to me, probably new to the world at large. Scary? Yes, but not nearly as disconcerting or serious as a trip up the Cathedral Trail on a stormy day.

The immersive unfixing that the trail offered up almost every day was perfect training for navigating the unfathomable novelty of being alive in the world that we all stumble through. I don't think I have ever lived a minute in the last four decades saddled with any sense that the space and time around me were routine, that the earth wasn't a bubbling cauldron of grand strangeness and boiling power.

Nothing to it, really.

Finding your backbone might take off your head

"You're gonna help me unload this truck, then I'm gonna drive home and have some lunch and lovin' with my nasty wife. All done, maybe I'm gonna weld up your ragged knapsack and you can go back to playing Sitting Bull."

As I geared up for the hike, I saved a few dollars by attaching a much-needed new pack sack to an old Kelty-style external frame that I'd already carried for years. Two weeks into the hike, that clever frugality almost took off my head.

In spite of its scary reputation, the 100 Mile Wilderness is actually a fairly easy wander through the countryside, if an unusually remote countryside for the eastern half of the United States. Tracking along old logging roads with occasional climbs of a few thousand feet, northern and central Maine might—in some parallel universe—act as a bit of friendly, woodsy gym where hikers, newly released from the sapping comforts of civilization that were marching them inexorably toward that life of mice-squeak desolation, could build endurance and strength. But it's more complicated than that.

Your body—it is true—is steadily building muscle, and your psyche is bathing in the beauty of the walk as you become comfortable with being a stranger in the strange land of the Maine woods. But that truth is simultaneously wrestling with other mighty and unrelenting forces. The constant bug irritations, the slow starvation, the constant armies of angry gerbils fighting it out in your stomach, the nights of uncertain sleep, the ankle turns, and the steady punishment of lifting the pack weight six inches and pushing it three feet forward thirty thousand times a day are in stout battle with your growing stamina. Most long distance pilgrims spend four hundred miles or so in this nether world of conflict before the champions of strength and health finally claw themselves on top.

A south bound AT hike adds another compelling force to this equation: two weeks into the walk somewhere just past the Kennebec River, the trail deadends into the brick wall of relentlessly steep mountains that is the rest of Maine.

The AT in the southwestern part of its first state is an unending series of bone-smashing Katahdins in a row. Three thousand, four thousand feet up. Three, four thousand feet down. More times than I can now remember, over and over. All laid out with the Mainer's forthright insistence that the best way between two points is straight up or straight down, over rooted and eroded trails fit best for goats or golems. Across wet, weirdly canted granite that rasps and shreds your skin when you inevitably lose your footing. Around not a single thing, no matter how big or formidable, that Father Time, the crunching of continents, or Ice Age glaciers have savagely hurled in the way. By the time I dragged across the six peaks of the Bigelow Range (tagged by *Backpacker* magazine as one of the ten most difficult hikes in North America), 150 miles into the hike and still thirty miles of the dreaded Sugarloaf and Saddleback ranges in front of me, I was exploring unplumbed nations of exhaustion. And Rangeley, my next resupply rest, was still days away. The "you know you could just hitch out at Route 16 and be at home in 24 hours" devil was steadily singing in my ear, and I was swaying in tune to His Evil Holiness's song.

The drop from the last Bigelow peak was 3,500 wobble-kneed feet of loose scree and dancing rock, so I knew a howling surprise slide or two was undoubtedly in my near future. But I still wasn't ready for the handclap speed with which I went down. In my daze, I initially assumed it must be some phantom defensive tackle from my past, maliciously returning to clip me off at the knees from behind. One minute I was picking my way carefully along; the next I was wrenched on my back, with blood oozings starting to map the backs of elbows, calves, neck, and head.

Spewing curses and spitting pieces of bitten lip, I rolled over ready to fight the bastard who had cowarded me from behind without warning. After a few seconds of cartoon arm flinging, it registered that there was nothing but me, the wind, and the rocks out here on the mountain. A little more careful investigation and it became embarrassingly clear that the nasty attacker was, in fact, my own backpack.

Decade-tired welds had given way on the frame's top support bar, unleashing fifty pounds of gear in a long, force-multiplying arc through the pivot of the pack's waist support cleanly into the rear of my lower legs. Now wised up to the true source of my disaster, I wiped off the gobs of blood I could reach, wrapped whatever jumble of string and rope remnants I could dig from my pack around the ripped joint of torn aluminum alloy, and hobbled on south.

An hour or so later, I was down at the road, getting the bad news from the attendant at the gas station near where the trail crossed. "Ya have a wicked hum-digah of a problem, kid. Ya need a Heliarc sahda on that stove-up mess, and nobody around heeah has a rig for that. Best just to get ya a new pack downt at the ski shop in Kingsfield." He stepped out to pump up the tank on a delivery truck loaded way past capacity with propane containers the size of bath tubs, exchanging a few laughs with the driver as he pointed in my direction. I sat in full desperation in the filling station office, brain wrestling with the catastrophic truth that a new pack would cost me a fourth of the money I had left to get me to Georgia.

"Nice job, hippy dip."

On his way to the rest room, the truck's driver stopped just a second to rap his knuckles on the mass of boot string I'd used to jerry rig my pack straps to what was left of the frame. "That should get you about twenty feet. Good luck with that jack, bud."

A minute later he was back. I doubt he'd washed his hands.

"Today's your lucky one, Natty Bumppo. Turns out I got Mr. Heliarc himself chained up down in my basement, and I'm completely his freakin' master. You're gonna help me unload this truck, then I'm gonna drive home and have some lunch and lovin' with my nasty wife. All done, I'm gonna weld up your knapsack and you can go back to playing Sitting Bull out there in the woods."

Later in these stories, you'll meet several characters I initially misjudged, people who started out rubbing me wrong but turned out to be wonderful. Mr. Gas Guy is not one of these. Maybe over the long course of a dark and rural lifetime, he had his better days. On this one though, he showed himself to a textbook case of stupid brutality. Over the next two hours, in an smoldering display of unfocused anger, he called one of his customers "a squaw," constantly nosed juicy mucus onto his slimy cigarette while navigating mountain roads at ninety miles an hour, mostly watched as I lugged and unloaded five dozen propane canisters by myself, and fought a volcanic battle with his "bitch" wife over the woefully overcooked nature of the hamburger she served up to him at noon. I heard exactly no evidence of any "lovin" while I waited on a rusty folding chair in his moldy basement.

However, he did know his welding, and I did leave his underground workshop with a newly intact pack, an unexpected outcome I celebrated with a trip to the ski shop across the street in downtown Kingsfield. Lewdly eying the clean, undamaged, new Keltys on the wall, I ended settling for a much less expensive wide-mouth plastic jar for my honey, mainly because the incredibly nice and heart-tuggingly attractive owner had been so polite to me as I smelled up her store for an hour. As I shuffled reluctantly out the door she called me back. "You look like you could use a jump start, my friend," she said, handing me a tube of Life Saver-sized "energy boosts," the highly concentrated dextrose/sucrose pellets that climbers and high-altitude mountaineers favored at the time for lightweight shots of enthusiasm.

That's when I lost my head.

Play this one in your imagination in slow motion. If you don't savor it enough, you won't get the point. Doing it in the slowest of slow motions will be best.

I wearily step out into the quiet main street of this dozing Maine small town, pack thrown sloppily across my shoulder, eyes red and legs unsteady. I step off the sidewalk and the first of the energy pellets gets unwrapped. A step or two into the street without a whole lot of thought to the matter, and the chunk of sugar is slipped past my weather-cracked lips.

Three more steps, and the sun halts in its path of revolution. The winds off the mountains cease to whip and agitate. Babies the world over pause from suckling. No tree falls in the forest; no sound stirs any tympanic membrane in any ear on the whole globe. All stops.

In my tailbone I feel something akin to the birth of a new star, a sudden, steadily fission of comfort and warmth and bliss that blooms at the bottom of my back, then unfolds and mushrooms steadily up my spine for three delicious seconds. Reaching the rear of my skull, it thunders and roars to a Beethoven climax, resonates and echoes for seconds, rushes back down the spine, smoothes its way once more slowly up the middle of my back, then climaxes again just at the hair line at the lowest part of my neck.

Shattered with pleasure and joy, I stand quietly in the middle of the road for days, for years, for undetermined centuries, until sometime in a freshly born eon the village of Kingsfield slowly begins to whisper itself back into view and I begin to once again feel my feet in my boots, my boots on the street, my body pushing down on the macadam underneath me. A jeep honks. I hear two teens laughing.

I collect myself, move the ten more steps across the road, and make my way, shaking a little but totally open eyed, to the inexpensive hotel room that I've rented for the night.

A good neurologist could easily explain the physiology of this moment. Blood sugar severely depleted by poor diet and exhaustion. Rapid rise in glucose levels. Release of a stream of endorphins that stimulate an unusual number of neurons in spinal cord and pleasure centers. Her analysis would be unassailable.

But I chose to freight this experience with a much more mystical weight. It's been useful to me in that form for the past forty years.

The 19,000 or so folks who have hiked the entire Appalachian Trail in the four decades since my head burst in Maine have done the walk for a wide range of reasons. You get bragging rights to an epic accomplishment; you earn the status that attaches to a determined feat of quirky athleticism. Girl Scouts and Boy Scouts admire your skills.

But the real reason most of us go out there for five or six months is to live immersed in a world of inspired beauty that only high peaks, falling water, and deep forest reliably bring. I won't talk much about this part of the hike in this book. I wish I could, but I don't carry the right equipment. Only a poet much more crowned with glory could enliven words enough to make that part of backpacking stand up, animate with flesh, and take on life.

In my mind though, here's what happened on the Kingsfield street. Somehow the shopkeeper's magic pellet took all the glory and all the beauty of the Maine wilderness and condensed it into a small, perfectly compressed nucleus. In that core were rolled all the strength and all the sweetness of the mountains, rounded into a single, compacted, potent charge of pure joy.

And that joy hasn't gone away—not ever. It left me with a memory I can summon up at will and feel as strongly in the moment as I did four decades ago. Like everyone else, I spent much of those forty years in the ordinary, necessary business of earning a living, paying for educations, buying houses and cars and vacations and other daily breads. But when the world was too much with me and I could feel William Wordsworth's famous getting and spending beginning to lay waste my powers, I could pick whatever time I wanted (I swear that I actually do this), close my eyes, summon up the taste of that sweet moment, and live for a bit in the proper splendor that is always available to us. It is a sweet skill to possess.

GasMan's weld collapsed 200 miles further down the trail, so I finally bought a new Kelty pack frame in Hanover, New Hampshire.

Sometimes the bird's in your brain.

Materializing out of the very dirt itself, she locked her steelies directly into my horror-show pupils, whipped herself to the center of the trail, screw-corked her mass round and round to build the proper mortiferous momentum, and then launched her full mass directly at my face, an unstable chicken-sized nuclear core of beak and claw.

I can't remember the exact point on the trail where this next confrontation happened, but somewhere in that nation of physical suffering that is western Maine I became certain that I was about to enjoy a cerebral hemorrhage. It didn't help that I was already living in a moment of great weakness when the head pain cracked and split into my brain—weak because I had already, early on this day, endured at least six reruns of the cruelest optical hallucination that darkens a backpacker's vision.

You might not as yet have had the joy of experiencing this distinctive Mainiac phantom on you own. So let me give you a little context to help you understand.

Mainers are a very direct people, and their mountain trails are created in their own proud and stubborn image. Back in the beginning, back when that first plainspoken, job-doing, simplicity-loving Maine backwoodsperson out dutifully tending his flock of moose first came across a mountain in his path, his most powerful impulse was not to go motorvating sideways, diagonal, gradually, or easily up a bunch of crybaby switchbacks. He had, after all, a wilderness filled with moose to milk, and his time was too valuable to wait for Moses to put on his knee pants.

So he lined up his eye with the Bullwinkle standing up there on the hill crest, and he went there, straight there, not bothering to step aside for anything mortal, vegetable, or stone. And the AT now follows those original trails, all agonizingly straight up. And this leads to some quite severe topographical illusions.

Even if you've never cranked a pack up on your back, you know a famous parallel version of the scenario, albeit from a different part of the world. Think the last movie you saw with desert scenes. Summon up in your mind's eye the cinematic cliché where the hopelessly lost, sun-jerkied soul in the desert sees his deliverance, the water-rich, palm-laden oasis on the horizon, only to collapse in bitter defeat hours later as he bellies up to the once distant point, knees scorched and eyes fused down to slits by the sun, only to discover that his destination of fondest hope is a chimera, just another cruel acre of scorching grit. The scene always fades with our hero drying out toward death, feebly mumbling to himself as he stretches out his pitifully basted hands into the parching sands, spasmodically kicking out the last of his life.

Its corollary up in Maine goes like this: sweat spurting, legs howling, lungs jet-engine-takeoff shrieking, and head thumping, you at last spot the long-sought height of land two hundred and fifty impossibly long meters straight up the trail. You at last see sky. You pause for a second, rally your very last reservoir of strength, dig deep into your final threadbare pocket of self worth, summon patience and self-flagellation worthy of your favorite medieval saint, and topple off those last four hundred impossible steps.

And when you at last crest the holy of holiest, you break into inconsolable weeping as the grains of your foolish illusion leak through your gorp-stained fingers. There before you, commanding the very horizon, is the real summit, a half mile and thousand vertical feet ahead, hidden up to this point, of course, by the rude steepness of the trail you've just crawled. By the third or fourth time this trick eats our lunch, even the most dull of us fully understands that the "real summit" you now see might itself well be just another cruel deception, with another ever receding high point just behind it.

So I wasn't all that surprised when my brain suddenly went into full scale, bring-out-the-guillotine, let's-start-the-Russian Revolution, burn-the-place-down, thundering and violent rebellion. Forty or fifty strides into the precious flat area before the trail began its climb toward the once hidden peak, my skull filled with an impossibly loud, barbaric hammering, as resonant, deep, and present as the air horn from some lost train that had somehow found itself in a small, tiled restroom, a noise as dark and consuming as the space between solar systems.

Totally panicked, I dropped to my knees, intent on making sure that when the artery in my head erupted I'd collapse the least possible distance to my death. I might be quite dead when they found me some days into the future, but my quick actions could insure that my corpse, all gnawed by the beasts of the wilderness, would have no bruises from an unnecessarily long fall.

On the other hand, being twenty-three and an English major, I had not the slightest clue about the proper way to forestall sudden doom by intracranial aneurysm. So when all symptoms abruptly disappeared a few minutes later, I applied the backpacker's universal medical solution: checking around to make sure no one had seen my abject, cowardly prostration, I pulled the pack back on and kept walking.

But two hundred yards up the trail, the terror returned, drumming violently away inside my head, a mad and energetic pep band at the last big game of the season. Noting very rationally that my earlier prophylactic grovel hadn't seemed to make much difference in outcome, I kept walking. The next shelter was only three miles away (over the next false peak), so I determined to die there with dignity, in my sleeping bag, with my boots off, among my own kind.

The head banging continued at irregular intervals, each time taking me to the edge of hysteria, only relenting a bit when I topped out above tree line. By the time I came down back into low shrub after the final climb before the shelter, I was a wreck, wired as tautly as Barney Fife at a big-city traffic stop.

Without warning, the chicken attacked.

At first the bird merely staggered onto the path, looked me in the eye, and marched southbound a bit in front of me. "That's cute," I said out loud. "I now apparently have a partner, a fellow creature to watch over me with kindness and concern when I faceplant into the dirt and die." Then, in perfect concert with my own mental state, it began erratic spinning, nervously completing a series of ever widening circles thirty feet in front of me, dragging a limp wing in the dirt and churtling away in deepest pain. I could relate. And then, a wild plunge into the bush and it was gone.

"That was diverting, for sure. Quite the entertainment. Sorry to see you go, old friend."

The trail exploded wings. A cavalry charge done up in claw, beak, feather, and bird saliva half flew, half skipped down the trail, mounted my head, ravaged the territory, dismounted abruptly, and retreated back, gasping heavily, to occupy the center of the path in front of me. There was a brief truce, several tense seconds, as we both regrouped and contemplated new strategies, the only sounds a series of "Christamighty" and "Jesusgod" spit out from my guppy mouth.

Her eyes met mine again, mine quickly averting lest I give any indication that I had intent to challenge or intimidate. She raised her wings, inflating herself to twice the size any bird should ever attain, rotated slightly to fulcrum more force into her next volley, and began visibly pulsating, some avian energy force pumping in vast, untapped streams of evil potential, building toward bird thermonuclear critical mass.

I raised my hiking stick, thought better of it, and tore off into the ragged heather to the left of the path.

Ten minutes and a quarter of a mile later, I climbed a rock and triangulated a course back to the trail, carefully choosing a route with the least cover available to hide a bird in treacherous ambush. Looking back on it, I guess in the next few minutes I did not actually hike several hundred yards of the official AT treadway, my only trail cheat of the walk. But at the time there was no way I was approaching that bloodied ground again without a squad of Marines and a skilled UN negotiator.

A few minutes later, I dragged into the shelter, muttered a few "glad to meet you—I'm not feeling so hot" to the three chipper Canadian guys already boiling up their suppers. I climbed into my bag, and rolled over to face the wall and begin summoning the courage for what I assumed would be a lifelong, soul-brave road to recovery. Sliding off toward what I was sure would be bad dreams, I overheard something like this:

"Dude, that partridge party was definitely the high point of the day."

"She reminded me of your crazy mom."

"Not taking any crap off anybody, eh? Nobody will ever schlep around her chicks with impunity."

"Love the little act where she lures you away from her nest by acting vulnerable and wounded."

"Leads to brutal conclusion if you don't go along with her act."

"Like your sister, eh?"

"You'd know, my friend."

"The partridge dudes were all amped up and randy out there too."

"That's God's truth, for sure."

"Feels just like the noise is boring right into your brain, right inside your head."

With a doomed sense of what was bound to come next, I began to pay closer attention.

"My dad said they do it by rubbing their legs together really fast."

This all led to a volley of teen snickering, some uneasy accusations about masturbation tendencies in the group, and a round of hearty, enthusiastic, but not very accurate imitations of a male bird slapping his legs about in sexual invitation.

But by then I didn't really need to listen to their bird parodies. I already knew what they would—each and every one—sound like: a loud and dramatic cerebral hemorrhage, of course.

So while their imitations propelled them upward into paroxysms of hilarity, I climbed quietly out of the bag and started cooking up my macaroni for the night.

There's plenty of real evil out there. Even the most sheltered of us eventually runs into it, the psychopathic monsters driven by creed, greed, anger, and certainty, an unsolicited cancer that eats away things beautiful.

But since my afternoon in Maine, I've always found it useful to spend a few minutes calling up the partridge test before I blow my chest out and cavalierly curse some nasty or another by slapping on the "wicked" label.

Might be something a little more understandable going on. Don't think like a child. Dig a little deeper for motivation. Understand the context. Sniff out the history, natural and otherwise. Follow the money.

Walk a mile in the other fellow's claws. The noise in your head means that you're trying.

NEW HAMPSHIRE

Devoting oneself to the lessons of agony

It's no mystery how mud gets in the Mercedes

The car was a huge one, just short of the length Sir Paul McCartney might command for a languid whisk around London on a night of celebrity drinking. It was—and this is not an exaggeration—gleaming a white so magisterial that heavy New England cloud masses evaporated in its path. Its chrome pulled vigor from the hidden powers of the Universe itself and beamed heavenly energy back at the rain, banning all storm from its elegant presence. It was obviously brand new and just as obviously not meant for me.

I think that I was walking at least shoulder deep under water as I left Maine and crossed into New Hampshire.

Earlier in the morning, a handwritten sign near the border announced the grunty news that the bridge over the Androscoggin River was out. "If he likes you," a helpful north bounder had added, "the foreman at the hydroelectric plant just upstream will sometimes let you cross inside the plant's dam. You need to be nice to him. Company rules say he can't let you in." The alternative was a ten-mile boot-powered detour up river to another highway bridge. And a ten-mile walk back down the other side to Gorham, New Hampshire, where I planned on resupplying, getting a hot bath, and celebrating the completion of my first state on the AT.

I usually do "being nice" pretty well.

But I had several negatives in my column as I walked up to the dam to make my plea. I smelled, for instance, like last month's road possum. My nasty, uncut hair was not likely to endear me to a crew-cut master of electricity. It had been raining off and on for a week; after the inevitable stumbles, trips, and wallows I was packing a multi-pound combo of Maine dirt, moose poop, and bodily fluids in livid and possibly permanent streaks up and down my arms and legs.

And with every step, my shredded cutoffs swung unwelcome, obscene views into the eyes of anyone unlucky enough to be looking in my direction. Like everyone else at the time, I started my hike in blue jeans. But a decisive removal of everything below the knees eased the heat early on, and then daily falls slowly eroded snatches of material until my denim loin covering wouldn't begin to pass muster any place on the planet other than among my fellow savages on the Appalachian Trail.

On the other side of the ledger, I had just spent the last few years doing construction work and had a sincere appreciation—hero worship, really—for the talents of the people who get up every day to imagine, build, and maintain the places that keep us warm, dry, and fed. That appreciation only grew when I was on the trail, usually cold, wet, and hungry. So I screwed up my courage, knocked on the metal hatch just below a huge sign mandating "no entrance, except by authorized personnel," and was soon explaining myself to the guy who opened the door.

"Boss Man, you got a skinny Tarzan up here wanting to see you."

A large guy in a blue twill shirt, matching pants, and well-worked boots whipped and skipped up a short set of metal stairs and gave me a quick once over. "Hi, son. Name's Don—what can I help you with?" As he smiled his greeting, he pulled me out of the drizzle with the huge hand he stuck out to shake mine.

It was time for rhetorical strategies. One of my most long-held personal goals, I began by explaining, had always, since I was a little boy, been dying to see a working industrial dynamo up close.

He snorted just a bit, looked at me the way a new father looks at his baby's first staggering experiments in walking, and cut eyes at his assistant.

"Tony, I think this young man here might be a plant. Most likely a federal inspector from DC. Maybe somebody the state sent up from Concord. It might be prudent to give him the full tour, top to bottom, show him the whole thing."

"And I suspect he might want his educational junket to end over on the other side of the river. Right, young man? Bring him one of those hot teas, and let's get started."

For the next hour I learned a lifetime's worth of lore about water flows, pluvial pressures per square foot, wildlife remediation, riverine ecology, tailrace and forebay rates, and core turbine copper wrappings, from two men who took imperial pride in sharing what they knew. The three-hundred yard stroll across and under the Androscoggin River was one of the high points of the AT walk.

At the far end of the plant, Don shook my hand, wished me well on the rest of the hike, and walked me out under another "No Admittance" sign, back into a steady New Hampshire rain.

"It's a three mile trudge into Gorham," he said at the end of the parking lot, where the plant road intersected with NH 16. "I'd drive you down, but my ride's in the shop. Wife dropped me off today. Don't think you'll have much luck on the thumb. You look like you were brought up in a latrine." He shook my hand and turned back toward the dam. "You be good, young man," over his shoulder.

He was right. There was nobody on the road, and the first three cars that splashed by slowed a bit, took a quick sniff, and never downshifted.

Then the Mercedes pulled over.

And not just any Mercedes. A huge one, just short of the length Sir Paul McCartney might command for a languid whisk around London on a night of celebrity drinking. It was—and this is not an exaggeration—gleaming a white so magisterial that heavy New England cloud masses evaporated in its path. Its chrome pulled vigor from the hidden powers of the Universe itself and beamed heavenly energy back at the rain, banning all storm from its elegant presence. It was obviously brand new and just as obviously not meant for me.

The tinted right front window came slowly down. As I awed my way closer, I could see acres of white leather, a manor's worth of virgin, alabaster carpeting. An intricately crocheted white pillow on the passenger seat announced that "Paula adores Stephen" sewn in white ribbon resplendent on a red satin heart. New car smell swirled out the open window to bless and consecrate this work of cushioned adoration.

"Hop in, my natty friend."

The driver was about my age, sporting an English driving cap, a neatly cut beard, and, if my nose was not mistaken, a marijuana cigar stabbing around precariously on his lower lip as he handed out the invite.

"You don't want me in your car, not like this."

"Not my car. Not at all, my mud-footed buddy. This is the boss's automobile." He sucked a huge pull on the cigar. "And just today I've officially proclaimed my fearless leader the newly crowned turdhead of this great land, the northern kingdom of New England. Dump the pack in the back (*the rear door locks popped*) along with this piece of embarrassment." The Paula/Steve pillow was frisbeed toward the rear, and a long ash broke free and floated down on the wood console.

I hesitated. This didn't seem right.

Then my eyes snapped to the creased and crumpled McDonalds' bag that shared the backseat with the pillow, greasy ketchup and mayo streams staining their way downward into the rear upholstery. In my perpetual defense, I saw the sack at a moment of great moral weakness. Through an unfortunate misunderstanding with a temporary hiking partner, the only food I'd eaten for the last thirty-six hours had been a cup of partially cooked white rice. The fragrant Quarter Pounder wrapper defiling the car's floor flipped the scruple switch in my brain as decisively as a needle pushing in an addict's poppies. Whatever gripe my driver had with whatever authority, I was totally in—if the rebellion led quickly to an oleaginous meat patty.

"We were supposed to start my training today on how to grade pine and fir for the secondary market. It's what he said he hired me for a month ago. Right out of community college. Seemed like a great opportunity for around here. Not many jobs in this bunghole. But when I got in this morning, he sent me out to wash the car again." A long, thoughtful pull on the cigar.

"I reminded him that I'd spent most of yesterday squirting, scrubbing, and shining. Then I politely pointed out this torrent squirting out of the sky and suggested that we maybe do the wash on a nicer day."

A toot on the horn apropos of nothing, and another inhalation and sustained hold of fragrant smoke.

With surprising skill, he then metamorphosed into what I took to be the nasally voice of his boss, snarling out a condescending, high-pitched order: "I didn't hire you to run the show. Paula likes a clean machine."

Then effortlessly back into his own voice: "Then he handed me a lunchbox, a pink one with Karen Carpenter on both sides."

Back into the boss's squeaky menace: "Paula's little bastard forgot her turkey and milk tits. Swing by first and drop this at the kid containment facility on your way. After lunch, we'll try to box up something else important for you to manage."

I could hear rocks drumming hard against the bottom of the car as we pulled back onto the highway and headed down the mountain toward Gorham.

"Don't mind doing my share of the grunt work. But this guy's jerkwad enough to run for senator someday. Didn't really sign on as head driver and delivery boy [giving his joint a jaunty tip for emphasis] for the Esteemed and All Powerful Sire of Specialty Toothpicks and Other Assorted Small Wood Trinkets and Accessories for Greater New Hampshire and Surrounding Areas. I'm through. Starting over tomorrow. Just signed on as lumber and hardware buyer for my uncle's building supply."

It might have been the onset of effects from the oceans of second hand smoke bouncing off the warm, dry, white leather. Or maybe it was just his black chin beard, worried face, and spider eyes crinkled up under the vapors from the joint. Then again, my view of him was out the side of my eyes, focused dead forward as I was, trying by force of will and intense concentration to keep us at least partially on the mountain road as he accelerated, two fingers on the wheel, through every curve we approached. But as my driver calmly reasoned out this considered announcement of emancipation, I could see, as anyone who was present could easily have, that he bore more than a passing resemblance to President Abraham Lincoln.

A few minutes later we pulled into the McDonalds lot. Abe popped the trunk, threw in the keys, shut the lid, and told me with deep solemnity: "I hid the other pair. Shit-ass." Head back and shoulders square, he strode out of my life, off down Gorham's pleasant New England main street. I stepped into the land of dry linoleum and bright lights, quickly finished off five dollars of food mass (as a point of reference, a Big Mac cost sixty-five cents in 1973), and, with great class, stepped outside and threw up five dollars of food behind the post office next door.

For many of the years of my post-trail career I managed groups of very bright, ambitious knowledge workers for a multinational corporation. The business constantly tried to help out fellow managers and me by bringing in impressive streams of organizational theorists and human resource consultants who specialized in motivating excellence in the work place. Their degrees were usually from Wharton or the Harvard Business School, and they were often employed by the likes of McKinsey or Arthur Andersen. They migrated to us in great stately formations, dozens to a flock, during a time of unprecedented downsizing, off-shoring, and layoffs. We all needed their help.

Every one of my hardworking, passionate colleagues—and me—flew in at dawn each and every morning knowing that we could be gone by lunch if any one of the masters of industry in our executive suites could dream up a way to increase his or her bonus a nick of a percent by slipping one of our jobs out the door.

In spite of the consultants' good intentions and great PowerPoints, none ever really added that much to what my Mercedes driver taught on the road to Gorham. If you're clueless about respect, you're going to end up scraping a gob of sticky mess out of your gleaming white leather, usually not that far down the road.

If you get yourself into enough trouble, a nap is probably best

My shorts and shirt were soaked, the temperature was somewhere near freezing, the shivering was constant, and options were limited. I had no way to create a viable shelter; I had no dry clothes, and I wasn't sure that I could get off the mountain. My very best idea was to continue walking and to count my steps out loud on the theory that as long as I could count, the hypothermia wasn't really all that bad.

Every trail headed toward the top of Mount Washington walks a hiker up to and around a series of huge signs only the dim of brain can ignore. Things like "Danger: weather can change abruptly on the summit. Turn back if it's bad." "Danger: Mt. Washington has the worst recorded weather on the planet—if it's raining down here, there's a hurricane up there." "Danger: a surprising number of jaunty walkers don't read these signs and end up piling rocks around themselves in a sad effort to keep warm in the last few minutes before they join the ancestors."

It was raining hard when I passed them in July 1973, three hundred miles into my hike and considering myself a seasoned veteran of all dangers the wilds could conjure. So, late in the day, I wound around the signs and headed above tree line. It was 75 degrees, and I was a strong, experienced hiker who knew all the tricks. I had, for instance discarded my wool sweater to save a pound. Within a mile, the trail became thigh deep with runoff from the heaviest rain I'd ever walked in, so with a hearty "bother" I compassed my way over onto Mount Washington's famous toll road, pretty proud of my mental agility at the change of plans. What bad could happen on a road? It was now 50 degrees.

At about 4,500 feet the rain mixed with light, wet snow. At 5,000 as the road traversed the Huntington Ravine and the winds scooped toward the summit, the snow turned to sleet, and the winds dialed up to bursts the summit weather station measured that night at just below 100 miles per hour. The road was now glass ice and my thick

Vietnam-era Army poncho made a perfect wing. I was soon sliding—sometimes quasi-flying—into large rocks carried down from Canada during the last ice age.

Disoriented by a sound knock on the head, I realized at one flat place on the road that I no longer had any idea which direction led toward the top. Out came the map and compass again, the map immediately ripped from my hands and deposited some seconds later in the Atlantic, a mere eighty miles away. I randomly picked a direction to stagger off into, unsure if I was even still on the unpaved road.

By now my shorts and shirt were soaked, the temperature was somewhere near freezing, the shivering was constant, and options were limited. I had no way to create a viable shelter; I had no dry clothes (but my pack was admirably light), and I wasn't sure that I could get off the mountain. My very best idea was to continue walking and to count my steps out loud on the dubious and probably deadly theory that as long as I could keep computing, the hypothermia wasn't really all that bad. In the film version of the next few minutes, the audience would see a wet, iced-over guy randomly shouting out numbers in no particular order, happy with his survival strategy as he wandered toward a brief mention in the local paper about another dim bulb who died in summer on what isn't even the biggest mountain on the East Coast.

At some point, a gust blew me into the side of a hut set up a century earlier to warm tourists as they buggied up to the summit. After an indeterminable period in which I struggled—giggling all the time—to remember how to operate a door handle, I was inside in my down bag, eating chocolate. After a nice nap, I headed ignominiously back down the road to the trail. In a moment of uncharacteristic clarity, I had registered my plan with the Pinkham Notch rangers before I headed out that morning, and when I hadn't arrived at the summit station, they came looking for me. Near the bottom of the trail, I introduced myself to the rescue team coming up for me.

It's a prudent lesson, one that I draw on every time I contemplate invading a foreign country or spouting out exactly what I think of some misbegotten idea at the office. It's possible to be stupid enough to create a situation that you can't walk around or through. Read the signs.

A penny's worth of mineral may trump a million of magic

I turned on my pack, dragging it down the length of the grave, heaving it time and again against rock and earth, at some point even getting a well placed, strategic bite or two into its waistband. A homemade leather tie-on I'd sewn onto the top with high-tensile fishing line was soon flapping a flag of surrender. The rage only lessened when I realized that it wasn't wise to have pulled my prized down bag from its stuff sack and begun to stuff ripstop nylon into my mouth.

The huts of Appalachian Mountain Club—and a pinch of salt—saved my hike.

Almost every AT thru-hiker agrees that New Hampshire is the crux of the walk, its most difficult section. But the pain isn't equally shared among all hikers. With 1700 miles of calf brawn and lung capacity onboard, north-bounders have the hard-won advantage of reaching the state in the best shape of their lives. Us southbounders, on the other foot, are totally grinded, both up and down, by the time we slog our way through the sawblade notches, staircase ascents, and exposed weather dodges of the Presidential Range.

I, for one, was ready to throw in the noodles and go home. The trail was beginning to seem like a tedious argument of insidious intent, and I had been heaving forward a full pack of fatigue for a month at this point.

Three things kept me lifting legs and moving south. First, it was going to be really hard to give up on the glory of the surroundings. I've already pleaded a lack of poetical talent, the kind needed to spread out on the sky anything like the beauty that the AT winds through. Just put down this book a second and swallow a virtual handful of Kingsfield magic pellets. Wait for a minute for them to kick in, and then conjure for yourself the most beautiful landscapes on planet, saga scenes in every direction, epic eyeball gulps that would energize the soul of even the most hardheaded bean counter.

In New Hampshire, the mermaids sing their songs for everyone.

And rumor had it that the topography was about to give me a break. I'd assumed that Vermont's Green Mountains were going to be a muscle crushing extension of New Hampshire's Whites, one color just inevitably blending into another, white to green. "Not so," said hiker after hiker headed north. "Vermont is equally as wonderful, but the beauty is draped across rolling hills instead of Himalayan sharks' teeth." "Hang on—it gets more manageable" was the chant of the knowing.

Most importantly, the AMC huts in the White Mountains were there to soothe both the body and soul. Spaced periodically down the spine of the trail, they provided an oasis (real this time) of good food, warm bunks, and like-minded people gathered together to enjoy the mountain life. At $11 a night—approximately a twentieth of my entire trail budget—they were far out of my economic grasp, so I'd initially planned to avoid them. But when I made my way down Mt. Washington with my own personal rescue party and safely reached the AMC Pinkham Notch command center, I walked into a full-panic state of emergency. The storm that had staggered me on the way up had now closed all roads into the area and trapped hikers all over the mountain, some with serious medical challenges.

Faced with a ton of need and no way to bring in more seasoned crews, the rescue director marched me into a corner, called me a few well-deserved and unflattering names, loaned me a wool sweater, and deputized me to spend the next two days going back up with experienced teams to help pull other equally dim folks to safety. In return, I was given three free nights to stuff my belly at the daily breakfast and dinner feasts at the Pinkham Notch lodge at the bottom of Mt. Washington.

But even the two days at Pinkham and the next two nights I paid for at AMC huts further down the trail weren't enough. I had one additional bitter pill to swallow.

The beef stew dinner at the Zealand Falls hut should have been a perfect end to my AMC tenure, the fourth great supper in a row that I'd shared with great people. But I ate it in an ungrateful funk of attitude, nagged by another of the headaches that had been colonizing the top of my neck almost every evening for the past week. The headaches shared the emotional spotlight with a nitty irritability that had been greying up life for days. When an attractive, bright Harvard student came over after dinner and sparked up a conversation, I quickly slimed up the mood by snorting at her sophomoric enthusiasm for E. E. Cummings. Even my toothpaste managed to offend. What idiot food engineer had decided it just had to be so friggin' minty and sugary? A perfect example of how Americans had to drown themselves in sweetness.

My mood had made base camp in a mental field as incorrigibly rotten as my long-wet socks.

At least tomorrow's walk would be an uncharacteristically easy one, I decided as I looked over the topo maps for the next day. The contour maps promised as smooth, level, and pleasant a walk as I'd seen in weeks.

Didn't turn out that way.

To begin with, the morning was misting, cold, grey, and fogged in. No views. And the trail's flatness? A mathematical illusion fostered by criminally negligent, statistically challenged scribblers who (I would have said at the time) threw together the pathetic ATC guidebooks I was stuck with. On average, yes, the trail stayed around 5000 feet. But at the boot level, I found myself was walking the back of a restless dinosaur, a series of bucking and heaving pointless ups and downs (PUDS to those initiated to AT linguistics), each perhaps too small to register on my map's contour lines, but each very real to the weight on my back, legs, and mental state.

The headache bored in with a hateful dig each time I came to another of what I began calling "the graves," geographically inscrutable gouges into the ridgeline (I guess I was still on the ridgeline; the fog made it impossible to tell) that the trail initiated over and over by sliding six feet or so down a roller coaster incline of pulverized rock and scree well lubricated by centuries of rain. It would then rattle forward several dozen yards with its walls inevitably reaching out once or twice to snag the pack or rasp raw an arm or thigh. At one point, a troop of martially inclined rats marched by hugging the wall to escape bombardment and singing lustily about

Tipperary. At least I'm pretty sure I saw this. At the far end of the grave, the trail would climb back up another six feet of nasty treadway, snicker a bit, and shove me on my way back out into the wind, cloud, and drizzle.

The headache continued to detonate, and my feet began to aggressively pursue their own cherished destinies and dreams. Sometimes they obediently did just what I asked. Sometimes they would angle a bit further left or right than I had ordered. Or maybe just snag the ground a bit sooner than I'd planned. Feet, boot, and leg take offs and landings became as unpredictable as Delta flights out of Atlanta on a sleety day. Every unexpected jolt ramped the pounding in my head a notch higher, the pain a little more intense. So I profaned my way slowly south, spitting a Niagara of clever curses. "Shit." "Shit on this." "Shit on you, butthead." "You piece of shit." "Butt rash."

The inevitable crash came with a particularly disturbing quiet. A wandering right foot cleverly caught a six-inch root that corkscrewed across the floor of the grave I was currently occupying. The stumble didn't even drop me to the ground, just rubbed a scraped arm across a rock wall enough to pull me out of an ugly musing involving an elaborate revenge fantasy on an insurance company employee who I was convinced had once wronged me.

I looked hard at the offending root, pondering the strangeness of its presence in this place. I was hundreds of feet above timberline; no tree massive enough to need an appendage this large had grown here since dinosaurs hunted down their macaroni in this latitude. I knelt down and pulled off a bit of bark. Yep, it was wood; nope, wasn't petrified. Clearly this root should not, could not, be here. Clearly a wrong was being done, to all fellow hikers, perhaps even to the Earth itself. The headache thrashed on, fueled by cruel injustice. A cosmic violation was at my feet, the two of them obviously delivered to this spot to set the universe straight. Music swelled in the background score of my life.

Calmly, I popped the waistband on the pack and propped it neatly against the tomb wall. Off came the poncho. I placed it squarely aligned on top of the Kelty. With dignity and purpose, I untied the bandanna I was using as a sweatband and folded it compactly beside the rain gear.

In a holy hurricane of righteousness, in the true name of all that blocks the way of virtuous men and women in their pilgrimages through the world, I then turned planets of power and wrath on the great root of the White Mountains. My war whoops rocked its foundations, a mighty imitation of the trumpets that brought Jericho to ruins. Booted toes and heels stomped, parried, and kicked until Vibram parted from leather. Fingernails and fists rained blood against the root's madding form. Tears galed down to flood away the tuber's dull physicality. On bare knees, with bare hands, I wrestled the wood as Sampson wrestled his lion and grappled the pillars of the offending temple.

Then I began the holy work on my pack, dragging it down the length of the grave, heaving it time and again against rock and earth, at some point even getting a well-placed, strategic bite or two into its waistband. A homemade leather tie-on I'd sewn onto the top with high-tensile fishing line was soon flapping a flag of surrender. The rage only lessened when—in a moment of insight—I realized that it wasn't properly wise to have pulled my prized down bag from its stuff sack, torn its waterproofing garbage bag to confetti, and begun to stuff ripstop nylon into my mouth.

I don't remember much about how I made my way the mile of fog and rain to the next shelter and climbed into my sodden bag. But sometime later in the afternoon two men stopped by for a snack, and I woke up enough to start up a wobbling conversation about my activities from earlier in the day, one that apparently set off alarms to this father and son out for a day hike in the drizzle. As my luck would have it, they were both physicians, partners in a nearby Vermont primary care facility.

"Young man," said the younger of the two after a brief examination, "You have a fever of 104. You been drinking adequate water?"

"Tons of it," from me.

The older of the physicians picked up the rest of the education: "Replacing your electrolytes?"

A blank look from me.

"Getting lots of extra sodium?"

Another blank look from me.

"Fever, irritability, headache, confusion, fatigue, loss of muscular control. Son, you have the classic symptoms of hyponatremia."

A really blank look from me.

"You're losing salt through the sweating that you're doing. Might not notice it up here in the wind and chill. But it's happening. Then you're making things worse by flooding your blood levels with liter after liter of water. At some point the unsalted membranes start to get stressed and water begins to infiltrate brain cells, causing them to swell and push against each other. The next step can be some really dramatic seizures."

Another blank look from me, tinted with the beginnings of fear.

The younger of the two brought my lesson to a conclusion: "Swallow two of these for now." He handed me a couple of salt tablets. "Take two every four hours for the rest of the day." He put the bottle on my sleeping bag. "Get two of these into you every day for the rest of your hike. You might try cooking them up with your supper to keep them from upsetting your stomach."

I did. And I've been a model of clarity and reasonableness for all the decades ever after.

During the rest of the trip—and for the rest of my life to this point—I have continued to eat my peck of weariness, anger, and confusion. But I earned these in the usual and fair ways, by walking long distances, doing difficult things, or trying to work and live with the few people on the planet who don't share the same opinions I do. The bad days happen.

But I've also been surprised by how often I can step out of my messes by assuming I merely possess, at least metaphorically, some mineral catastrophe whacking around near the stony roots of my ill-placed disposition. So before I start ripping up the useful things around me, I find it worth a try to halt the mindless march forward for a minute or two, take a couple of thoughtful breaths, and gulp a thoughtful swallow in memory of the power of a pill of salt.

VERMONT

Finding the perfect pace to wobble down the path

A good deed is sometimes never punished

When a rain burst interrupted my reveries and I ducked back into to the trail shelter, I wasn't at all prepared to meet a young woman about my own age, still a bit stinky looking even after her river bath, but charming nonetheless. I was immediately smitten, already planning a life of adventure together, only wondering which of us was going to happily choose to change directions so we could travel down the trail together in the morning, hand in hand.

I met hundreds of people on my hike—dozens of northbound thru-hikers, multitudes of day hikers, and locals (both good and bad) in towns along the way. After forty years, I remember the full names of only a few, at least of the ones who I haven't seen regularly since. I remember Kara's, however—though for the sake of delicacy, given the wonderful night we spent together, I won't repeat her last name here.

I was headed south, just into Vermont, with two fairly unsavory characters (their hiking partnership later ended in a brief, ineffectual, but spirited knife fight) who I'd watched heavy-handedly shoplift their way through a series of stores in Hanover, New Hampshire, during a resupply layover a few days earlier. We had been hiking together fifty miles or so at this point, and I was growing tired of the company. So when we passed a shelter stuffed full with Girl Scouts and my hairy-faced companions decided, despite nasty glares from the uniformed Scout leaders, to stick around and (as they said) "try to snack on a few of those tasty little cookies," I was happy to leave them behind and put in some more miles for the day. The older and more sociopathic of the two, I never saw again. But years later, I met his partner for a few beers, and he told me the tale of Kara's good deed.

Here's how it went.

When I reached the next shelter—a beautiful place twenty feet back from your typically stunning Vermont river—there was already a pack in the corner, and I could just see the movements of someone downstream bathing. So I went upstream, skipped a few rocks, had a few dreamy thoughts, washed off, gathered water, and headed back.

In 1955 Emma Rowena "Grandma" Gatewood—Ohio farmer, mother of eleven and aged 67—became the first woman known to thru-hike the AT. She did it alone. Carrying an over-the-shoulder homemade cloth bag for a pack, a shower curtain for shelter, and wearing through many pairs of Keds, she later made the trip twice again, the last time at age 75. Within a few years another woman, Dorothy Laker, completed it too, again as a solo trip.

Grandma Gatewood finally got the book she deserved in 2014, but no one has yet written the story of how, over the last century, women backpackers have leveraged the AT to make a determined feminist statement and to carve out their own well-deserved place in the history of courage.

Female technical climbers and mountaineers have long battled a certain smirky condescension from their male counterparts. But they have traditionally done so in a fairly closed community, one where the objective risks are shared by all and played out on stages generally populated by like-minded folks who at least aren't, most of the time anyway, physically threatening them. Women AT hikers, in contrast, follow a trail that winds through many an isolated road crossing or hamlet, past the eyes of all sorts of characters, again both good and bad. And in the early days, before the AT attracted thousands of thru-hikers onto its treadway each year, the original pioneers often walked their lonely walks on long stretches of largely deserted paths. While over 25% of today's thru-hikers are female, in 1973 America's long trails still largely belonged to men and boys.

So when a rain burst interrupted my reveries and I ducked back into the trail shelter, I wasn't at all prepared to meet a young woman about my own age, still a bit stinky looking even after her river bath, but charming nonetheless. She had, she explained, spent the last month walking up from Connecticut and planned to finish in Maine before she went back to her senior year in college. And of course, she was an English major. And of course she loved the British Invasion, Whitman, Yeats, backpacking, and Gibson guitars (all my favorites at the time).

I was immediately smitten, already planning a life of adventure together, only wondering which of us was going to happily choose to change directions so we could travel down the trail together in the morning, hand in hand. We chatted, smiled a lot, sized each other up with sidelong glances, fixed supper together, then headed separately back down to the river in a gentle drizzle to brush our teeth and get ready for the sleeping bags.

I have never quite understood what happened next, never quite parsed it out completely to my satisfaction. But I've come to carry it lightly.

When I came back up from the river, my teeth all clean and spearminty, Kara had pushed our sleeping bags and pads from their chaste and prudent opposite corners into the middle of the shelter, in a neat but nonetheless conjoined pile of goose down. She quietly explained: "I've had some run-ins with porcupines that have unnerved me." In the middle of the night, a porc—crazed to get at the salt that hikers' legs and bottoms impregnate into the wood of an AT shelter—howls out the sound you might expect a clumsy farmer to make as he accidentally slips his hand inside a combine and feels himself being slowly chipped up and pulled inside. "Would you mind if we slept near each other?" But she had arranged the bags so that, in fact, they weren't "near." They were side by side, touching.

And so we slid into our sacks, quietly chatted about the stars and the incredible earth- and fir-perfumed smells of the Vermont forest at night. And then—at about the same time, both on our backs with our elbows sometimes lightly rubbing together—we went to sleep. I woke up several times during the night, all dizzy and disturbed from being so close to her. But as far as I know, she slept soundly.

In the morning it was raining too hard for even long-distance hikers to accept the punishment, so we made a ridiculous card deck out of birchbark (ridiculous because every card was a slightly different and so recognizable by size and shape that cheating was inevitable) and then played "Go Fish" and flirted for an hour until the weather began clearing.

At about midmorning, Kara gracefully hoisted on her pack, and we both hesitated in front of what could have been a kiss. Instead, she turned to head north, stopped a few yards down the path and said, "Thanks for not making a big deal about my porcupine insecurities. You are a very nice guy. I'll remember you."

I tugged my heart back together, picked up my thirty-five pounds of burden, and turned south to continue my own walk.

I don't know if she remembers me or not. Recently though, following up on trail rumors that she'd completed her hike, finished college, joined the military, and retired a colonel, I put Google through its paces and phoned up the most likely candidate. The "Kara" I reached was twenty years too young —a colonel in the US Army but on her way to Afghanistan instead of retirement. And, no, none of her relatives from the right generation had hiked the AT as far as she knew. When the real Kara turned toward Maine and the rest of her life, I guess I'll never know where she was eventually headed. But part of that journey was not an awkward romance on a dirt floor with someone she barely knew.

I hope her memories of that night and morning are as good as mine, full of promise and innocence. But most of all I'm hoping that she still enjoys remembering the way the meeting with my two buddies went later that morning.

They were sullenly eating cheese (probably stolen) on a trailside rock, red-eyed and spiteful from sharing a campsite with whispering teens who had rewarded their ardor with nightlong giggles and a halfhearted moon or two. Neither lad could quickly come up with a clever line as this handsome, strong woman powered up a long approach, gave a cheery "good morning," and started to pass by out of their lives. "Wait," Branson called. "Did you see a blond-headed guy about our age going south? We're trying to catch up." What he didn't add, of course, is that they weren't really all that interested in partnering up again with a shrimpy guy who didn't carry a large knife, didn't slip a whole bag of chips under his fleece without paying, and had little interest in little girls in uniform.

She briefly turned back, gave a shiny smile, and replied, "Oh yes. You mean David. We spent the night together. He's pretty far ahead and was pretty amped up when he headed out this morning. I don't think there's any way you can ever catch up to him. But if you somehow manage to match his pace, please tell him for me that he was amazing." Then she headed out of their lives too.

It was a moment of easy grace that cost her nothing. But it meant the world to me years later when Branson told me the story.

The last thing I want to do is to tie up this story in too neat a bow. But you can be sure that I thought of Kara often, especially in the business world, when I met someone navigating tricky, even dangerous, currents with courage, cunning and aplomb. But mostly when he or she could pull it off and still make me smile.

An easy trip is probably just a detour (especially on the road to your desires)

"This will freak them out. Watch." She walked deliberately out through the crowd, stopping about half way to remove her sandals. Carefully placing one bare foot directly in front of the other to achieve maximum gyration, she did the most perfect parody of a high-fashion runway walk ever celebrated on the planet. Everyone who wasn't militantly not looking away from her was now looking directly at her.

Every long distance hiker has at least one all-consuming, gnarly obsession about a particularly enticing food. It inevitably happens. The unfamiliar demands on your body are stirring subterranean chemical and hormonal needs, and your constitution is crying out for satisfaction. You have lots of time on your hands (on your feet, actually) to feed the obsession, and any practical satisfaction is usually a sufficiently long enough distance down the trail—the very recipe for boiling up longings of legendary intensity. I've observed through wide study that the most frequent reverie for trekkers in warm weather involves half a cantaloupe and full scoops of blueberry ice cream.

My own personal burdens were elaborate fantasies about bread. A competent dietitian could perhaps explain the need. I can't. The food of Roman legions on the march hadn't featured prominently in my pre-hike world, and hasn't been an important destination on my pilgrimage of desires since. But on the AT, I pursued it without shame or proportion. At the height of my need, I once traded four strawberry Pop Tarts, just recently bought with a covetous desire of biblical proportions, for two tiny Pepperidge Farm mini-slices. I was, at the time, delighted by the bargain. Alone that night in my tent, I feasted upon the small squares of rye with the intensity that Gollum gives to gold rings and that Satan visits on human souls.

I hadn't planned to stop and didn't really need supplies. The trail through Vermont passes close by dozens of villages and small towns, so for the first time on the trip I could eat well and keep the pack weight down by dropping into a store every three or four days. I'd just visited a well-stocked minimarket a day earlier, in fact. But I'd finished that trip's loaf of wheat bread in two sittings. So when I crossed State Route 11 and noted that Manchester Center was only a short hitch away, warm rivers of grainy appetite canyoned through me and I stuck out my thumb.

I'll tell you right at the outset that I obtained the object of my lust. But satisfaction came at a hefty price.

Most of the expense was exacted by the cashier at the small grocery in town. Bread went early into the cart as expected. But the pack was light, Vermont was feeling like the land of milk and honey, and I had other needs that I decided to indulge. In went a bag of Chips Ahoy!, a substantial square of Danishes, a half dozen Hershey bars, a couple of Almond Joys, and a pound of semi-sweet baker's chocolate. And likely more that I've since forgotten.

The woman behind the cash register was young. From a distance, I took her to be in her late twenties, but when I reached the front of the line I saw she was much younger, apparently one of those teens who had developed early and energetically and who had likely been attracting unhealthy attention for years. In the spirit of the times, no underwear conspicuously graced her deeply cut tie-die t-shirt, cinched up around her waist to present her firm tummy to all who looked in her direction. Her peasant skirt was far too tight to allow for the comfortable pricing and bagging of dry goods, its length somehow not a balance to the lack of clothing above but incendiary in its own right. She had the first tattoos I'd ever noticed on anyone who wasn't at one time a sailor or Marine. The bold coarseness of the handiwork made it likely she had done the needlework herself.

But most of all, I had trouble keeping my eyes from the dozens of partially healed scratches that ran up both arms, disappeared under her shirt sleeves, reemerged around her chest and neck, and then disappeared again down her back.

She caught me looking, grinned knowingly, and moved a handful of candy down the conveyor. Coughing the theatrical cough used to quiet an audience before a toast, she picked up several chocolate bars and held them out like a drum major might hold a flag. "Ladies and gentlemen of this most excellent store," she trumpeted to the half dozen customers in the grocery. "Gather round, my friends, for I have yet another of my wise observations to proclaim." Stepping out from behind her counter, she bowed deeply and swung the upraised arm out to point at me. "This somewhat unclean gentleman in front of me, my dearest neighbors, apparently has a dangerously intense interest in all things sweet and delicious." There were snickers.

She then turned to me, spread her arms out like she might give me a motherly hug, and asked with exaggerated concern in a loud stage whisper, "You get all the sugar you think you can use today, sir?" Her gum smacked. More snickers, some enthusiastic, some uneasy.

I didn't let her catch me a second time. Quickly gathering my purchases, I regrouped in a shady place outside on the curb and began stripping off the excess packaging and placing my goodies in waterproof bags.

Bread is too big and bulky to fit in a pack. It's why no one carries it. But addiction, as they say, is the mother of invention, and I'd found a way to make it work. I'd done the routine enough times by this point that I went through it without much thought. My brain was, in fact, still stuck back in the drama in which I'd just played my uncomfortable part. Off came the twist tie, and I opened the end of the bread bag. Then, putting one hand at the front of the loaf to hold things steady, I slowly, systematically, and lovingly twiddled and caressed the other against the loaf's rear until all the air was forced out.

Back went the twister around a wheaten slab that was now a third of its pre-squeezed volume. From great experience, I knew that over the next few days I, when the need became insistent, could carefully massage each slice back into something like its original size and consistency, no appreciable harm done.

"A man of intrigue, a man of skills. Nicely done, Master Sticky Buns." The cashier was standing on the sidewalk behind me, clapping. She applauded by holding her left hand out straight in salute and tapping it dramatically on the very bottom of her palm with the three bottom fingers of her right hand. The thumb and index finger held an unlit cigarette.

"Look, give me a minute. That bastard will fire me if I don't deal with him, would have done so already if he didn't like looking at my shoulders so much. Desperately, pathetically, very sadly hoping that one happy day I'll take an interest in his floppy butt. Never, never, ever happen. Though it might be interesting if for no other reason than to stir up stuff with his horrible wife." She ended the applause, dropped her arms thoughtfully, sighed, and then hugged herself across the waist. "I hate people around here."

For the next few minutes I could see her through the store window pointing and shaking fingers at a frightened looking middle-aged man. She was soon back on the curb pulling her hair out of its pigtails and, without asking, hoisting on my pack.

"Gotta be back in thirty minutes. Should give us plenty of time. You hiking the AT? Thought so. Cool. Will do it myself someday. Bet you're looking for a shower, eh?"

No word from me during this onslaught.

"Could do one at my house, but dear Mom is home and she's probably at least half sober this early. Don't want to deal with that mouth. Besides the water system or something is down in the whole town. Out for three days now. Kinda cool. Everyone's washing in the river. Real scene. Every pop-veined Ma and Pa Kettle in the whole place is hanging out there."

We had crossed Manchester Center's beautiful main street and were now down by the Battenkill River where, as she'd predicted, a hundred or so contented looking villagers had spread out towels, lawn chairs, and picnics for a quiet Saturday afternoon on the rock slabs that wandered down into the water. Old guys with sunburned arms and faces but fish-vanilla legs, chests, and bellies. Older women with their hair in buns. Young families with toddlers wading in small scoops in the rock where the water was warmer. Pre-teens learning how to make themselves noticed by their peers.

"This will freak them out. Watch."

She walked deliberately out through the crowd, stopping about halfway to remove her sandals. One couldn't help but notice that she was apparently forced to spend an inordinate amount of time bending over during this process. Carefully placing one bare foot directly in front of the other to achieve maximum gyrations, she did maybe the most perfect parody of a high-fashion runway walk ever celebrated on the planet. Swinging and twisting, she slowly closed the twenty last yards to a large rock on the edge of the water. Everyone who wasn't militantly not looking away from her was now looking directly at her.

She climbed up the natural stone platform and began working some mechanism on the granny dress, her eyes patrolling the crowd like a sentry on night duty in hostile territory. Even the militants were now staring. When the dress finally came off, I'm sure that everyone was as relieved as I to see the bottom half of a quite proper swim suit, navy blue with red porpoises frolicking across the curves of stylized white waves. A few minutes on the rocky stage swooping up a pony tail, straightening the tie-die, and doing a few exaggerated stretches, and she was back through the crowd, back beside me.

In the meantime, I had reclaimed my pack.

"I skinny dip here all the time. Been arrested twice already this summer. The cops luuve that duty, my friend. When I want a little peace and quiet though, I go to my own special place further down the river. We'll go when I get off work."

The invitation felt like an act of vandalism.

"Look," I said, probably the only words I'd spoken in a half hour. "How old are you anyway?"

"Twenty-two."

"Where'd you go to college?"

"OK, nineteen."

"What college do you go to?"

"Stop it. I'm seventeen, almost eighteen. Just graduated. I've always been big for my age." She grinned an aggressive leer. "Been accepted to Middlebury for next year."

"Wow, that's a nice school."

"Who cares? Not into it. Not gonna go."

"What's your plan then?"

"Run the register, get high, try not to get pregnant again."

"You ought to go, you know."

"Probably will, dumbass. Just acting out. But right now I've got to go back to making sure these folks can feed themselves, wipe their bottoms with quality product, and have squeaky-clean dishes. I'll be off at four. There's some guys in town today selling weed, already been by twice trying to score me. I'll hunt them down. Meet you here."

Ten or so strides down the path, she turned back. "My bike's in front of the store if you need it. No lock on it." Apropos of nothing, she did a little spin to some rhythm only she was hearing. "You're welcome to ride it all afternoon, any place you'd like, my friend." She turned again and left. And so did I.

A massive traffic jam seemed like the last thing you'd have to deal with in a small Vermont mountain town, but that's what I found when I climbed back up to Main Street. Later when we passed a four-car fender-bender a mile up the road, I learned the cause for the line of cars idling irritably in the sun. But my first impression was that the cosmos was throwing up evil barriers to keep me from getting out of town as quickly as I felt necessary.

"Hop in." It was a nasty, huge, much assaulted old Pontiac with 700 hippies inside. But I wasn't particular. When I opened the back door though, there were already four large guys on the seat. I moved toward the trunk with my pack, but the driver shouted, a bit stressed, I thought, "Its full of shit. Just hop in already, dude."

The sun was hot, and my manual dexterity had disappeared. I kept looking over my shoulder to make sure the cashier wasn't following. And the guys in back just looked at me cow-eyed instead of taking any action to rearrange themselves. A few whacks of the clumsy pack as I tried to shove it in on top of Crosby, Stills, Nash and Young, and we had a pretty good Three Stooges episode going. Nobody was laughing though. Sweat flowed freely.

"Jesus Christ, dude. Just get the hell in the car." As if by some magic twinkling and twitching of the nose I could make it happen. Through the driver's window, I could see two policemen walking down the line of cars.

"Now, man. I mean it. Holy shit, get your ass in here. Jesus."

The car rolled forward a few feet, and my bovine-eyed friends in the back seemed to stir a bit. Hands came out mauling clumsily around, grunts were grunted, and I found myself on someone's lap with a door only partially crushing my right leg.

Another "Jesus Christ, man," from the driver.

One of the policemen stepped over to the front left window. "Everything OK with you boys."

"Absolutely, Officer."

"Kinda crowded in there. And hitching isn't allowed inside city limits in Vermont."

"Sorry, Officer. We didn't know. We're dropping him off just outside of town."

"That's fine. Have a good day. You boys be safe."

"Neil, you think he saw it?" whispered the guy whose lap I was puddling, leaning forward toward the driver. He was looking down at the line of plastic bags under the feet of my fellow backseaters.

I had found the cashier's travelling merchants.

That night I shared the shelter with two nice, uncomplicated fifteen-year-old boys out for the weekend. We ate my entire bag of Chips Ahoy!, shared their hoard of Hostess Cupcakes, and admired the stars. After they left in the morning, I had bread and honey for breakfast.

Go fast enough and you'll never get there

I was going full tilt, eyes on the prize, when I passed him late in the afternoon on a wide, grassy pass somewhere in southern Vermont. He was sitting on a downed tree, hat off, pack against a small fir, looking out over the valley in front of him. It looked like he might have been there for a while.

Set in a high glen filled with acres of ferns and a thousand firs smelling like every Christmas from my childhood, the Vermont lake was way too beautiful to leave, even though it was only mid afternoon. And the two Green Mountain Club caretakers stationed there for the summer had homemade pie and good conversation. So I stopped walking early for the day, shared a bottle of wine over dinner, and later cowboyed outside on the ground next to their tents, falling asleep to an incredible sky above the dingle starry. It was one of those ends of day when Time, for sure, let me climb golden in the heyday of his eyes. Down the rivers of the windfall night.

One of the GMC guys came over as I was putting down my sleeping bag and handed me a letter. It was written on cheap, lined school paper. But a summer of longing, lots of free hours, and some epic and heartfelt crayon labor had transformed it into a work of art to rival a medieval prince's illuminated prayer book. Never has woman's name been so ably celebrated midst a hand-drawn heart pierced by Cupid arrows. His girlfriend was serving two days down the trail at another GMC camp, and he thought it would be a nice touch to have his note carried by hand. Would I mind dropping it off when I passed by?

Moved by his ardor, I embraced his burden and upped the ante. I took a solemn vow. Not only would I put the token in her hands, but I'd do it by tomorrow night. Though affection of this depth surely would not alter with brief hours or even weeks, I was determined that my slow pace would be no impediment to this marriage of true minds. It would be my first (and last) thirty-mile day on the AT.

He was right about the effect. The Intended swooned over both the letter and my own Pony Express gesture, and her rosy lips (and those of her female co-workers) were wonderfully generous to my cheeks at the exchange of the token late the next afternoon. But I also ended the day knowing that Time had, in its way, made me His fool, using his unbending sickle to teach me something sad about the value of a day and the tricky, unyielding tradeoffs among which minutes and hours force us to live.

I rose that morning at dawn to get the early start I would need. The lake had transferred its mist over my sleeping bag in crystalline patterns of fragile beauty. I hardly noticed. I was, instead, pissed that my bag was wet, requiring me to waste a few seconds lashing it on the pack to dry out on route. My first stop that morning was a shelter seven miles down trail, where I mixed water, dried milk, and granola into a slimy mess for a gulped breakfast. A few just-waking Bennington seniors from a ballet class out for a bonding overnight hike wandered over while I was eating, but our talk was quick and perfunctory. I was in a hurry. "Wonder where the Lone Ranger thinks he's off to now?" I overheard one say as I loaded on the pack and headed back out. I'm sure that the distance between the lake and the first shelter had any number of points of interest, Vermont in green and hill. But I have no memories of them.

Forty years after my five months on the AT, I do have hundreds of brain shots that routinely circulate into my consciousness in a sort of reverse PTSD, benign, even celebratory, tiny spots of time that play like flashbacks and give me a vivid second or two of some glory, either substantial or not, of a fully blossomed moment from one of the days on the AT. I treasure them.

But I have only two from the rest of this morning and its afternoon. One is a tiny flash snap of an empty pool fed by a waterfall just off a segment of road walking around a small town. The water hole had achieved some notoriety because it was part of the village's water supply, and trail rumor had it that locals, including several past retirement age, had been arrested in the past week for "fouling the water," relaxing there without hindrance of clothing, floating streaming hair and body parts with complete disregard for hygienic propriety. My mini-memory is of passing, looking quickly right, and noting that there was nothing to see. Perhaps because it was ten in the morning and all the offenders were still home with their dreams and water-birthed wrinkles?

My other visual snap is of the Quaker. He was in his very early twenties, maybe a year to two younger than me, tall, very lean, quietly muscular, sporting the round, wide-brimmed, honest felt hat that announced the Friends' radical belief in the dignity and equality of all. He wore it without irony, proud that it traditionally was never removed to bow to worldly power.

I had stayed at the same shelter with him earlier that week, but he'd apparently passed me when I took a day off in Rutland to visit with relatives. The rumor whispered around him was that he'd spent time in federal prison for refusing to be drafted during the Vietnam War, even though his religious beliefs entitled him to an easier choice of alternate service teaching school or working in a hospital. He carried himself with dignity and grace, but still clearly enjoyed the loud, coarse farting antics of the group of Scouts we shared the camp with. The only slight affectation I noticed was an almost instinctive tendency to slip quotations from Whitman, Jesus, Dylan Thomas, and others into the conversation. They seemed so naturally a part of how he experienced things that the quotes usually didn't receive any attribution. I didn't get to spend much time with him that night, but I liked him a lot.

I was going full tilt, eyes on the prize, when I passed him late in the afternoon on a wide, grassy pass somewhere in southern Vermont. He was sitting on a downed tree, hat off, pack against a small fir, looking out over the valley in front of him. It looked like he might have been there for a while. With a quick glance in the direction he was looking, I noticed lights starting to glint and glimmer out in the far distance. Following a physics that I've never understood, a semi-transparent half moon was showing against the still-blue sky, the way it sometimes does.

I said a perfunctory "hello" as I puffed past, elbows and knees going like a sewing machine in a South Asian sweatshop, and then churned down the trail off the high point the path had carried me over.

That night at the shelter, at the end of my thirty-mile day, I avoided him, knowing in good conscience that I could no longer really look him in the eye.

I'd like to say that my discomfort taught me something profound. That decades later when I was at home at night ripping about in a presentation for an important meeting the next day, I wouldn't hurry through my son's bedtime story, hoping he wouldn't notice that I was skipping pages that he loved. That I pushed out of my cocoon of worry and responsibility and fully savored his kisses and the light whisper of his sleep.

But I didn't always. When the days go away, all we are left to carry are the memories we've packed in. I have almost none of thirty beautiful miles in Vermont.

MASSACHUSETTS

Discovering how to know what is scary, what is just a fright

On occasion, indiscretion might be the better part of valor

"Yep, out here all alone, no friends, small guy too."
The driver squeezed my right arm. I pulled it away.
"Anything could happen."

I didn't know where exactly I was going, but I was really hoping to get there before it got dark and the rain started.

Leaving the college town of Williamstown on the Vermont/Massachusetts border, I couldn't help but notice how the aggressive bulk of Mt. Greylock filled the skyline like a great whale gnawing away at the horizon. At least Herman Melville thought so as he sat nearby at his writing desk a hundred years earlier looking out at the Berkshire peak while conjuring up the violence-scarred malignity at the dark heart of *Moby Dick*. Greylock wasn't as high as Mt. Washington or Katahdin, but it was still impressive, spouting its own cloud system, one that rivaled anything north of it.

But the truth is that I didn't know how high it was, at least not its exact elevation. In fact, I knew almost exactly nothing about what was ahead. I didn't have my maps or AT guidebook for Massachusetts.

Earlier I'd checked into the local post office to pick up my usual care package from home. But nothing was there. Taking pity on me, the postmaster had made a few calls, found my resupply at another Massachusetts office, and promised to send it along to Dalton, a town a few days down the trail. He kept his promise, and I was soon back among the land of the knowing.

But for the next fifty miles I was on my own, with just AT white blazes and the ATC *Mileage Factsheet*—a thin, stapled list of shelters, roads, and distances—to keep me on track. All I knew as I thumbed out of town toward the trail was that the Wilber Clearing Shelter was 2.99 miles from the road crossing (a precision that made me instinctively doubt the accuracy of anything within six inches of the entry on the page), two-tenths of a mile off the main trail.

"This ought to be interesting," I remember thinking as I headed up into deteriorating weather. And I was more right than I could have wanted to know beforehand.

The fun started when I hit the crest of the Greylock ridge after a steady 2,800-foot climb. On a hike on Vermont's Long Trail many years later, I remember topping a mountain graced with an antique fire tower that dominated the peak, one of those Civilian Conservation Corp-era beauties whose stout-hearted iron girders and beams wove artfully together to elevate their function and design into a rousing piece of simple backwoods sculpture.

You could see it miles before you reached it, crowning the bald top of the tallest mountain around. The trail broke out of the trees a good hundred yards in front of the tower, situated in a cleared area with the kind of unobstructed approaches you might find in a Walmart parking lot. It was near the end of the day, and I was tired. So I crossed the hundred yards of low grass in front of the tower at a measured pace, eating up the beauty of the eighty feet of vertical art in front of me. Twenty feet in front of the old lookout, I sprang the catch on my hip belt, anticipating the burst of hover boost that always comes to exhausted leg muscles at the day's end dropping of the pack. At ten feet I was totally focused on the stairs just inside the crisscross of muscular beams that I had been admiring for a good five minutes at this point.

Then I found myself on my back, not quite out cold, but blinking-brained, feeling the blood runnels start their slow meander down from my forehead into my not-so-reliable eyes. At a nice, steady pace of three miles per hour, I had walked with confidence, conviction, and considerable inertial force forehead first into the iron beam I had been following with unrestricted gaze for the length of a football field.

Here's the point for this particular story.

The AT generally marches you right up to its shelters. The trail most often passes within yards; it would seem like you couldn't possibly miss them. But you can—and you sometimes do, especially at the end of a long day when the feet are leaden, the eyes have riveted their focus on your boots, and the mind is slowly shutting down important parts of itself. If you are dependent on the shelter to keep dry and warm, you are hyper vigilant in the last mile as you approach. And all bets are off if your maps tell you the shelter is some distance off, right or left, on a blue-blazed side trail. If it's possible to miss a structure the size of a FedEx truck (or a beam the size of a dinosaur spine), it's way too easy to haze past a couple of six-inch blue blazes and a thin dirt path. And if a storm has taken down just the right tree or trail maintainers have gotten a little behind on maintenance, the blue blazes might not be there at all.

After a half mile on the backbone of Greylock, I'd gone way past *hyper vigilant* into full-blown, hysterical *hyper*. Full-blanket dusk was starting to settle, the rain had started in earnest, and the wind was shelling cloud fragments through trees in that moaning, spooky way that is the glory of the mountains when you're in a fine mood, but the sound track of a slasher film when you're not.

And every twenty feet or so yet another trail veered off the AT toward who knows where or what. The first three or four that spun up on the left I turned down only to find that these, now clearly just animal paths, petered out in fifty or sixty feet—or worse, in a several hundred wasted yards, sometimes downhill. Here's the thing: I knew every one of these paths except one—even the ones marked by inexplicable boot prints—were dead ends. But one wasn't. I didn't want to miss it and had no reliable way to guess which was the treasure.

Soon I had galloped and galumphed down dozens, not the best plan on rooted, slippery footpaths in the assembling darkness. I didn't think I was in any particular danger, as I might have been facing a night out on Mt. Washington or Katahdin, but I was beginning to fortify myself for an uncomfortable ten hours balled up under a damp poncho. Little did I know.

I had just sprinted off yet another blind alley, made a sharp left back onto the AT, when I slam, kneecap first, into the rear end of a late model, nicely polished, bright blue VW Super Beetle. I'd naturally assumed since leaving Williamstown that with every step I was trekking a bit deeper away from roaded civilization. But in the heat of the moment the oddity of two thousand pounds of misplaced steel in the middle of the AT wasn't what my mind seized to puzzle through. Why, I wondered instead, were the brake lights pumping so rhythmically on and off, so far from any of the usual dangers of the trafficked world? Refreshingly festive to have all these red bulbs strobing up here in treeland. But why?

And why was the back Super window all foggy when rain surely could not be finding its way inside the cozy, newish auto? Why, as I disentangled myself from the bumper and spun past the right passenger window, was that fifty-year old gentleman looking at me so intently from out the circle of glass that his well-trimmed beard was rubbing free from condensation? Why were his eyes so wide and popping? Fear of me? No way. And what sense could I make of the tangled maze of feet—some socked, some bare—pressed hither and yon across the inside of the car window, one set of pink-nailed toes, I could see now, planted firmly against the windshield?

As I rounded the front bumper, I for a second met the eyes of a young woman, perhaps twenty, her hair a hurricane of brown and blond tangles. Through the steam heat of the front glass, I could see her mouth forming into the universal four-letter cry of alarm and confusion that the Anglo Saxons long ago bestowed to help beget resolution and acceptance in the climactic moments of the frustrated, the scared, or the angry. I croaked out my apologies—probably not heard in the churning chaos of hands, elbows, buttons, and textiles inside the VW—and hurried south.

Two hundred yards down the trail, I came to the Wilber Clearing lean-to, not two-tenths off the path as advertised but planted right beside the footway. Within minutes, I had my gear unpacked, my supper boiling, and a dry change of clothes warmly in place. All was well.

I only got ten seconds or so of warning from the groaning of steel on steel, tire against dirt and rock, before leaves began parting twenty yards in front of me. Small trees went down; the rain and growing darkness was slit by wildly bouncing stabs of headlights; and a rusted, much abused small pickup bullied up in front of the shelter.

I could see two ball-hatted thirty somethings inside conferring, arms jabbing and gesturing at me, before the truck lurched back a dozen yards, pitched just as suddenly back to its original resting place, and shut down with shudders and coughs. The driver swung out with a large Navy duffle over his shoulder and bolted for the shelter. His passenger did the same, laboring to control a case of Budweiser he was trying to use to keep some of the rain off the action of the deer rifle pivoting sloppily around under his underarm. Halfway to the shelter, he did a stumbling Wile E. Coyote double back, the rifle barrel drawing an erratic loop under the beer, jerked open the back gate of the rust bucket, and let out three unusually stupid-looking coonhounds. The dogs launched off into the woods without a second of thought or hesitation.

Twenty seconds later, another ragged truck bulged through the forest and two more guys blurted into the lean-to, their cadre of gape-mouthed, tongue-lolling dogs setting out to catch brethren. I couldn't help but notice that all four humans sported pistols holstered on wide leather belts. The driver of the first vehicle rounded out his look with a Bowie knife strung upside down across his chest, anchored there with jaunty, piratical flair.

All went well for a few minutes as they sorted gear, popped a few cans, snorted a round of snouty laughs, and passed a mostly empty Jack Daniels bottle among themselves.

"Hope you don't mind the company, bud. We're just up running the dogs." A significant look to his companions. "And getting away from our women for our fair share of red neck jubilation. Don't worry though—we're harmless as last year's dead Bambi." More laughter. More pulls on a second bottle making the rounds.

My gear was now mostly over in a far corner. I'd moved some of it there myself, but the bulk had been pushed over, not very carefully, by shoves—some just the result of clumsy jostling by too many people in too small a space, some very calculated—from the boots of my new companions.

"You hiking the AT?"

"Yessir."

"I'd appreciate you not calling me 'sir,' bud. I ain't your daddy." He pushed my shoulder like we were sharing the funniest joke ever conjured by two drunkish frat boys.

"See many snakes?"

"A few."

"Rattlers?"

"Some, but mostly black snakes."

"You scared of 'em?"

Another push on the shoulder, this one from the back. I could smell a potent mixture of beer, toxic tobacco, and unattended dental hygiene.

"Bet he's a lot more scared of tough ass, scary bastards like us." From the shoving comedian behind me.

"Under every rock." The passenger from the second truck dropped on his belly and slithered dramatically across my sleeping bag, stopping every other spasm or so to leer up at his buddies.

More laughter. And more slaps to the head and shoulders, some aimed at me, some exchanged among the three jokesters, many of them connecting too hard to be all that funny. Out of the corner of my eye I saw that their other friend was standing on the edge of the shelter floor, looking out into the rain, ignoring his companions, clearly not comfortable with the script playing out behind him.

"Yep, out here all alone, no friends, small guy too." The driver squeezed my right arm. I tugged it away.

"Anything could happen," he continued. "Real brave guy. Or maybe just stupid." He used the thumb and ring finger of his right hand to thump my forehead. The other two gallant buddies leaned in from the circle they'd formed around me and added a series of thumps of their own. Lots of laughter.

"We're not that brave ourselves, right my friends?" Nods all around, and more laughter. "Shit, I wouldn't ever come up here by myself, not with a blond girly mane like that anyhow." Their hair was longer than mine, but I sensed it wasn't the time to point this out. He reached out toward my hair. I took a half step back. More laughter.

"But he's got these muscle-man arms," said someone behind me, knocking my right elbow hard enough against my side to draw a wheeze out my mouth.

"Nope, nobody would dare throw sand in his face." The driver looked around the shelter for a prop he could heave. Not finding anything to fit his fancy, he instead kicked one of my boots out into the rain. "He's got these shit stompers too. Big man with big shoes." I got a kick on my bare left foot.

Looking around for a feasible way to bail, I met the eye of the fourth guy standing quietly by the shelter entrance.

He turned toward our ugly knot: "That's enough, Rob. Just cut it out. We're not up here again for that sort of stuff. Remember last time?"

"Fuck you, Saint-man. We're not hurting anybody." He gave me a shove, aiming for my chest, I think, but knuckling dead into my throat instead. I shuffled backwards, but a hand from behind pushed my face into Rob's.

"Step back, hippy slime. Nobody gets in my face like that." The thump to my right jaw was an unmistakable punch this time, no room for humorous interpretation. More laughs and another enthusiastic shove to the back of my head from behind. I had little choice but to begin reconciling myself to an unpleasant beating.

"I'm guessing that's about enough of that for now, Rob."

The driver of the VW was standing just inside the circle of light, fully dressed now, sandals on his feet, by himself, drawing on a fashionable wooden pipe as he spoke, the way you imagine Einstein might have done when facing down some particularly vexing math.

"Professor Benson, haven't seen you in a coon's age," from my tormentor. A pause for thought. "How's your wife doing?"

"I miss you too, Rob. Especially miss you since you never came back to finish the screen porch."

Laughter from Rob's companions.

"Just up for a drive," the professor continued. "Nice night. Thought that was your truck. Heard you guys hooting up here. Thought I'd drop by to see what the joke was."

"We're up running the dogs." Another pause for thought. "Saw your car back in the clearing on our way up. Looked like you were busy, so we didn't stop for conversation."

Some snickers from the truck crowd. Professor Benson stepped a yard or two closer.

"I saw Homer and Ulysses pass back at the car ten minutes ago.

Looking good. Homer's over that limp. Also saw this gentleman a little earlier." He looked at me with a canary smile. "Thought you might run into each other. Figured I'd let you know there was a hiker up here before you had another accident firing your hardware out into the trees. Now that I see you all here together I feel much better. Now I've seen him with you, all partying with you guys, I'm sure no nasty accident could happen."

He took a few steps back north toward his car, then turned back to me: "You like a ride back to town? I've got room in the back."

"No thanks. The shelter's a little crowded, but I'm going to camp on the trail and get an early start in the morning. Thanks, though."

So I did, after all, end up spending a damp night out huddled under my poncho, carefully triangulating myself between three large pines so my misfortunes would not include being run over by a drunken bully in a hundred-dollar pickup. For the next few hours, my dog-running buddies hooted and hollered, punched clumsily at each other instead of at me, and incessantly called for the deer dogs, who never came. Near dawn, after the fire they lit in the wooden shelter got out of hand and burned long enough to dig out an ugly divot into the floor, they packed up and bounced back out through the dripping trees. Without the dogs, as far as I could tell.

I tramped back to the shelter, got a few hours of sleep, and left early the next morning, shivering in my wet clothes. Within a few minutes, I had crossed the two-lane park blacktop that parallels the trail on its approach to the Mount Greylock summit. I checked my guidebook when I picked it up days later and the map shows the road quite clearly. At the end of the road I found Bascombe Lodge, a red spruce and stone beauty built by the CCC in the 1930s as a centerpiece for the Veterans War Memorial at the top of the mountain. Again, it's easily spotted on the map.

While I was drying off by the huge fireplace in the lobby, the director walked over, handed me a cup of hot tea, and placed the final period on my first day in Massachusetts: "You know, we often let AT thru-hikers stay here for free. Wish we'd known you were in the area. We cooked up hamburgers for a big party of folks here last night. Had plenty left over."

I wish I'd been there too.

The easy learning here is that you should make sure you prepare enough to always know exactly where you're headed and how to get there safely. But I want, as is my habit, to go more metaphorical than that.

After finishing the trail, I also traveled much of my professional life without much of a map, working in the unprecedented churn of the high-tech communications and Internet revolutions, navigating booms, busts, vicious downsizings, and windfall expansions through years of woozy, unpredictable economic and societal turns, seldom knowing if there was anything like a well-engineered road anyplace nearby.

I don't want to make too much of the role that the college professor played in my mental wellbeing during these adventures. But he did have his place.

In the business world, purity often competes with a long list of other admirable virtues. Corporate life is often way too nuanced to find a set of clear blazes pointing easily to absolute right or absolute wrong. Let me give one example. It's a bit long, but it has to be—we're talking nuance here.

In the early 2000s, the executives who ran my company (into the ground, it turns out) decided to deal with a harsh turn in the market they hadn't anticipated through one of the most predictable and pitiful go-to moves in the executive playbook.

"We screwed up," it goes. "But let's earn our huge compensation not by addressing that sadly unfortunate reality. Let's, instead, lay off 10,000 of our loyal employees. This will spike the stock price for a couple of weeks, letting us cash in our stock options and bank some ill-gotten proceeds before we take early retirement (we'll say in the press release that we plan to spend more time with our families). Our successors can deal with the angry customers who won't get what they need any more because so many of our employees are gone, now drawing unemployment while desperately figuring out how not to lose their houses to the banks."

"Great strategy—tried and true," echoes the Board of Directors that hired the clever executives. "Call in the minions of vice presidents and make it happen."

My senior vice president was leaning toward axing his web team, which I managed. His last job before joining the company, I might add, involved selling horseshoes and dog harnesses in rural Venezuela. That was before his best friend, our new CEO, hired him to direct our path through the tangle of engineering and physics that created the high-speed optical lasers that made the Internet possible. Our internationally prominent web team, I pointed out in an early conversation with him, gave us decisive credibility with customers who expected us to practice what we were preaching.

He didn't buy it. We were just, he insisted, a drag on his bottom line.

So my managers and I went into the climactic meeting knowing his executive mind was already made up. And as expected, the meeting initially went very badly. Until one of my managers stepped out of the back of the room and hijacked the discussion. For every negative proof point on the VP's charts (created, of course, by his executive assistant), she marshaled an incontrovertible, exquisitely detailed avalanche of metrics and statistics demonstrating our absolutely critical value to his market success. I'd never seen these stats before. In fact, when I'd asked for ones like them earlier, the whole team had to concede we didn't yet have the technology to gather them.

After trying to dodge his way out of the business logic that flowed around him in colossal waves of irrefutable truth, the VP abruptly ended the meeting and asked me to come see him the next morning. I knew him well enough to know that he had changed his mind, that some other group of undeserving unfortunates would instead take the hard thumping he'd planned for us.

On the way back to my office I caught up with Barbara, shook her hand, thanked her a hundred times, and asked her to come by later and show me how she derived her metrics. They were perfect, and I wanted to make sure I could marshal them the next time they were needed.

"Can't," she said. She tapped her temple with the perfectly sculpted nails of her right hand. "Made 'em up when I saw what a jackass we were dealing with. Air. Total bullshit. And he bought it." I recoiled instinctively, considered things for a minute, and then gave her the most sincere hug I ever doled out in the workplace.

Parked in a clearing beside a mountain road, the good professor was in a morally compromised position. Compromised position indeed, if what I think I saw through his VW windows was what he was indeed in the act of doing. His partner didn't seem to be the appropriate age to be his wedded wife. And even if he were a blameless bachelor, I suspect many of his colleagues would not approve of his recreational trip into the forest with a much younger student.

It would have been prudent for him to start his car and flee undetected into the lowlands, his slimy indiscretion hidden by dripping pines and darkness. Instead, he walked over to my rescue, knowing that four of his not-too-wonderful neighbors might likely make significant trouble for him in the wake of his gallantry.

I'm glad he made the choice he did, and I here take the opportunity to give a seedy but grateful salute to his peculiarly tainted courage.

Treat your water well

That night I slept like a baby.
Woke up like one too. Only on this particular morning I had no diaper to hide my shame and no protective parents to clean the mess.

Outfitters didn't carry water filters in the early 70s, so I didn't pack one. I drank straight from nature's clear, cold streams. So naturally, I was twice gutted with dysentery (*dysentery* has a nice British imperial ring to what would now be diagnosed as giardia). For a week each time, I'd get max three seconds warning before the explosions. I did my business in front of snickering groups of Girl Scouts—more than once. Forty years later, I'm still sometimes struck with nasty surprises in the intestines.

Let this serve as a belated apology to the middle-aged woman who was witness to the onset of these disasters. I could blame it all on all those nitwits who stumble through the world letting their dogs run free around the water the rest of us have to drink. But, no. I was sloppy. I deserve and will embrace full censure for my carelessness. I'm sorry.

The night after my awesome experience with the fine gentlemen on Mount Greylock, I was determined to catch up on my sleep. The AT offered no shelter within a reasonable distance, but as it turns out Nature herself could not have done better by me. I was already in a great mood. Everything seems marvelous the day after you escape a beating.

Then, around four in the afternoon, somewhere on the mercifully flat and beautiful woods walk between the villages of Cheshire and Dalton, the stroll took me right to the border of a small paradise. The trail sauntered along a modest, shallow brook that swooped a leisurely loop around a tiny peninsula. The spot stopped me in my tracks with its perfect beauty. Frederick Law Olmsted could not have planned anything more perfect if some ambitious committee of New York vacation homers had given him double the budget he originally lavished on Central Park. About the size of a suburban living room, it was an arcadia of fir and pine needles, guarded by a half dozen wise old trees whose gentle canopy of shade had long ago banished any sign of bothersome weeds, nettles, or poison ivy. I could easily imagine Adam, having been babbled by the stream to a long, liquid catnap on a snoozy afternoon, waking here in this magic circle to first see Eve all unclothed and sparkling with dew among the ferns.

I stepped across the brook into my own personal chersonese, pitched my poncho, cooked, washed, brushed teeth, and slept through the night like the legendary baby.

Woke up like one too. Only I had no diaper to hide my shame and no protective parents to clean the mess.

Years before, I had made a wrong turn on an Air Force base and found myself standing just barely on the protective side of a huge metal blast deflector, only fifteen feet away from a giant B-52 as its pilots revved up the plane's eight massive turbojets to accelerate down a very short runway. That volcanic experience is the closest I have had to the convulsions that were being visited on my stomach in my first seconds of consciousness that Sunday morning. I launched out of the bag and made three paces before the first detonation cracked the ribs of the earth, broke the back of the sky, split the channels of earth's rivers across the land. I crouched where I was, and the crude of all-powerful biology ruled all my systems.

Shaking in my labors, naked in my shame, bent in primal humiliation, I looked up in a brief respite from my groaning to meet, just across the three-foot stream, the huge brown eyes of the kindest looking motherly type on the planet. Hair nicely washed and combed, Eddie Bauer outfit clean and neat, birding binoculars at her neck, day pack most likely carrying a healthy treat for lunch, cheeks rosy from her walk, she was just leisurely rounding the southern end of my land of misery when my first cries tore the foundations of the Massachusetts morning. Walking at, say, two miles an hour, her speed gave her, I would calculate, fifteen seconds to pace the boundary of my peninsula before her momentum would put the sight of me (and my behind) behind her forever.

It was an agonizing quarter minute for us both.

"Do you need help?"

"No, Ma'am (a southern upbringing rising to the occasion). But thank you for asking." And she was gone.

I now always carry a filter.

A relatively short time ago a pipe owned by my local energy company, our nation's largest, ruptured and dumped eight million pounds of coal ash mush into a nearby river. For the previous two years, company engineers had asked their superiors to budget $20,000 to do proper maintenance on the pipe. Eyes on the bottom line, the superiors had declined the repeated requests.

Coal ash is what's left when coal is burned in large quantities. It is generally laced with deadly smidgeons of arsenic and selenium, toxins that in the smallest portions encourage cancers and block normal growth in young brain and nerve tissues.

For thirty years the utility was the employer of my state's governor at the time, one of those noisy politicians who lament all the regulations breaking the defenseless backs of our civic-minded job creators. Nearby, an additional five billion tons of similar liquid toxic ash sat behind earthen dams built during the Eisenhower administration, three miles from the water intakes for Charlotte, North Carolina's biggest city. My state's Supreme Court recently ruled that the energy company does not need to be in any particular hurry to begin the clean up. Other state courts have already decided that ratepayers will eventually pick up the Everest-high costs of the mess. No utility executive was prosecuted. No utility executive lost any well-earned compensation. No utility executive lost a smidgen of his or her professional reputation. All was forgiven and largely forgotten.

I suspect similar stuff is going on in your state. I can only imagine what we're packing into children's genes and asking them to carry into their futures.

From little acorns sometimes slightly bigger acorns grow

"Now, Mr. Hiscoe," as she poured the tea, "tell me about your history."

I had not, up until that minute, thought of myself as someone with a history, only a somewhat shaky future. And up to that minute I don't remember anyone ever calling me "Mr. Hiscoe" without the rancid stink of irony in the air.

Through the early 1970s all aspiring thru-hikers took it as solemn obligation to stop at a certain house just beside the trail in the tiny village of Washington, Massachusetts, where the Appalachian Trail guidebooks told them to knock on the front door of Mrs. Fred W. Hutchinson and ask for water. Though the visit had a sound practical reason—the stream at the nearby shelter was noxious—its real import took on an almost biblical feel, like a scene from parable you were sure came from a authoritative testament but that you couldn't actually find when you looked in the book itself.

The outlines of the fable were clear enough though: a respite at a house along the pilgrimage to ask sustenance from a wise woman conspicuously named to call attention to her widowhood, a significant waypoint along the journey gated by a Socratic examination over ceremonial refreshment. It probably wasn't an accident that before I met her I often confused things and referred to her as "Mrs. Washington." At least unconsciously all the trail stories I had heard of her colonial-era home, her stately manner, and her land-grounded wisdom had inevitably conjured up a talk with a Founding Mother herself. When I learned much later that her first name was Genevieve (close enough to *Guinevere* for me), the myth layered itself further with a bit of Arthurian weight.

At her door asking only for water, I apparently passed some sort of first trial and was invited into the parlor.

"Tea?"

"Yes, please."

She returned in a few minutes with a silver tray, navigating her ninety years with only the slightest wobble. The tea was British, warm, and came in pot and cup, rather than iced and sugared as I had expected. On the tray with the two cups were several baked sweets.

"Now, Mr. Hiscoe," as she poured the tea, "tell me about your history."

I had not, up until that minute, thought of myself as someone with a history, only a somewhat shaky future. And up to that minute I don't remember anyone ever calling me "Mr. Hiscoe" without the rancid stink of irony in the air. I was turning twenty-four in a few months, but I looked much younger. When most people first met me, they assumed that I probably wasn't old enough to legally drive a car on public streets. Just before leaving to hike the trail, I had dropped by my university's Registrar Office to get an undergraduate transcript. When I walked up to the counter, the attractive twenty-something behind it had looked up from shuffling her papers, popped her gum, and announced to all, "Sorry son, you're in the wrong office. Admissions is down the hall on the right."

So "Mr." sounded nice to me. I sat up a bit straighter in the chair.

I told her about my early plans to be a military officer and about how learning a little history about the long, vicious, bungling European colonization of Southeast Asia had shaken that ambition out of me. About how during my first college class I met a Marine and naval corpsman just back from Vietnam who threatened to damage me if I signed up—and then sent me off to the library with a list of history books to check out. She nodded. Reading her obituary the spring after we met, I learned that her son had been killed thirty years earlier during the Normandy invasion.

"Then what?"

I told her about quitting the engineering program in my freshman year (I later learned that Mr. Fred Hutchinson had been an engineering professor), about becoming an English major and loving my college years, and about my aborted start at graduate school.

"Why did you leave?"

"I'd been in school for sixteen years. I wanted something more, something real." I ended with an embarrassing display of sophomoric learning, spouting out a mishmash of what I could remember of

Thoreau's explanation of why he went Walden: "I wanted to live deliberately, to front the essential facts of life so that when I died I wouldn't discover that I hadn't really existed."

She smiled, and I detected not even the slightest whiff of either condemnation or condescension.

"So what did you do when you left your graduate studies?"

"Construction work, usually fourteen hours a day, seven days a week. Travelled around the United States during the summers with the money I saved. Then started trying to save up to hike the Appalachian Trail."

"And now that dream is over one third done. What future do you have planned once you reach Georgia?"

I liked her certainty that I would finish the walk, but begin bouncing all over the chair nonetheless. I had suspected that this question would eventually pounce, but when she asked it I had no better answer now than I did before I knocked on her door. Or before I boarded the plane to Maine. Or before I started college. Neither of us, of course, had any idea that she would be three months dead when I reached Springer Mountain the next May.

Earlier, when she was out of the room preparing tea, I'd walked around the parlor in my socks. My muddy boots were out on the porch. Aside from three chairs and a table, the room had little furniture. But there were shelves of books, stocked with copies of novels and poetry that I had read in college. None of my parents' friends had books like these in their houses. One slim volume, *Substance*, shelved in with the rest, had "Hutchinson" on the spine. I meant to ask her if it were hers but only remembered hours too late, when I was making supper in the October Mountain Shelter.

I had no plan. But looking past her shoulder to her books, I quickly developed a tactic.

"I think I want to be a writer."

She smiled. "No profession is more noble, nor more important. But, as you know, it is a very difficult one with which to earn a living.

A pause.

"Did you write much while at university?"

"Well, just term papers." I decided not to mention my

masterwork, a poem about the harsh inconveniences inflicted on society by traffic stoplights, crafted in the manner of George Herbert, a 17th century English religious mystic.

"Are you keeping a journal on your Appalachian Trail journey?"

It was an idea I had fully intended to implement when I was planning the trip back home on my ragged couch. But the plan had petered out into an occasional couple of cryptic words and phrases in the margins of my trail guides. Beside the entry for Mrs. Fred Hutchinson, Washington, Mass, I now find the Nobel-ready, "nice lady, visit, cookies"—wisdom I had gleaned a month earlier from a north bound thru-hiker up in Maine.

"No, Ma'am. I'm usually too tired at the end of the day."

She smiled again, a long smile that bought enough time for her to package a strategy, one part New England practicality, another personal graciousness.

"Have you considered returning to graduate school for some additional training and a chance to gain additional experience with your craft?"

That in fact was my plan, as hobbling as it was, and I said so.

"Well, Mr. Hiscoe, you have shown an admirable dash of both ingenuity and perseverance in your journey thus far. I talk to many ambitious trekkers who stop here. Many of them are young, and most are walking this path in hopes of finding their way. They travel on their feet in order to find their voices. Most find them, I think, and many write later to tell me of their many accomplishments. I hope that you will too. Remember what W. B. Yeats wrote late in his life."

I was surprised when she seemed to choke up a bit at this point. It wasn't what I expected from her, and I didn't at the time understand where the emotion came from.

"Even the wisest man grows tense," she continued, "Before he can accomplish fate/Know his work or choose his mate."

I knew the quotation. It was from Yeats' great funeral poem, "Under Ben Bulben."

I shared the shelter that night with a guy about my age who drew his water from the stream that slugged in front, in spite of the admonition in the guide book that the creek was polluted and that

Mrs. Fred W. Hutchinson would supply water at her home, six-tenths of a mile north. "I went by her place," he said. "But I didn't have time to stop."

In the back-and-forth in the trail community after her death that March, I learned that Genevieve Hutchinson had indeed authored several collections of well-received poetry, including *Substance.*

I wasn't, of course, able to write her when I finished my walk or later to tell her how the rest of my life went. I did, in fact, become a writer of sorts, accomplishing my fate by writing annual reports, marketing literature, ghostwritten articles and speeches for corporate executives, and scholarly pieces on medieval literature. It never was Hemingway, but it was mostly honorable work and provided a good living for me and others I cared for.

I suspect Mrs. Hutchinson would not entirely approve of all that is carried in this particular book. She would most assuredly not be pleased with its liberal dash of snark and irony.

But I hope that she would be pleased that snarcasm had little place in the way I tried to raise my children or in the ways I worked with my employees and colleagues for forty years. The implacable respect with which she treated the skinny, dirty, clueless young man she invited into her home left a huge impression on me. I have tried my best to honor it.

CONNECTICUT

Understanding the trials of following a wide path

Judiciously share your juice

If, as I was hoofing the road to Salisbury's town center, Alexander Hamilton had bounded out of a nicely appointed roadside colonial, straightened his powdered wig, and sniffed dismissively at my untutored opinions on the National Bank, I would have taken it in stride. No one, in fact, stepped angrily off the sidewalk as I passed. But no one extended a hearty welcome or friendly smile either.

I took the half-mile road walk into Salisbury, Connecticut, without much enthusiasm. The word out from NOBOs was that this beautiful, quintessential New England jewel had gotten long tired of the likes of us, that no one was going to be laying out any welcome mat, no happy parade planned for yet another dirty stranger in town hauling around a backpack.

1973 was, in fact, a very interesting time to be hiking the trail. The butt end of the hippies' "back to nature" fashion and a couple of best-selling books were dramatically ramping up the number of hikers wandering through the tiny, mostly rural towns along the AT. In 1970, when I first started thinking about doing the hike, fewer than seventy people had hiked its entire route since it became a continuous Maine to Georgia pathway in the mid 30s. In the next two years alone, 1971 and 1972, that number almost doubled, with slightly more than sixty hikers registering their completion with the Appalachian Trail Conference. In 1973, eighty additional folks snowballed the list. Facing this exponential growth of wanderers, the small communities that line the trail were beginning to feel the growing pains, especially since a disproportionate number of the hikers were of that tender age when a few rowdy beers in town seem a birthright. And after a week or two on the trail, everyone looks a little disreputable and scary.

In the north, the trail sat on land that was growing more valuable every day as nearby urban areas eyed it for expansion and second homes. In the south, federal civil rights legislation had reawakened a hostile anti-government heritage. In this super-charged atmosphere, the 1968 National Trails System Act was beginning to stir a degree of paranoia among some landowners, even ones who had long welcomed the AT on their property. The law now established the AT and the Pacific Crest Trails as national treasures that could and should be protected forever, with federal dollars and with federal power if appropriate. Rumors were flying about among the easily spooked that any day now Lyndon Johnson might spring from his grave and show up with a host of federal marshals and lawyers to seize the family farm. Facing an invasion of alien walkers and uncertainty about how the Trails Act might be implemented, even some judicious and friendly landowners were pushing the trail off their property onto nearby roads. For hours at a time in the early 1970s the most colorful scenery on the AT might sometimes be the red, white, and black "NO TRESPASSING" signs tacked up every hundred feet or so along the pavement you were pounding around a small town near the trail.

As it turns out, the National Park Service and other government agencies partnered with local trail clubs, rural service organizations, public-spirited and savvy landowners, and non-profit groups like The Nature Conservancy to turn the AT implementation of the Trails Act into what is now considered one of the most successful private/public projects in our history. In a few nasty cases, eminent domain and other legal maneuvers were used, but on the whole most landowners ended up being proud of their part in protecting what has become maybe our most beloved national park. And in the last few decades of the 20th century, as seasonal thru-hikers surged through these small towns by the thousands and reached a critical mass, everyone would get more comfortable with each other. Few hikers roll into town with their pockets overloaded with dollars, but as our numbers swelled, the money incrementally accumulated to make a nice enough pile and became a huge boost, even salvation, to the economies of many a mountain community. Dozens of these wonderful places now proudly pull the trail and its hobos to their bosoms.

But in 1973 the verdict was still out.

Even back then, I wasn't expecting any sort of stridently unpleasant reception in Salisbury. And I didn't receive one. I did expect to feel a little out of place, though. And I did.

The town is not only archetypal New England; it is archetypal New England toney. As an easy commute from New York City and a comfortable Berkshire destination, the village tends to attract people with deep pockets and mountains of sophistication. The road into town is lined with perfectly restored colonials, one of which, I was told weeks earlier, was summer home to Barbra Streisand. That particular rumor turned out not to be true, but the town has been harbor to, among others, Meryl Streep, Jill Clayburgh, Rip Torn, and Laura Linney. Margaret Hamilton, the Wicked Witch of the West in the original *Wizard of Oz* movie, spent her final years there. Predictably enough, there was a big ballyhoo when some telecommunications executive of pedestrian taste first recommended an unsightly cell tower for hills around Salisbury. No wind power there, for sure, not in their sculpture-rich and manicured backyards.

If, as I was hoofing towards the town center, Alexander Hamilton had bounded out of a nicely appointed roadside bungalow, straightened his powdered wig, and sniffed dismissively at me for my untutored opinions on the National Bank, I would have taken it in stride. No one, in fact, stepped off the sidewalk as I passed (much less raised a shirt to reveal a pistol in his belt, as one gentleman did a week or two later on the main street of Duncannon, Pennsylvania). But no one extended a hearty welcome or friendly smile either. I felt ragged and uppity as I headed to resupply in the village's small grocery. It wasn't my sort of town, and I hardly expected to be nourished at the font of community while there.

I was wrong once again.

After a quick hump through the store to select my groceries, I claimed a stately wrought iron bench in the small shady park across the street. The intent was to promptly sort my supplies and head smartly out of town. But the huge, ripe peach I had splurged on lulled me into sitting for a little longer, and with food in the belly, sun filtering through old elms, and a break from the usual labor of slogging large weights along ragged paths, biology quietly seized the rudder. I was probably snoring softly and contentedly when the bench moved a bit and I realized I had company.

I didn't catch his name that day, and I have only the sketchiest sense of what he looked like. By the time I was fully awake, he was seated next to me, which made it awkward to look to my right to see his face. What I could see was a sack of groceries on the ground next to a pack that instantly made all the important identifications. It was worn and stained, to be sure, with the zipper missing on one outside pocket, no doubt teethed repeatedly by dozens of marauding shelter mice. But it was also put together as neatly, pure and sleek as a wild pony, its form following its functions as closely as if Frank Lloyd Wright had showed up at Amicalola Falls and architected it himself. That's what I saw on the ground in front of me, and that's what immediately let me know I was sitting next to a thru-hiker. That and his boots, which were the huge Tyrolean mega-stompers that we all wore then, five pounds of leather and Vibram, ragged and whacked but oiled so carefully and thoroughly they looked like something you might stuff in the oven for the mainstay of a holiday dinner.

Neither of us said anything. We both well knew the liturgy of the service that should unfold next. With the fluid moves of synchronized Olympic swimmers, we simultaneously dipped into our respective grocery bags. From mine, a cheerful bag of twenty four bite-sized miniature cake donuts, each brightly coated with enough powered sugar to mask the emulsifiers and pyrophosphates that anchored the fine arc of lard that circled around their dainty center.

From his, a glass gallon bottle of orange juice, sweating down its sides, watery trails of cool streaming down a banner proclaiming, "made fresh from pulp proudly harvested and frozen in Immokalee, Florida."

For the next fifteen peace-filled minutes, the bottle passed back and forth, the bag shuffled between us.

Then I started up the ritualistic conversation: "When did you start in Georgia?'

"March 17th. You?"

"June 5. Took two days to get over Katahdin though. See much snow?"

"Two feet in the Smokies, just rain everywhere else. Lots of bugs for you?"

"All of Maine, most of New Hampshire and some of Vermont. A nightmare. Should be mostly gone by now though," I assured him.

A nod, a pause, and then he picked up the conversation: "You like the Dunham boots?"

"Heavy, but comfortable. Would like to try to find something lighter if I had the money."

"Yep."

I asked the first question every thru-hiker gets from almost every weekender, day hiker, or townie: "Seen many snakes?"

"Four hundred and six, mostly copperheads. Partnered with one, in fact, for about 500 miles down south."

"Yeah?"

"Taught her how to walk. Had to first get her off her belly and then step it up to keep up with me. I'm a thru-hiker, and Maine's the game."

"Yeah?"

"Turnabout's fair play, though. She taught me how to crawl like a champion."

"Good for the long uphills in Virginia?"

"Exactly."

A few seconds of quiet and then he picked up the story again: "Made her a very nice pack of her own. From an old sock."

"Carry her own food?"

"Exactly."

"Shelter mice?"

"Exactly."

"Taste just like chicken?"

"Exactly what she said."

"She here in town?"

"Nope, got off the trail down in Pennsylvania. Plagued by a sore stomach, huge blisters mostly. Think she's staying with an aunt just north of Lehigh Gap. Probably sitting in the den right now, both of 'em, feet up, glued to *Wild Kingdom*."

With a heart full of compassion, I tried to steer him down the path toward some consolation: "You part friends?"

"Yes and no. Truth is, she ended up sticking her fangs in my very last nerve."

"Happens. Hard to be with anybody twenty-four hours a day."

"Yep."

"Poor hygiene?," I continued.

"Yes. But that wasn't the core problem. You know that Beatles' song, 'Paperback Writer'?"

"Sure. A favorite."

"Wouldn't be anymore if you'd spent time with her. Hummed it all day, every day, every step, every slither of every foot north."

"Annoying," I sagely concluded.

"Not the worst part though."

"Yeah?"

"She also sang it."

"Couldn't carry a tune?"

"Had a beautiful voice actually. Harmonious as Eden. Miss that voice a lot, actually. Nope, it was the words. Got 'em wrong. Over and over again."

"That can be annoying."

"DAMMMMN straight. Sixty or seventy times a day, over and over: 'DII A AH MOND BACK—da da da dum da dum da dum de dum—RATTLER!—da da da dum da dum da dum de dum."

"That's pretty evil. She doing it on purpose?," I asked.

"She was a cold-blooded reptile, dude."

"Play air guitar?," I asked, throwing out the worst of all sins in my book.

"Every time. Looked stupid. Annoying as hell."

"Did Hendrix too, I bet."

"Yeah?"

"'Scuse me while I hiss at the sky?"

"Exactly. Annoying as hell. She'd grin at me every time like it was the newest joke ever. Place an imaginary guitar up behind her head, then whip it around and play it with her fangs, squirming down on her back in the grass, looking stupid."

"Once it reaches that point, best to go your separate ways,"

I wisely advise.

"Absolutely." A pause and a painful, scattered, thoughtful look off towards the Connecticut hills. "But I really miss her sometimes, man. Some days two-thirds way through a long climb I'd give anything to hear her go through one of her Monty Python sketches again. Cracked me up. Word for word, nailed it every time. 'Bring out your dead, bring out your dead.' Or 'Ah'm French! Why do you think I have this out-rrrageous accent, you silly king?' She'd have me on crawling on the ground, spittin' out my water."

We were quiet for a minute, working on the orange juice and donuts.

He picked up the thread again: "Nice town."

"Just what I was thinking."

"Might want to visit here someday after the trail."

"Maybe not alone the next time?," I suggest.

"Exactly."

"Write her, dude. Don't let her slide away that easily."

"Guess you're right. I'll think on it."

Stomachs full, bodies rested, souls at ease, junk food gone, we both finished packing and headed off back to the trail.

You'll probably want to know what happened to him. But I can't help.

The storybook ending to the Communion on the Bench would have our families exchanging Christmas cards most years for the past four decades, maybe even vacationing together up in Banff a few times as we got settled in our careers and had enough money for skiing vacations. But as it does (but shouldn't) life got busy and complicated for me after the trail, and I never saw him again. I do know one detail from his life though.

I received a single letter a year or so later. As was probably inevitable, he spent much of the rest of the trek suffering from giardia. It may not have been the best of ideas to have shared orange juice with him. Drinking from a mutual container is not prudent.

So we didn't see each other ever again. But for me at least that thirty minutes on the Salisbury bench has been living itself out fully alive, fully real, somewhere in the DNA of every day in my life, informing the possibilities of what friendship can be.

The connection people can share when they travel a similar path is as powerful as the nuclear bond. Especially if getting there is hard, and especially if the compensation has little to do with money or prestige.

In every job I've held the last forty years, I've tried to duplicate that bond with those I work for and with. It hasn't happened every time, or even very often. But when it did, it was as full of power as a parent grizzly in protective charge, a rattlesnake in its coil.

Maybe not let your blankie get too comfy?

Connecticut was like that job that you are doing just fine, after surviving a challenging time of apprenticeship, one where you have settled into the rhythms and have mastered the panics, pushes, and pulls of the learning curve. One that has its quiet satisfactions and that repays your efforts nicely, one you feel contented with.

This will be a short chapter. It has to be. Because the truth is that I can't remember much from the rest of the fifty AT miles in Connecticut. Except that I was deeply contented for the next three days. And that itself is an interesting story, though necessarily a brief one.

It's not that the state isn't filled with the stuff of Sierra Club calendars and classic walks. I do remember an hour or two in several mini-gorges where fairy-fable brooks drove time in little, magic circles of beauty and perfection. If two tiny blue, furry gnomes, a couple of small angels with gossamer wings of light, and a miniature, overly wise mastodon had joined me for a sit on a smooth rock beside one of the pools in these ravines, it would have come as no surprise to me. And somewhere along the way there was a titanic stand of 150-foot white pines—later destroyed by tornadoes in 1987—that were growing strong long before the American Revolution. Then there were the hour-long saunters on old woods roads beside a classic New England river, where once I popped momentarily back into normal consciousness to notice that all the huge trees along the road were in rows, lined up in straight lines, perfect diagonals, exact right angles, for hundreds of yards, as geometrical as a well-drilled infantry battalion on a parade ground, a lumber farm turned cathedral by being left alone to grow by the rules of its own nature long past the years when it might have normally been harvested. And at the south end of the state, the terrible beauty of a large tract of land completely denuded by gypsy moths, as efficient in their hunger and destruction as high explosives on a European battlefield.

But my favorite memory from the state is a literary one. May all the deities in all the universes bless the army of volunteers who laid out the trail decades ago and who now spend their weekends, vacations, and retirements keeping it in shape for the rest of us to wander. And a special shelter in the heavens must surely wait for the literate ones who prepare the maps and guidebooks that try to keep us on the right path.

Except that sometimes what they produce is as about as useful as a box of rocks.

One example, and I'll move on (probably in the wrong direction if I choose to actually follow the exact words from many AT guides): my 1972 edition of the *Guide to the Appalachian Trail in Massachusetts and Connecticut* promises that "on the forest maintenance road between Falls Village Bridge and Bunker Hill, the forest growth… is especially fine." I'm sure that it was, and I was glad enough to be reminded to pay attention to it.

"Next pay attention at exactly the five-mile point in the section," it earnestly exhorts, though not in these exact words. Not at 5.137 miles into the section, mind you. Not at 4.8654 miles either. Exactly at five miles.

I tried, but I wasn't worthy.

Problem is, the Appalachian Trail doesn't have mile markers like federal interstates. I did, at some point, get pretty good at judging distances, say maybe within a tenth of a mile or so. This eventually happens by some inexorable natural process at some point when you slow down and walk everywhere you go for months at a time.

They got my interest, I'll admit it. The promised tree they wanted me not to miss became an obsession for a good hour and a half. Walking that stretch of Connecticut backwoods, I wanted to see that tree as eagerly as my grandchildren and nerdy friends await the latest rollout of the *Star Wars* franchise. As my inner GPS began to light and blink, I looked to the right, I looked to the left, my eyes eagerly pierced the pines fore and aft, reset, and then pierced again.

But, alas, my arbor ardor was never requited. Somehow I must have just walked right past "twenty-five ft. to the right… a native Norway (red) pine."

Not that I'd know a Norway pine if it was growing out my cooking pot. If anyone finds it though, I'd really like to have a photo (david.hiscoe@gmail.com).

So, at any rate, I do still carry memories from Connecticut. But they are not imprinted in memory with bright colors and sharp lines like the days on Mt. Washington or Katahdin or the night on Mount Greylock. They are soft, an imprecise blur of cozy and snug. They are not the memories I call up each night as I drift off to sleep calibrating the day's this-and-that.

Seven hundred miles down the trail and I had become fit, capable and efficient, the walking largely pain-free and automatic. Cooking, washing, resupplying, putting out the sleeping bag, ignoring unfamiliar night sounds, repacking the pack in the morning? I did these economically now, without particular challenge or ordeal. Heading down the AT had become a job—not the worst job in the world (more about this later in Pennsylvania), but not the best job either. Not one of those jobs that slowly kills you with boredom, or that job where someone else's cruelty, thoughtlessness, or ambitions ground you for hours while you are at work and for hours later at home as you stew in your indignities.

Connecticut was more like that job that you are doing just fine, after surviving a challenging time of apprenticeship, one where you have settled into the rhythms and have mastered the panics, pushes, and pulls of the learning curve. One that has its quiet satisfactions and that repays your efforts nicely, one that you feel contented with and happy for.

But also one that promises no great excitements, no heart-pounders on most days. When you go in each morning you know that nothing will happen for the next ten hours that you will remember ten years down the road. This particular point in the inevitable trajectories of a job can be exactly the right place to stay for just the right amount of time, a time for building strength, compassing out another path, or just enjoying the coast of life. But it's not a good place to linger.

After leaving Salisbury, I can't remember talking to another human being for the rest of the entire state of Connecticut. This can't actually be the way it really happened, but I've thought about it a lot while I worked on this chapter. It may as well be true.

I was glad to be moving on to New York.

NEW YORK AND NEW JERSEY

Living in the wilderness doesn't necessarily require you to be a beast

Smiles are nice, but trust those who stand and deliver

"My daughter told her mother that you may have the absolute whitest butt in the state of New York."

My first twenty-four hours in the populous state of New York were, in fact, the least solitary time of my hike.

For most of the AT trip, I was alone, or at least as alone as one could be on the eastern seaboard of the United States in the late twentieth century. I had started in Maine with a long-time hiking buddy, but a family emergency (as well as size fourteen feet, as flat, long, and hard-smacked as the landing deck on an aircraft carrier) had sent him home after the first one hundred miles. Later I'd occasionally team up with someone for a few days or even a week. But when I wasn't in the Smokies or the Shenandoah or the White Mountains, it wasn't at all uncommon to see only a handful of people in a day. Several times in the south in the frozen days of April, I went almost a week without running into anyone at all. Sharing a shelter at night with another hiker or two was cause for an excited celebration on my part, a mini-party marked usually with me obsessively running my mouth until my new best friends took to their bags and pretended sleep.

Ironically enough, though, I avoided the AT for decades after I reached Springer Mountain, thinking—with a staggering lack of context and proportion, given my own solitary experience—that the trail was in danger of being overrun with the likes of me, that I'd had my share of a scarce resource and ought to let others have their chance at it. The eighty some thru-hikers who swarmed the trail in 1973 seemed at the time like some sort of latter day, woodsy Normandy, albeit without tanks, mortars, heroes, or mass early death.

Then in the mid-1990s on vacation I happened to drive through a New England trail town in July and discovered what an invasion really looked like. On the outskirts of the village, we passed a couple of clean but raggedy types eating ice cream on the sidewalk, all cares gone for a day back in civilization. "Look," I excitedly shouted to my wife, "thru-hikers," like I'd been the first to spot a Carolina parakeet since the last one chirped its final song back when Woodrow Wilson was president. In the next block a half dozen of the same, all in shower clogs, were huddled around a pay phone. A block later the public square bloomed with at least thirty, some with packs, some with the happy grins of those who have put on their town clothes and left all burdens back at the hostel. At this point I pulled over and struck up a conversation with an overly slender, overly tanned guy, all happiness, Gore-Tex, face hair, and calves.

"Yep, we tend to travel in waves these days. The AT marching band. There's probably seventy-five of us in town already, most taking a zero day to get ready for New Hampshire. I've personally seen at least forty-five that I know myself, and I've heard a dozen others are kicking it to make town for pizza tonight at the Episcopal church."

And that in a rain shell is the most profound change in AT sociology since Earl Schaffer carried his painfully uncomfortable army rucksack up Katahdin in 1948. For 124 days Schaffer was largely alone with his war ghosts and his highway maps. Current trekkers are likely to meet dozens of new brothers and sisters their first day on the trail and then move north or south with a core group of familiars ready made to share both the nasties and the glories of the trip. Even if a most cherished goal is to find a chunk of time alone to sort out whatever put them on the trail to begin with, today's hikers have the option, whenever isolation starts cuddling up toward desolation, to choose to slip easily into a social life as full of possibilities as that first day when you check into your freshman dorm.

It wasn't like that for the class of 1973.

When I hit the first road crossing in New York and ran into a local trail club out for the ten mile walk into Pawling, I had apparently become way more similar to that awkward kid who didn't get out much in high school—the one you know is going to ruin the happy vibes at the first dorm party, the one who drinks too much, talks all night about his awesome collection of entomology photographs, and ends the evening either throwing up on somebody's shoe or peeing in the closet.

Unfortunately, this is not a comparison that I invented for myself.

It was—the leader of the club's outing told me at the end of the day—the picture that forged in her head as soon as she invited me to tag along and I started spouting a soup of desperate "thank-you's." I had the dreamy look, another clubber revealed, of the two-year old you used to see standing out under the clothesline on wash day, one hand on his favorite blanket still drying on the rope, the other hand with a thumb in his pathetic mouth.

"You were a little scary, but we couldn't figure out how to politely disinvite you."

That being said, they turned out to be an incredibly nice crowd to walk along with, though most were at least thirty years older and all, unlike me, probably had more than $75 in their bank accounts. A mechanical engineer, a couple of pediatricians, several practicing lawyers, an international arms dealer/sometime privateer (just kidding), a building contractor, two plumbers, and a half dozen retirees, they were a good mix of interests and professions, and filled with good conversation. And it was pretty heady that a lot of that conversation turned out to be about me. In 1973, thru-hikers were still a rarity, and none in this crowd had ever met one, though their club walks went out every week, with snowshoes in the winter if necessary. Earlier in the hike, I'd met folks who were interested in what I'd been doing. But now I was nearing the halfway mark, had some credibility, looked the part, and we had a whole afternoon to fill. There were the usual questions about food, equipment, motive, and animals. But, especially when I was walking with the doctors and lawyers, the conversation was often about how I paid for the trip.

"How can you afford to take five months off?"

"Doesn't cost much. I worked a lot of overtime to save up."

"No, not that kind of cost. The cost to your career. How can you just leave your job?"

"Sadly, you have to choose a job where nobody cares if you disappear, one with a lot of turnover. Helps to work where alcohol benders and parole revocations aren't uncommon. Lots of times nobody much notices if a carpenter's assistant doesn't show back up on Monday morning."

The contractor snorted.

At this point we were all largely grouped together, walking in a large clump, the AT now on a little used two-lane through the countryside. At least ten people heard the next exchange.

"What's your biggest worry?"

"An injury serious enough to stop the trip. I couldn't afford even a couple of days in town to recover, much less a doctor's visit. One x-ray would wipe me out at this point."

The doctors didn't snort.

"But so far so good. Mostly though, it's becoming clear that I'm going to run out of money before I run out of trail. My father's patience with the construction work and vagabonding mountain summers is exhausted. No hope for rescue there. My friends have already done all that they can. We'll just have to see."

This became the recurring topic of conversation over the next few hours as we strolled through some of the more beautiful valleys and pastoral highlands on the Appalachian Trail. I haven't seen the survey yet that shows this, but I'd be willing to bet one of the biggest surprises for most thru-hikers is just how handsome the trail is in New York and New Jersey, everything from the crossing of the Hudson to the rugged palisades and ravines just forty miles north of New York City, to the pine wildernesses in New Jersey, to the miles of granite outcroppings over Greenwood Lake. The trail now largely files through the woods for the day's walk north of Pawling, but in 1973 it was mostly beside restful open fields on old woods roads or rural paved lanes not troubled by more than ten cars a day. It was easy walking in a gentle, romantic terrain, the sort that well-heeled folks travel to rural France or northern Scotland to ooh over before retiring with a nice glass of white in a restored castle or pricey bed and breakfast.

Had we turned past the dusty antique shop over there at the intersection of those two forgotten roads to find Albert Bierstadt or some other painter of the Hudson River School dipping brushes into the pastels on his palette, no one would have blinked. It seemed like the 19th century (or maybe 16th century Flanders?), and it was great.

The consensus was that maybe I could stop a week or two in a trail town in the South and find enough carpentry work to refill the coffers and finish the hike. At this point, this was my best stab at a plan too, though I'd have to be lucky enough to find a cheap place to stay to make it actually work. And it didn't help that the US was in a crippling recession at the time. At any rate, the problem gave us something to mull through together as we walked. And the back and forth created a sense of community that was nice, if not quite as wonderful as the moments when the cherished blankie finally used to come out of the dryer and I got carry it to my son just as *Sesame Street* came on.

We entered Pawling just at dusk, all glowing a little with the comradeship that gels around group walks through the woods.

"We're going to have dinner at a nice Italian place in town before we head home. Please join us."

An awkward silence in the parking lot at the trailhead.

"I can't really. Have to watch the cash flow. But thanks so much for asking, and thanks for sharing your day."

"Don't be ridiculous. Don't worry about the check. It's no problem. Come along."

And so I did, to the perfect ending for the afternoon. Great lasagna, bowls of fresh greens, endless calorie-rich baskets of buttery bread, and a glass of wine. The bottle came by again.

"Have another. We all agree you need it! Relax a little."

That's when they all told me how crazy lonely I'd seemed at the beginning of day. We all laughed.

A quick word on alcohol and my younger self. I come from a family where gushing fountains of scotch, bourbon, and the like had regularly created uncomfortable dramas. Drinking had little romance for me, and I skipped most of the usual debaucheries others waded through in high school and college. So at twenty-three I had exactly no physical tolerance. One glass and I was ripe and happy. Two, and I was well on the way to a lop-mouthed, grinning nap.

That may explain a little how I was completely sucker punched by what happened next.

The waitress smiled one last time, the checks were deposited in front of plates now empty except for tiny islands of smeared tomato goop, and everyone else briskly picked up his or her bill, expertly scrutinized the additions and multiplications, put down a generous tip, and headed for the cashier.

My bill remained in front of my plate as the table emptied, everyone else finished paying, and one by one stepped outside to continue the last little fragments of their after-dinner conversations, forgetful of their earlier offer and apparently oblivious to my predicament inside.

I turned the check over; it totaled a fifth of what I had left for the thirteen hundred miles to Georgia, a large part of the charge being for the two glasses of wine. I cashed a traveler's cheque (more on these later), satisfied my obligations to the restaurant, gave a ragged grin to the cashier, and walked out to join the mellow crowd in the parking lot.

"It was a great day, David. Thanks for walking with us and sharing your stories."

"Absolutely, a great time, wonderful day. Give our best to Springer Mountain."

"Send the club a card when you're finished. We'd like to hear from you. We are completely jealous of your walk. Keep dreaming, my friend."

More of these until everyone was in his or her car and headed toward home.

Still a little dizzy, but with the pleasantness of the buzz now sucked dry and spit out, I picked up the pack and started south down Old 55 to the Edward R. Murrow Municipal Park, where the town of Pawling then let thru-hikers camp, swim in the village's beautiful lake, and use the bath facilities without charge. The park was a mile wobble down the pavement in the dark. A light drizzle started on the way and grew stronger as I walked on.

Things seemed to take another sour turn when I walked through the park's entrance and into the circle of light and noise coming from the pavilion by the lake, the covered space where I'd planned to spend the night.

The beer cans, Dr. Pepper bottles, and abandoned paper plates shuffled around the area made it clear that the party had earlier been much more spread out. But now a hundred or so folks were crowded in together under the pavilion's roof, a space that looked like it was meant to cover probably no more than fifty. There were a few young children here and there, but mostly it was a crowd of older adults, the women in shapeless Bermuda shorts or summer dresses meant more for comfort than for show, the men to a person crowned with baseball caps, most embroidered with the name of a Navy ship, an army division, or a storied place of conflict from a past war. *Khe Sanh—Semper Fi* was blazed across the hat of the extremely large, extremely muscled man—the youngest I saw in the crowd, the only one who might be even close to my age—manhandling a smoky grill up under the roof as the lightning picked up. An outsized banner nailed to the front of the pavilion made it clear I'd stumbled into the annual gathering of a local veterans' group.

A brief word on my hair—because sadly enough haircuts were the chief way people quickly sized each other up in 1973, the most efficient way to tack a set of values to someone else, especially if you were in a hurry to dislike them. Think neck or knuckle tattoos today, but at a more toxic, explosive level. When I had announced before my sophomore year that I wouldn't be reapplying to any military academy and that, in fact, I would not serve in the armed forces at all, I had been disowned by my parents. It didn't help that I (a good Southern boy) also roomed with a black guy (the last I heard, now an executive with an American computing giant). So, by necessity, I paid my own way through the rest of college, mostly by working with the state prison system three days a week and full time in the summer. Which meant that, regardless of any Beatle worship I might have harbored, I kept my hair nicely trimmed. I loved college; college for me required a job; the job I had required short hair. End of that story.

I was a little past due for a trim before my hike, and fully intended to have one the morning before I left for Maine. Instead of visiting the barber though, I spent hours on the phone being questioned by a claims investigator from North Carolina Workers' Compensation about the medical procedure that derailed my earlier plans to start the trail in March. Then there was an hour frantically and impotently trying to contact my hospital and physicians to work out payment plans (more about this mess later). I barely made the plane, all hairs still intact about the ears and neck and sprouting for glory. Over the next few months, lack of money and absence of trailside barbers took their natural course. And by the time I reached New York I have to admit that I had begun to think I looked dashingly Tarzanic with a headband holding back my stringy golden locks.

Later in the summer I received a more objective take on my hippie look from a bunch of teenagers lounging outside a grocery in a small Maryland mountain town.

"What's your trail name?" they demanded as they watched me squash down a loaf of wheat bread. They had heard of the emerging AT tradition of taking on a *nom du pèlerinage* for the duration, a custom that lets hikers assume a new name that captures some core aspiration or personality trait they wanted to cultivate on the hike. The tradition wasn't yet much in practice in 1973. I only knew two people who had trail names, one—still a friend—who named himself *Peregrine* after the falcon celebrated for speed, endurance, and focus.

The other may have been the originator of the second trail naming tradition, the one where fellow hikers choose a name for you based on some dumb thing you do early in the hike. This young man was tagged his first week and henceforth universally known as the *The Eagle.* But not because of his soaring bravery, visual acuity, patriotic zeal, or general awesomeness. Rather, by day two on the trail he had irritated the total, complete hell out of everyone who had the misfortune to spend time with him. From the first handshake on, out flowed overblown, annoying boasts about his one-time exalted leadership status in the Boy Scouts.

In all fairness, I'll admit upfront that I never actually met The Eagle and have no reason to wish him ill or to blacken his reputation. I'm just passing along the wisdom of the masses. I heard his story many, many times from many, many shaken and embittered of his trail mates, good men and women all, but men and women to a soul who damned each day in which they were forced to endure his infantile, childish dreams of past glories. If all these legions of true and worthy hikers were wrong and I have slandered The Eagle here, I hasten to apologize.

Actually there was a third, but more about *The Squirrel* later in North Carolina.

"Your trail name, dude?"

"I don't have one. Haven't thought much about it."

"Well, we're calling you *Colonel Sanders*."

Manly puffs on their cigarettes and snickers by all.

"Please don't do that."

"It's perfect, dude. It's the real you, *Mon Colonel*."

His French pronunciation wasn't very good, a gratingly overblown southern version of the language of love.

"It's not cool to mock someone's accent," I reminded them.

"Nice try, but you know that's not it. You paying attention even a little bit? You talk fine [we were in Maryland, remember]. It's that Kentucky-fried, pathetic, scraggly white goatee."

His buddies laughed. One bent over in joy.

"And that hair. Tell the truth, my man. You stashing some Extra Crispy up in there in the grease? Gotta be. Share the wings, dude."

"Buckets of finger lickin'. Yum," enthused his friend.

The first week I returned to Raleigh after the hike my hair once again reared its ugly head, and another fond name was threatened. Seeing my stringy new coiffure, the construction crew I worked with immediately christened me, "The Straw Man." I gave up, folded to conventional wisdom, and got a good burring. My prized sweatband is still in my sock drawer to this day.

But when I stood out in the light rain in front of the Edward R. Murrow pavilion, the haircut was still months away, and I looked all the world like your generic hippie, a look that didn't necessarily inspire peace and love with many vets at the time.

"You lost?" It was the guy with the grill, the one whose hat, if it were to be believed, said that in 1968 he'd been running deadly Marine patrols along the DMZ or burrowing in Asian mud to escape murderous artillery barrages during the siege of Khe Sanh—just at the time I was back in college reading Vietnamese history and

English Romantic poets.

This wasn't starting well.

"Not lost, but maybe not in the right place. I'm hiking the Appalachian Trail, and the guidebook says that the pavilion is available for camping in bad weather. Didn't know that it would be occupied. Sorry to bother you."

"What's the Appalachian Trail?"

It was a question you used to get all the time in trail towns like Pawling. Like many of the people who lived within miles of the pathway, he had never heard of it.

Before I could answer, he stepped back out into the drizzle and shook my hand. "Help me pull this grill up here, and tell me what you're up to."

We got the grill in place, and I gave him the elevator speech about the hike.

"Joe, you know the Appalachian Trail goes by here?"

"Never heard of it."

"This kid is walking from Maine to Georgia."

"Dumb shit." Joe had a hat that said, *USS Independence.*

"Probably born dumb. Then worked diligently at it. Excelled at stupidity. Probably studied it in college. I wouldn't walk to the kitchen if Marilyn Monroe was hid behind the fridge, all dabbed up in Cool Whip." Thus saith a hat braided *Ranger, 173rd Airborne.*

"My grandson has been talking my head off about wanting to do that." This from an older woman with thin, purplish hair. I initially assumed she was talking about the bit with Marilyn, kitchen appliances, and delicious, sticky edibles. Couldn't blame the kid for his dream, but suspected he was in for a life of bitter disappointment.

The grandmother's hair was sculpted to great glory and held in place by a plaid scarf, perhaps the only person under the pavilion whose hairdo looked as scary as mine.

There was a crowd now. "You probably could use a cheeseburger," the Marine told me as he handed over a beer. The lasagna seemed weeks away now, and I was indeed hungry again. I never learned Semper Fi's name.

It was a great evening. I told stories about the hike, ate at least four more burgers (before consciousness shut up the suitcase and left town) and forty-three plates of potato salad, heard a dozen or so half-true tales about bear encounters in various national parks, and easily tripled my lifetime consumption of beer over the next three hours. At some point, the grandmother's kid showed up with his father, and we talked about how to plan a thru-hike, where to get the maps, how you didn't need to carry a pistol or an ax, all the basics. I enthusiastically and expertly danced through several Merle Haggard songs with somebody's wife, easily three times my age. That was after a blistering group twist to a Chubby Checker classic. Just before things went blank for me, some guy and I entertained all with a howlingly unmasterful a cappella version of "Rocky Mountain High." There was a lot of laughter, not all of it aimed at me. I have no memory of everyone leaving.

I woke up the next morning dead and in Heaven.

As my awareness gradually awakened more fully into this blessed new existence, I was facing a dazzling dance of sunlight, bedecked with ever changing patterns as it filtered through leaves on its way down to my sleeping bag hood, which rested gently on my face. Covered my face actually, I discovered as my level of alertness increased further, because the bag was upside down. My head rested on a muddy boot. Not my usual pillow, but why should things be done in Paradise as they were done on Earth? The angels, I supposed, sleep differently—choose to rest in whatever pattern and with whatever head support that their ethereal state desires. There was a heavenly breeze too, just what was needed to soothe a head that pounded away like a pod of celestial Harley Davidsons ripping down the road in first gear.

And hymns sung so sweetly. No harps (thank God), and not even the tinkling piano chording I was used to from the churches of my upbringing. Just human voices, lots of them, and they were beautiful. Singing "Nearer My God to Thee" voiced in harmonies from male and female, young and old, some in tune, some not, but beautiful en masse.

I hated to hurry along these first moments of my eternal reward, so I soaked (soaked soon to be the operative word) in them for a bit, watching the prance of radiance through down feathers (perhaps they were really just very small and delicate angel wings), now listening to "Rock of Ages."

Then came the insistent call to pee, really pee, pee in an epic way, in the way the Columbia River would push water if the Grand Coulee dam cracked into sections the size of container ships and fell away in thunderous tonnages of concrete.

I wasn't sure how urination was to be graciously handled in this particular place in God's many-roomed mansion, so I proceeded slowly, pulling back a corner of the sleeping bag hood for a stealthy reconnaissance.

To my left were two dozen folding chairs, with assorted bottoms, legs, and shoes stationed in front of each. A turn and peek from the other side of the hood. More folding chairs. A look backwards, done awkwardly, positioned on my stomach so as to least disturb the thundering bladder. Dozens of 20th century New Yorkers, all quite alive, and all singing lusty praise to the Lord, some intently looking forward above me, some—I couldn't help but notice—sneaking sideways glances at a host of covered plates stacked on a picnic table pushed to the right side of the pavilion. A quick look down and I discovered yet another picnic table, the one on which I apparently had spent the night. My normal tendency would have been to study over its cryptic command, "Eat it!—Dominic, 1964," elaborately carved on the bench below. But before I could adequately absorb the mystic depths of the commandment, my bladder once again swelled, roared, and demanded obedience to its fleshy laws.

In a moment of clarity and prudence, I took a quick look down into the bag to see how I might now be dressed, here in the Lord's house on the first day of the rest of my eternity. I wasn't. Not at all, nothing. Without the bag, all would be fully exposed to the eyes of God and all His creatures. The bladder spoke again, roaring with Old Testament earnestness.

Earthly instincts kicked in and ruled. In a spasm of punching, grabbing, and stretching, I wrapped my sleeping bag around my waist, hobbled off the picnic table, and—dodging among and between dozens of chairs and parishioners—coyoteed out of the pavilion up a path along the lake. Fifty yards out, I swerved into the trees, and parted water with the urgency with which God once saved Moses and all those he led into the wilderness.

Ten or so minutes later, I sat, shaken, embarrassed, my bag around me toga-style, on a nice patch of grass just up the hill from the picnic grounds and listened as the service ended with a fine version of "Just as I Am."

The last time I had been in a church had been Sunday, May 10, 1970, six days after the Ohio National Guard shot thirteen students at Kent State University and three days after I marched in my first ever anti-war demonstration. For years, I had pestered everyone around me with arguments about why the war was somewhere between a big mistake and a sorry betrayal of American ideals. I had long before stopped carrying my draft card and hadn't requested a student deferment for the 1970 school year, deciding to let the new draft lottery decide whether or not I would have to go to jail.

But I had drawn the line at marches. They seemed stupid to me, clichéd at best and at worst just pale imitations of the civil rights demonstrations that had so powerfully changed American history while I was a younger teen. I had often stood at the sidelines of anti-war parades, and they had always seemed too much like unintentional, low-grade insults to the African Americans and others who had put their lives at risk by having the gall to walk the middle of the street proclaiming the need for some small teaspoon of justice. The chanting and theatrics of my anti-war mates had little appeal. But the invasion of Cambodia and the killings of American students by American soldiers at Kent State made my squeamish distinctions seem foolish. So I had joined tens of thousands of local citizens and North Carolina students in a march down Raleigh's main street and onto the State Capitol grounds for a rally.

The roads, to be sure, were filled with the usual suspects, folks who had been on dozens, if not hundreds, of these marches. But I was particularly struck by how many other people I met had felt compelled by the shootings to come out for their first public demonstration.

One other twenty-year old newbie at the event—though probably not there by choice—especially sticks in my mind. "Sticks" being exactly the proper word because it was his bayonet that established the relationship between us.

I was a marshal for the walk, my job being to wear a special blue armband and try to keep everyone in line and peaceful. And all went well and orderly until the street we were on dead ended at the Capitol grounds and the back of the line began to drive up against those in the lead who had stopped and had nowhere to go. Things quickly started to get out of hand; folks at the front of the procession began to be pushed, then pushed harder, then crushed in ways that threatened to be serious. Near the front of the group, I was shoved steadily and inevitably forward until I was stopped, base of the neck first, against the extended rifle and fixed blade of one of the North Carolina National Guardsmen who had been called up and deployed to protect the Capitol.

He was about my age, just as scared, visibly shaking just as much as I was. I could hear marshals further back in the crowd shouting for people to stop moving forward. But the press of people continued inexorably, and there was no physical way, someone's chest against the rear of my shoulders, for me to back away from his bayonet.

I don't know what his orders were. Maybe an officer gave a command I couldn't hear through all the screaming, or maybe he just acted on his own. But he backed up a step, moved into port arms stance, and brought his weapon up against his chest. The line of troopers to his left and right did the same.

"I hate this shit."

He said it twice, looking right at me.

"Me too. I'm sorry. Thanks."

Speeches were made, and then we all turned around and went back to campus.

That Sunday I went with a friend and her family to the church I had grown up in, the church in which I was baptized and where I had attended my mother's funeral. The minister was new to me though—perhaps a vacation stand in, and I didn't like him much, put off by his corny jokes and his bitter obsessions with sex and socialism. I don't remember the core of his sermon that day, but I do remember his final prayer, a genuinely moving and timely request that his parishioners pray for our soldiers, sailors, and marines in Southeast Asia.

But then his prayer took a final turn that sent me leaping out of the pew with spastic and uncontrollable rage. At least I didn't seem able to control it at the time.

His final words began admirably, I thought, calling on Jesus to provide daily guidance and wisdom for the young Americans who were fighting our war for us. But soon he quickly turned his attention to the home front, in words so inflammatory that I remember them clearly to this day:

"We also beseech," his voice rose in volume and hysteria to ask, "You, Lord Jesus, to protect us from the deceitful Communists that we see this week in our own hometown, abandoning Your narrow way for the wide streets right here in Raleigh, abusing the blessings of the freedom that Your Father so freely gave them as their birthright."

I had been on those streets, and I had seen no communists, just a strange, lumped up mixture of concerned older citizens, students struggling to understand how the nation could continue to offer their generation up to meaningless, violent death, contingents of Baptists from the more liberal church down the street, and a small group of the drugged out sorts you always found at demonstrations at the time.

Then his knife pushed more deeply:

"Your word has taught us to forgive even Judas. But it is also true that You promised the sword to those who cry 'peace, peace' when our enemies deserve no peace. By your Grace, reveal to us who gather in Your house the right sword to close up the mouths of those whose deeds mock Your word."

Having branded us Judases and blasphemers, he then spat out a reference or two to traitors and stampeded to conclusion with a final request that our elected Christian leaders find effective ways to, as he said, "Cleanse our blessed schools and colleges from their errors. In Jesus's name, Amen."

In the version I usually tell about what happened next, I walk out in the middle of this peroration, striding proudly and erect past row after row of startled parishioners, holding my hands aloft to give the peace sign to anyone who raised eyes up from his or her prayers.

There is, however, a less flattering version that also makes the rounds. The father of one of my childhood friends, for instance, would insist tomorrow if you asked him that I was instead extending my middle finger to at least some of my neighbors as I sashayed up the aisle and out the door.

If his version is true—and I deeply hope that it is not—I am at least three-fourths deeply ashamed and embarrassed by my childish and churlish behavior. But I'm not too ashamed to admit that just a little of me would also be a little proud of my younger self.

And now, back to Pawling, New York, and my nakedness displayed among the holy.

As the crowd at the pavilion shuffled folding chairs, pushed picnic tables from the rear of the shelter back in line with the one on which I'd apparently passed out, and began setting up an after-service lunch, I watched with trepidation as three middle-aged men broke off from the crowd and headed up the hill toward me, one carrying my sleeping pad and boots, another holding at arm's length a wad of my clothing, and the third shouldering my pack.

"My wife says you have the whitest feet she's ever seen." I learned later that he was the pastor.

I did. My feet hardly ever saw the sun, earning their fishlike, zombie hue from months inside of socks that were always some place on the spectrum between damp and soaked. I wondered if the feet had been hanging out the end of the sleeping bag throughout the service, or just particularly noteworthy as I made my retreat.

"I'm really sorry about all of this. I'm not usually this way. I'm really embarrassed." I paused to try to come up with some witticism to defuse the awkwardness. "At least, unlike Lot, my nakedness was fully covered by my bag when you found me." Not really Johnny Carson material, but the best I could do.

The three looked at each other, telegraphing something of significance that I couldn't read clearly just yet.

The grey-haired man with my boots broke the silence. "Well, son"—he paused and smiled, and I knew some joke at my expense was on the way—"my daughter told her mother that you may also have the absolute whitest butt in the state of New York."

They all laughed.

"You weren't in the best shape this morning when we came in to start setting up. Bet you also don't remember anything that you said to us—or to John's daughter." The truth was that I didn't remember saying anything at all, and wasn't sure I had, especially to anyone's daughter.

"I am so sorry. I just wish there were something I could do to make this all go away."

"We understand," said the guy I recognized from his Ranger hat and his enthusiastic Twist at last night's party. "To be fair, I'm not sure that the vets around here are the best influence on young people. I'd avoid them in the future if I were you."

"There is one thing we'd like you to do." This from the pastor.

"Please join us for lunch. We have fixed way more than we can eat, and I think you'll enjoy yourself."

"Yes, please," seconded John. "But you may want to avoid trying to strike up any rapport with my daughter. I pretty sure that she's seen all of you she needs to for now."

I did join them. It was a wonderful lunch, and they were wonderful people. I never was introduced to John's daughter though.

In fact, I'm not even sure if she ever really existed. I suspect that she was probably just thrown in to make it a better story.

Sometimes you can't climb high enough to escape how low we are

A fox in a chicken wire box the size of a refrigerator. Her neighbor, a very bored, disturbed black bear in slightly bigger display. And a large group of children crowding around, completely delighted to be seeing a real fox, a real bear.

The AT crosses the Hudson River less than forty miles north of New York City, dipping to its lowest elevation where the trail crosses the Hudson River, just below where Benedict Arnold betrayed the details of the Great Chain across the river, the defense that was supposed to keep the British from bringing their warships up to attack West Point during the Revolution.

The river is a half a mile wide—wild, powerful, and as beautiful as a leopard. Drop a stranger on Anthony's Nose on its east bank and she'd probably guess she was closer to the Karakoram than to a major American metropolis. And crossing it is especially profound when done slowly on the pedestrian catwalk of an auto bridge two hundred feet over the water. Cars blew past me at seventy miles an hour, but I couldn't walk more than fifty feet or so before finding myself drifting to a stop and gaping at the cliffs that channeled the river through this geography of strength and awe.

On the bridge's south side there's a huge statue of Walt Whitman with incredibly trail-worthy lines from "Song of the Open Road":

> Camerado, I give you my hand!
> I give you my love more precious than money,
> I give you myself before preaching or law;
> Will you give me yourself? Will you come travel with me?

Perfect. Then fifty yards to the south, the trail enters a state park that provides recreation to the same New Yorkers Walt Whitman so enthusiastically celebrated. The crowds and the swimming pool were strange enough lined up beside what the Appalachian Trail Conservancy used to call "a footpath through the wilderness." But the trailside zoo was the real stomper. A fox in a chicken wire box the size of a refrigerator. Her neighbor, a very bored, disturbed black bear in slightly bigger display, no longer actually black because he had long ago worried off most of his fur with his yellowed teeth. And a large group of children crowding around, completely delighted to be seeing a real fox, a real bear—still too young to take in the monstrosity their elders had put in front of them.

I've never been able to carry this one comfortably, but there it is: the universe gives us wonders, and we build bear cages.

We'll walk through fire pits if you just tell us we're good at it

Don't waste breath trying to kiss someone who won't pull the snorkel out of her mouth.

The teenager manning the concession stand at Lake Tiorati seemed a little overwhelmed before I even started ordering.

I pulled up full-gallop in front of the booth's serving window a few minutes before he opened, propelled by thoughts of a lunch that didn't include mauled bread or week-old cheese slimed with the mysterious juices that always ooze it up after days of mucusing in a plastic bag tucked deep into a warm pack. It wasn't often that the trail routed itself within a few hundred yards of an opportunity that I was sure would likely be as tasteful and perfect as state fair food. I meant to capitalize to the fullest stretch that my stomach and budget would allow.

It probably didn't help the guy that he first had a struggle getting the window's rattling steel barrier to rise and shine. Crashes tore the mountain quiet, squeaks cried for oil, and chains hopped, leapt, and clattered for long minutes. Then silence for a bit. Then "stinkin piece of pig dump, Mary and God" from a muffled voice behind the plywood walls. Then tennis shoes scuffing and scrapping, followed by desperate bursts of breath that built to a sound I knew all too well. I had often made it myself in the final seconds before I was pinned in high-school wrestling matches. The window's metal grate began to jerk upwards, and then screeted to a rusty halt. "Mary's mother's peanuts" from behind the wall.

Standing there for the ten long minutes that all this took, my feet ached out the screams they always did during the hike. But I didn't dare look for a place to sit for fear of losing my place in line. Well, there wasn't a line—the only other semi-sentient beings around were two red squirrels screaming at each other over some squirrely quarrel or amorous arbitration. So while I waited for the young man to triumph over his mighty struggles, I stood rocking from foot to foot just outside the window, a practice thru-hikers adopt to ease pain when flinging themselves to ground isn't possible or wise.

With a final hoggish squeal, the metal barrier gave up resistance, ratcheted jerkily upward, and I was face to face with a seventeen-year-old guy who could have stepped directly off the streets of Mayberry. Wide, unwrinkled face, good grooming, big smile, more Andy than Barney, but with enough Barney to be noticeable under the pressure of a morning not going well. Arney shall be his name. "Crap, sir. Sorry. Didn't know you were there. Give me a second. Please. Sorry."

The collar on his uniform was several sizes too large, the jacket itself was jilted way too far to one side, and several large sweat blossoms hung just barely from the piece of narrow skin that divides human nostrils. But he was still all smiles, the push-and-shove redness on his face not even beginning to dim the seven or eight sizable freckles lined across his nose. A sleeve started to make a dab at the nostril precipitation, but the other hand quickly brought up a paper napkin and mannered the problem away.

There were a few more dramas with mustard and ketchup bottles; a number of relish packets escaped momentarily out of their box and skittled over the counter space; and then another series of wide-open smiles. "Let me crank up that register and I'll be glad to help you. Thank you so much for your patience, sir."

A few more minutes of intense activity with a green bag that held the petty cash. Out came a penny roll. I could see disaster coming. But I wasn't quick or bold enough to intervene before a flourish of the hand snapped the roll against the cash drawer in the way we've all seen the cream of cashiers accomplish flawlessly. Flawless style, imperfectly executed somehow. Coins orbited to all corners of the stand, and Arney bounded off to retrieve them.

He was hands and knees in a corner in earnest pursuit of a few of the more energetic pennies when his better instincts and customer service training apparently kicked in.

"Sorry for the delay, sir. This place is a mess this morning. But I think we're ready now. What can I get for you?"

I'd had plenty of time to study the menu and was ready to go.

"I'll have four hot dogs, all the way, a large order of fries, and a lemonade."

"Whoa, sir, I have to say you're pretty hungry this early in the day."

"Starving."

"OK, we'll get right on it. It'll take me a few minutes to warm up my buns, and the fries take seventy seconds after the oil starts boiling. They're the real things though—made right here from Idaho potatoes. Says it right on the bag." He showed me the packaging. "Cooking with gas now, sure thing—shouldn't be long." He finished a few dashes around the receipt book. "The total will be $3.75."

Hoping to move things along as quickly as possible, I'd already pulled my traveler's cheques out of the plastic bag that served as wallet during the hike. It wasn't a gesture I enjoyed. Every time I'd snapped open the cheques' pseudo-leather cover since I'd left Raleigh that snap had triggered a growing sense of concern. There had been twenty of the $20 cheques when I left home; there were now only nine left, and I had a lot of wheat bread and noodles to buy before the hike was done.

The marketing department at my bank had labored mightily to package up the cheques to create a sense of unperturbed substantiality. The formal dignity of the expensive looking leatherette cover, the high-class British spelling for the *cheques* themselves, the ornately designed, parchment color of the paper, and the special majesty of the line where I would co-sign with the signature of the bank president—they were all fashioned to convey the solidity of a sound and prudent banking system, one that I practically became a partner in when I sat in the wood paneled office in my local Wachovia bank branch and did the initial signing of the checks back in May. All was meant to convey calm and security. But now even a quick look at the cheques produced a minor panic, and each signature a mark of doom across the hike's completion. There were hot dogs to be had in the near term, however, so I was prepared to shake out the consequences later.

"Do you have a pen?"

"Sure, here you go."

I pulled a cheque from its imitation cowhide and started in on my signature.

"Wait, sir. You can't do that."

I looked up.

"Sorry. Not you. I mean, I can't do that. Really, sir, I can't take a check. It's not allowed. Completely against park policy. No checks."

"Well, it's not really a check. It's a traveler's cheque." He looked at me blankly. "It's the same as cash. Everyone accepts them."

He stepped a little to the left, moved back the same distance to the right, moved his book of receipts around a little on the counter, opened his mouth to speak, and then said nothing. My impeccable arguments weren't as persuasive as I had hoped. A cheque, despite my assurances, still seemed a check to him. He was the one swaying from foot to foot now, his beauty-pageant smile courageously trying to stave off the beginnings of panic.

"I'm really sorry, sir. Never heard of a traveler's check. I just can't. I'd lose my job."

I tried a different tact. "They are issued by the bank itself." I showed him the one I had begun to sign, pointing to the bank's name. "I've already given them the money, and they gave me these official certificates in return. They are certificates, not really even checks. They are totally guaranteed. It's what people who are travelling use all the time so they won't have to carry lots of cash that could be stolen or lost. Really, it's just like I am giving you a $20 bill. Your boss will be fine with it."

The back and forth rocking had stopped; the way of duty and conscience was clear to him now.

"I'm really sorry, sir. We're just not allowed to accept checks, not any kind. It's policy, and I can't change it."

I could smell defeat as clearly and strongly as I could smell the fries just beginning to boil up in their pot of oil. A freethinking heretic standing before a non-reformed priest, I was cooked. Folding up the cheques, I turned to walk back up the side trail to the AT.

"Wait, sir."

I stopped. "I'm really sorry about this. My boss usually comes by around 12:00. If you want to wait, I'm sure she'd be glad to talk with you. She's a really nice guy."

So that's how I ended up taking the first of the only two mid-day naps I'd enjoy on the Appalachian Trail. A policy, by the way, that I've since decided is as shortsighted as not accepting traveler's cheques in a park where, by definition, every guest has to be a traveler to even get there (not that anyone still uses traveler's cheques—if you're under forty with a credit card in your pocket I'm sure you've never heard of them). If you're not taking regular lunch naps, you're not enjoying your day enough. Don't get so tangled up in the walking that you don't have time for a nap; don't waste your breath trying to kiss someone who won't take the trouble to pull the snorkel out of her mouth. Same thing.

I slung my pack over one shoulder, walked over to a nearby bench, stacked the pack against a tree, and drifted off.

"You the hiker who needs to cash a check?"

"Yes sir." Though just that second I had been deep into a vivid dream of riding a large French fry pony, I was totally awake and sitting up immediately. "It's not really a check, a traveler's cheque. They're not the same thing."

Standing in front of me was a thirty-year old, uniformed in the ranger outfit of Harriman State Park, complete with the park's version of a Smokey Bear hat. Tall, straight-backed, resting easily with her feet almost exactly eighteen inches apart, lots more Andy than Aunt Bea.

"You're right. Of course, you're right. I try to go climbing in Nepal or India each fall, last year in Chile though. In places like that traveler's cheques are the only way we can buy locally without a lot of hassle. Use them all the time. "

I waited for her to swerve off from personal experience into some officialdom dead end and crush my dream of a high-fat lunch.

"No problem. We can cash yours if it's for $100 or less."

"It's for $20."

"Absolutely OK then. Done. Don't hold it against the kid. Headed for an Ivy in the fall. Deserves it.

He's new though. And he had enough good sense to follow up

with me. Let's go talk with him."

She turned and headed for the stand, but then stopped and put her hand on my pack.

"You're an AT thru-hiker, right? Headed for Maine?"

"Yes. But started in Maine, headed for Georgia."

Then she changed my life—in a couple of sentences, in less than a minute, doing more for me than legions of teachers, hosts of preachers, and a half dozen coaches had done in the last twenty-three years.

"I see a lot of Scout troops up here," she began. "I'm always a little stunned to watch them march past with their sleeping bags careening sloppily off the bottom of the pack, bouncing toward an escape someplace down the trail, ricocheting straps slapping around like snakes popping out from under rocks. Jackets, cook pots, Coke cans, raisin boxes, and stuffed parrots plastered and poked higgly-piggly here and there.

You folks are different, as easy to spot as albino deer on newly paved macadam. We don't see many of you, maybe two or three a year. But it's always the same. It's the pack." She patted mine again. "I've climbed with world-class guides and mountaineers who don't put their stuff together as carefully as you people do. It's impressive. Everything in its place, everything streamlined, functional, and ready to go. No messes."

She thought about it for a minute and then continued. "Might just be prejudicing the data, I guess. I'm not seeing the ones who drop out earlier on. You don't get this far if you don't know what you're doing. You folks are pros. I admire that. Great work." She shook my hand.

In the past forty years, I've received my share of honors, awards, degrees, promotions, raises, and bank deposits from Nigerian princes. But having this stranger take the time to praise something that I had worked hard to master opened up the skies for me. I've never forgotten it.

Managing people, building a team, helping raise a family? I humbly suggest that you could do worse than to remember the woman in the Smokey Bear hat.

Pay attention to what your people do well, what they do better than anyone else. Then make absolutely sure that they know you have noticed. Tell them over and over. The brightest ones will ferret out what they have that produces this excellence and exploit it in all they do. The more average will beam like newly forming suns; and in that light they will be much more ready to listen and act on advice you give about things that they aren't doing so well yet.

Praise. More nourishing than a hot dog, a cheque that can be cashed a thousand times.

Back at the food stand, the young man seemed genuinely happy to hand over my lunch and then expertly count out my exact change. The hot dogs were perfect.

Some people are just dogs

"Look." She reached over and touched just above the dog bite and moved her hand carefully and expertly in a circle around the tears. "This obviously needs a careful washing, some antiseptic, and a good, tight taping. I would never again feel right if you had to quit your hike because I didn't give you the care you needed."

A dog and his owner provided my warm welcome to New Jersey. Unfortunately, the warmth was almost entirely generated from the blood spurting across my thigh and down my leg.

I was just a few miles over the state line, mid-morning crossing one of those beautiful pastorals that are the big surprise for hikers new to this part of the trail. I could have just as easily been moving through one of the lower alpine passes in Switzerland, walking across the top of a gently rolling globe of pasture, no horses in sight but everything else saying that this was someone's prized gentleman farm, all neatness, charm, and pleasing two-mile views of the surrounding countryside.

Three hundred yards to the south a small speck appeared, headed in my direction. At 150 yards it resolved into a fairly good-sized dog, followed many yards behind by another dot that gradually focused into a woman giving determined chase.

At fifty yards the dog was all snout and flopping ears, maybe seventy pounds of something part Lab, part German shepherd, part prehistoric wolf, head down, legs hammering at full go. The woman pumped arms like a gold-medal sprinter, but fell several feet behind with each canine stride.

At twenty-five yards, the woman's streams of "no, no, no" and the Niagara of saliva roiling from Fido's mouth finally pierced my hiker's morning reverie and started pulling the levers on my alert system. But not very much. Or at least not enough. I like dogs; they like me. When Rovers, all attitude and hormone and aggression, would gallop up on me back home, I would drop to a knee, stick out a hand for a friendly finger snap, and inevitably cash in a premium of doggie kisses and wagging tail. I had a talent for dog charming, no question. So I knelt into the pose and confidently awaited a hug.

The dog plows in like a rear-ended NASCAR ripping through the crowd fence. As we slide backwards together in a mass of snarls, "no, no no's," and "oomps," Spot attaches teeth to the closest calf and begins the whiplash head snaps so effective in breaking the neck of the squirrel at center stage in all doggish dreams. I land a fist to his nose; he retreats two steps and growls his way back in, aim somewhat off as he attaches teeth to my pack's padded hip belt. More nasty shakes from him, and a cannonade of whacks to the head and nose from me as I try to find his eyes with my thumbs. He steps back to amend tactics, reconsidering how best to apply wolfish skills to multiply the carnage. On my knees, I raise fists to prepare for tooth and claw.

At this point, the woman arrives, grabs the dog by the collar, authoritatively cries, "sit, you little bastard," and—amazingly enough—he does just that, stepping back a couple of yards, planting his bottom, and—looking at the woman—beginning to wag his tail, just a little, just the tiniest arc of flipping joy.

"I am just so sorry. Please forgive me. He's never done anything like this before."

She appeared to be in her early thirties, older than me but not old enough to be my mother. Her hair was up in a 19th century bun perfect for the farm scene, but otherwise she was definitely an upscale child of the Sixties, uniformed in an expensive peasant dress, tooled leather sandals, and a tasteful collection of jade bangles and jewelry. A silver chain and peace sign ornamented her neck and the upper part of her chest.

"He's usually such a good dog. He just flew out the door as soon as he saw you. I just have no idea why he reacted that way." A long pause as her face drained from splotched, sprinting red to uniform, winsome paleness. "Oh God, look at your leg. We need to treat that."

I looked down, expecting to see Colorados of blood, Grand Canyons of ripped flesh, but delighted to find that the apparent damage was mainly a couple of bluish puncture wounds. They looked deep, but not particularly scary, considering the attention and enthusiasm that Bruno had just lavished on them.

"I'm fine. I'll just wuk it off around the gym once or twice."

I don't know why it happened, probably just habit from years of imitating him with my buddies. But, once again pulling myself in defeat off of my back and beginning to contemplate the licking of my wounds, I found myself uncontrollably lapsing into the accent favored by my high school wrestling coach, a hard-boiled Army vet who reacted to most injuries short of traumatic amputation by ordering a determined stroll around the ball field.

In practice once, a friend of mine caught his thumb between something hard and someone's foot and bent it back so violently that the thumbnail momentarily rested on his forearm. Straightening out the colossally strained and bent mess as best he could, but still holding it at an angle not usually seen in nature, he approached Coach for consolation and advice.

"Take it back to the locker room and suk it, Tate."

Tate looked like the solid earth had just dropped away, leaving him to tumble uncontrollably toward the emptiness of space.

Coach was hard and direct, it was true. But no one in the collective memory of the school could remember him belittling his charges, finding more positive ways to motivate us toward the dozens of football, track, and wrestling championships he had earned. None of his athletes—not even me, a competitor in whom not even this dedicated, clever man could ever find a smidgen of competitiveness—had ever been called a baby. No one was really surprised a few years after we graduated when he himself went back to school, got the appropriate training, and moved on from coaching and teaching Drivers Ed and Health Sciences to become one of the most beloved and effective elementary school principals in the state.

But out on the field or in the gym, we instinctively obeyed the coach with fear and trembling. So Tate, fully obedient, started to move his thumb toward his mouth as he headed for the showers.

"Being a smart aleck doesn't help, son."

Tate turned around, totally confused but having worked up the courage to argue the seriousness of his plight once more.

"It's no time for fooling around, Tate. You need to get that thumb back there and start suking it."

"I don't mean to be a smart mouth, Coach. But I don't understand how sucking could help, sir. I don't think it's broken, but it seems really hurt."

"Pay attention, Tate. You've had a sprain before. You know that the first move is to suk it in the whirlpool. So get back there and get it in the water for fifteen. Then get some ice on it."

So I'd seen good medicine work. And now I was sure that a few minutes of wuking around the field a bit would take care of the dog bites, and said so again.

"No, really, you need to let me nurse that some." She smiled. I was tempted to think there was just a little flirt in the smile, and my heart, still not quite back to normal from the dog charge, did an athletic flip flop.

I must have been wrong though, because immediately she was all commands and seriousness.

"Look." She reached over, touched just above the wound, and moved her hand carefully and expertly in a circle around the bites. "This obviously needs a careful washing, some antiseptic, and a good, tight taping. I would never again feel right if you had to quit your hike because I didn't give you the care you needed.

"We're going back to my house and I'm going to give this the nursing it requires. Stand up, lean on me, and let's get started."

So she and I walked a short distance over the hill to a perfectly restored farmhouse just out of sight of the AT, the dog quite happily bringing up the rear.

And she, indeed, did expertly dress and tape the wound ("I may have majored in sociology, but you can't raise prize stallions out here without learning how to take care of them."), fed me several oatmeal cookies that she had just taken out of the oven, served up a couple of cups of ginseng tea ("best thing around for building stamina"), and waved as I headed away back down the trail, sporting only the slightest hint of a limp.

Lassie followed me for a half mile south, his tail wagging a full flag of satisfaction and happiness every step of our walk together. The wounds never bothered me, and in a few days both the hobble and the bruises were gone, not even very firm memories.

This was the last I thought about the episode until several years later while attending the biannual gathering of the Appalachian Trail Conference (now the AT Conservancy).

Part of the fun of these conferences is meeting up with fellow hikers, especially the recent long distance folks, and spending an evening or two working through all the exaggerated tales we can muster.

Just like every weekender or townie suspected the whole time, these inevitably turn to animal stories. But among real thru-hikers all the snake, bear, and rabid bobcat episodes—at least the ones that have any remote grounding in something that actually happened—are hashed out pretty quickly. Then we turn to the beasts that actually did torment us, the shelter mice, the raccoons, bugs big and small, and, most of all, the dogs, usually ones that think they are loyally guarding some home that the trail marches us near.

Dogs apparently see hikers as the closest thing the woods have to postal carriers, and most of us eventually get bitten on our rounds. So I had my story, in fact, two of them.

First, I wowed the crowd with the legendary attack of the Tennessee Light Brigade, the pack that kept me awake most of one long nightmare of a night, canine to the left of me, canines to the right of me, repeated, sustained charges of snarling beasts. Having trusted the overly exact distance spelled out in the trail guide, I mistakenly tented down at dusk thinking that the small, pleasant valley I'd chosen was well into the wilderness but still close enough to the next road to make a quick resupply into town in the morning. When full darkness arrived and the lights came on in the large house less than half a league away, I realized I was, in fact, in someone's back yard. Doing my best to discreetly retreat, I apparently made just enough noise to excite the most macho of the neighborhood dogs—almost exactly six hundred of them.

Teeth bared, slobber flying, theirs was not to reason why, theirs was but to make me die. No bites this time, but they did keep me, with great skill and heroism, sabering away with walking stick for hours until they finally withdrew from the mouth of hell and went back to scratching their bottoms and enjoying their naps.

"Well done. Clever and brave, Hiscoe. But how about that nasty, rabid bitch up in New Jersey?"

At first, I didn't know what he was talking about. I'd just met him a few minutes before, a thru-hiker from 1974 that I'd somehow missed on the trail, easy to do if one is going north and the other south, and either steps off the path for a brief visit with nature. Up to this point he seemed distinctly laid back, a nice enough guy. The outburst of vile, marrow-anchored, heart-felt sexism came as an ugly surprise.

"Frau Adolph's friggin' dog bit me too." This from a 1973 NOBO.

"Got at least five of us over three years. Kept happening 'til she moved away." From a 1975 alumnus.

"Same story every time. Nasty bite from Rin Tin Tin; cookies and Neosporin from Mistress Crazy Smiles. We'd never have figured it out if we didn't piece together the pattern from the shelter registers."

"Wonder what her deal was?"

We all looked at each other for a good fifteen seconds, each expecting the other to come up with a motive, to explain the mystery.

"Maybe she was just evil. Maybe crazy." This from the 1973 NOBO.

Nobody thought this was a satisfying answer. Another round of silence, some desultory scratching, some shuffling foot to foot. And then we moved on to another topic.

I usually don't go for simple, obvious answers, but I don't have any better explanation this time around. I haven't thought about her all that many times over the years. But she does pop up when some motiveless malignity occasionally bowls headlong into my life. When one of my company's managers starts getting his jollies by making the new hire feel like she's stupid. When that guy on the project steals everyone's enthusiasm with his ceaseless "look at me" pettiness. When a lifetime of subterranean grudges nudges the idiot in my idyllic college town over the edge and he guns down the Muslim newlyweds next door. And the wife's sister.

When I do think of her, the New Jersey woman gives me a convenient reference marker for one of the more sad, inexplicable of our truths. Some days, some small number of us do indeed apparently erupt from our beds all driven to stir around the pot of evil and see what we can boil up.

Thanksgiving: not necessarily just another day off work

The two fifteen year-old boys out for the night at the High Point shelter watched me with the same caution and suppressed awe that the warden focuses on Hannibal Lecter at dinnertime, clearly puzzled, probably even a little repulsed.

It was the very end of July, and it was hot, hot for me enduring the several miles of road walking leading to High Point State Park—and especially hot for Richard Nixon a few hundred miles south in Washington. It was still four months before he'd go on national television to claim—erroneously it turned out—that he wasn't a crook. And still a year until he would drunkenly resign just before the Congress was sure to impeach and convict him of high crimes and misdemeanors.

But the miles were running out on his trail, the end in sight. Just that week the nation—eyes and ears sucked tight to TV coverage of the Senate's Watergate investigation—had learned of the existence of the trove of incriminating tapes the President had made of his day-to-day illegal dealings in the White House. And under relentless "aw, shucks" questioning from my senator—North Carolina's Sam Ervin, our own grandfather redneck suddenly loveable across the nation—other Nixon staffers were starting to crack, painting an ugly picture of the sorts of unethical, unlawful, and generally stinky shenanigans that my neighbors weren't used to seeing from their elected representatives. So at this particular juncture in his traipse across history, I suspect that the president was starting to sweat as much in the Oval Office as I was on this particular crooked New Jersey back road.

It was getting near cocktail time for all of us on the East Coast, so Mr. Nixon might well have been sitting down to wet his whistle and drown his sorrows with a nice bottle of his favored Chateau Lafite Rothschild (he was famous for surreptitiously serving two dollar reds to his White House guests, having the servers use wine towels to hide the labels so his boon companions wouldn't know they were being cheaped). I, on the other hand, had drained my canteen some miles back and was wishing that this particular Jersey two-lane was as shady as our national politics in the summer of 1973.

The nice ranch house that I was passing had a hose attached conveniently out front, and I was tempted to stop and ask for a fill-up. But the Lincoln Continental in the driveway had not one, but two, very conspicuous "Support the President" stickers, one on the bumper and one on the rear window. I wasn't at all sure I'd be welcomed in my current longhaired incarnation and decided it best to keep moving.

"Where are you headed?"

I had slipped totally and completely into the usual hypnotic mode I fell into when I was tired and the trail wasn't particularly taxing at that moment, epically lengthy, elliptical, hopelessly undirected reveries in which I would entertain myself by hazily wandering through and picking over some juicy mystery of the universe. In this particular meditation, I was wholeheartedly congratulating myself for being the kind of salt-of-the-earth soul who always assumes that people who don't agree with me politically are just sadly mistaken in their views, not necessarily bad people. But really, I went on to muse, Mr. Nixon was so obviously a dangerously disturbed creep whose disturbances were ruining the nation that anyone who could support him must be an unredeemable slimy dog, a criminally stupid fool.

So the question startled me, scared the crap out of me, if the truth be known.

"Pardon?"

"Head in the clouds. I salute that in a young person, especially you serious ones." My hackles instinctively started up.

"Didn't mean to break in without an invitation. Sorry." He was middle-aged, balding a lot, plumping up in the front a little, standing next to a band of pole beans strung up across the front row of a sizable garden that I had totally missed as I cruised by at maximum stride.

"We can start over if you'd like. Where are you headed?"

"Completely and totally daydreaming. Caught me. Sorry, too. Hoping to spend the night up at the shelter in the state park."

"You'll like it. It's a stone beauty, a piece of consummately American architecture, in my humble opinion, as they say. Built by the Civilian Conservation Corp in 1934. Still as solid as the Republic and as weatherproof as Christ Our Savior's best Sunday rain hat."

I had no idea what that meant but liked the sound of it.

"Best work that ever came out Roosevelt's first term. Kept a lot of young men working, busy, and fed during lean times; gave them the satisfaction of contributing something that lasted. Good for the soul. It was the first place that my daughter and I ever went camping. Great spot too, even has its own bear. And a beautiful brook. Water's pure, unless the bear has just plopped a drop of his work in it."

"I especially like the sound of the brook—ran out of water a while back."

"No need for that sort of suffering—let me pull this hose off and you can fill up from the spigot here. Hate that rubbery taste you get from the hose, though it does remind me of when I was a kid."

I contorted my right arm up and backwards over my pack and pulled my canteen out of the top right outer pocket. Early in the hike, when I was lapping up any trick that would save energy, I learned I could stuff the water bottle in on top of my rain cover and, with a few practiced moves, reach it, pull it out, and slide it back in without having to heave off and then wrestle on the pack.

"Nice move." He tipped an imaginary hat. "Wonder why they don't build all packs with a pouch for the water bottle? Certainly would make sense. Somebody will figure that out and earn their equipment a real competitive advantage in the marketplace. And what's the buckle in the front?" He was obviously giving my pack the once over, with a practiced, practical eye.

"It's a hip belt. They are selling them now as accessories at some outfitters. Lets you distribute the weight off your shoulders onto your waist. Just recently I've seen them come as standard equipment on a few of the new, more expensive packs. A lifesaver. Gonna kill the market for hernia operations."

We chatted a few more minutes as I repeatedly emptied and then refilled the canteen until I was satisfied. After shaking hands, he headed back to his garden and I took a right out of his driveway back onto the road. I had decided that he was a nice enough guy.

Forty-five minutes and two miles later, I was enjoying another satisfying reverie—this one about the young woman who had floored me with an unexpected, lengthy, and satisfyingly juicy kiss at the airport the morning I left for Maine (I must have still been just a little thirsty)—when two white AT blazes woke me to let me know that the trail was about to leave the road and head back into the woods.

Just as I stepped off the still-hot pavement, the Lincoln pulled up and the driver's side window purred down as smoothly as water flowing over well-grooved creek rock.

"Thought you might enjoy these. Your mother would probably like it a lot if you ate them every one. You came along at just the right time. My garden is a bounty this year. No clue how or why. But it's more than the wife and I could ever eat by ourselves." He handed me a grocery bag through the window, shook my hand again from his awkward position across the front seat, and headed off, the Lincoln's rear end still exhorting us all to stand firm with our leader.

A paper grocery bag is not the easiest load to carry uphill for two miles. I decided along the way that somebody ought to figure out a way to attach handles to the sacks. Probably a great business opportunity.

But the load was lightened by the overwhelming smell of green peppers. If you haven't put one to your nose in awhile, mark your place, put down the book, grab one, and bring a little paradise to your senses. You'll have to agree, probably sadly if you're a fan, that James Joyce blew it in *Ulysses.* Mr. Leopold Bloom should surely have followed his enjoyment of giblet soup, nutty gizzards, stuffed roast heart, liver slices fried with crustcrumbs, and fried hencod's roes by relaxing in the toilet to the earthy aroma of a fine ripe pepper. And given all the evidence, a madeleine is also a perversely odd choice. Certainly Proust should have tripped into the past remembering the bursting delight that a Swiss Army knife sets free on the first slice into a warm, zestful bell.

The two fifteen year-old boys out for the night at the High Point shelter watched me with the caution and suppressed awe that the warden focuses on Hannibal Lecter at dinnertime, clearly puzzled, even a little repulsed, by the hour of joy I spent sitting on the ground peeling and eating five dripping, sloppy tomatoes, a half dozen cucumbers, and a bag full of peppers. Only two eggplants went to waste, released unharmed. At the time, I had not the slightest clue what they were or what to do with them. They reminded me of footballs.

That meal is a joy I have carried with me almost every minute through my adulthood. I can smell it now. It absolutely always sits with me every time I belly up to the table. Five months of hard work fueled by noodles, oatmeal, mystery jerky, and other assaults on good taste totally inoculated me from the fast food culture that sprouted into maturity alongside me. Every meal I've had for forty years has been uncommonly delicious and elegantly holy, a squealed ceremony of orgasmic pleasure. Thank you, Appalachian Trail.

And to this day every person who doesn't share my politics is, of course, just walking down a different trail from the one I'm on. Except for Richard Nixon and his kind. They are idiots. It's just a fact. But sometimes I even waver a bit on him. After all, even Mr. Nixon supported the Environmental Protection Agency. And enjoyed a good glass of wine at the end of a difficult day.

Pride goeth before the donut

I stepped out of the woods with something of a troubled mind. Back where I grew up, local laws still let us Baptists and Methodists decide which stores could be open for shopping on our Sabbath, and bakeries weren't on the approved list for Sunday mornings in Raleigh.

Today's AT websites, YouTube videos, trail journals, and hiker memoirs usually don't mention Worthington's Bakery. It's apparently now just your typical rural roadside deli, operated under another name, probably shelved with the usual collection of disposable diapers, jars of peanut butter, bottles of Snapple, a sprinkling of overpriced laundry detergent, and, by all accounts, some pretty good deli sandwiches. Enough necessaries to serve the nearby lake community but now not particularly friendly to long distance hikers. These days a quick stop there definitely doesn't seem to rival, say, the wedding of an English prince or standing on the front row all covered in free beaded trinkets during the climax of your first Mardi Gras parade. I haven't returned to the bakery since a Sunday morning in August 1973, so if I'm misrepresenting the current experience, I hope that all current Worthington fans and aficionados will graciously accept a *mea culpa* from me.

In fact, I earnestly hope that I'm wrong. It would be a tragically sadder world if this and subsequent generations should be denied the bliss of anticipation that this legendary destination engendered for early AT pilgrims. I started hearing about it in Maine, five hundred miles before I arrived. Fresh baked blueberry turnovers, hot bagels with garlic cream cheese and salmon, strawberry-filled donuts with hot, liquified sugar running free and thick off the top, orange juice that still had the peel on five minutes before you walked in, huge sandwiches made on the spot. All of it right on the trail, the front door a vision waiting when you stepped out of the woods to cross Route 206 at Culvers Gap.

I stepped out of those woods with something of a troubled mind, however. Back where I grew up, local laws still let us Baptists and Methodists decide which stores could be open for shopping on our Sabbath, and bakeries weren't on the approved list for Sunday mornings in Raleigh. Maybe after all this waiting, the fabled Worthington's wouldn't even be serving when I presented myself? It was a fate I pondered for days as I drew closer. More immediately though, my stomach was enduring another periodic return of the dysentery curse, seething, burning, and fuming like the sun weathering an outburst of solar flares.

But there it was when I stepped out of the trees, cars in the parking lot, a good crowd visible through the front window, and an "open" sign cheerfully neoning a welcome. No stomach nonsense was going to keep me from this rendezvous with gluttony, even if I did have to double over a bit as cramps and rumblings intensified when I crossed the road. Pausing a few seconds at the door, I waited somewhat nervously as a few errant, sneaky farts pushed their way to freedom and then, combing my hair as best as I could with dirty fingers, I stepped inside.

An older couple at the counter was testily flip-flopping decisions over their toppings for a shared ham sandwich (I could see the bread, meat, and cheese waiting across the counter, and they looked like a million dollars to me, regardless of whether their destiny would eventually include regular or spicy mustard, shallots or red onions). I couldn't have cared less about the delay though—more time to mull over the choices in the glass cases in front of me, more time to build hoggish anticipation toward the climactic taking of my place at one of the small group of tables in the bakery's small dining area.

We've all had the occasional feeling that we're being watched, the sense that someone in the nearby crowd is surreptitiously checking us out, be it with good or evil intention. I now had it so strong that I was able, with supreme, heroic willpower, to pull my own eyes off the bounty of sweets and do a quick sneak sweep around the room. A family with three small children, not paying the slightest attention to me. Another older couple with their order now on the table, waiting for their friends at the counter to join them, should they ever finish paddling their epic journey across the great ocean of ordering. A middle aged guy reading the *New York Times* over a huge cinnamon bun and coffee.

Then I dead catch her eyes slying a look at me, at about waist level to be exact. She is thirty or so, brown hair, dressed nicely but casually, sitting at the table closest to the door cozily between two other women about her age. She looks away when she is caught and goes back to talking with her companions, now in a huddle of freshly washed hair and dangling, sparkly earrings.

Then it happens again. I turn quickly in her direction and she is staring. Eyes turn away. I straighten out from the slight hunch into which my torrid stomach has woven me and look again; she's whispering to her friends. One of them is looking towards me as they laugh a little at something that Ms. Curious is saying. The third now looks my way until I catch her eyes too and she goes back to the whisper assembly.

Never in my life had I ever been the sort of male that females congregate to look over. I'm average looking, at very best. And I was cursed at twenty-three to look much younger than I was. At the time, I could have—and often did—blended in seamlessly with any group of sixteen-year olds. Nothing special at all, that's what I had learned through over two decades of uniformly depressing feedback from a largely disinterested female world.

But maybe the trail has begun to change that, I can't help myself from thinking. Rock tight glutes, muscular calves and athletic thighs, shoulders sculpted by months of pumping a heavy pack. The dashing beginnings of a ponytail, its bold, pioneer masculinity only held in check by a rakish headband recalling the untamed manliness of the noble Plains warrior. Weathered and sturdy, a man of nature, that creature of the wilderness who strides mysteriously through your sleepy town turning heads and starting hearts to carom in uncontrolled thumping. Later in the hike, as a matter of fact, three older women in Virginia do spend the fifteen minutes it took to hitch me into town making lewd, smacking comments about my lower half, even suggesting in voices that I am meant to overhear all sorts of salacious activities that the four of us might complete, should I decide to go home with them for a night of free lodging rather than be dropped off at my seedy Waynesboro hotel of choice. I'll admit that it probably wasn't a legit offer; clearly part of the joy was getting to thoroughly embarrass an awkward, shy kid, trapped in the backseat as they sipped their Buds and puckered Marlboro smoke in my direction. But it was the thought that tallied, at least from my angle of vision. The offer, while scaring me to death, did me a world of good.

Maybe it's time to reassess my appeal, I posit to myself as I look again at the most interesting table in Worthington's Bakery on that Sunday morning. They are definitely paying attention. These handsome ladies are talking about me with clear interest, that's obvious. I pull myself even taller and adjust my best James Bond pose as the counterman asks if I'm ready to order. Had my eyes not hooked Ms. Curious's again just at that moment, I might have been tempted to answer him with just the hint of an intriguing British accent.

Before I can order though, she makes her move, standing up, slowly pushing back her chair and beginning to stride off the fifteen feet now between us.

Good manners require a trigger alert at this point.

I normally have no patience with female objectification, none at all. But just this once, I must throw myself on your mercy. I apologize in advance for any offense, however necessary under these circumstances. In my defense though, I do plead a fierce feminism that took hold of me as a teen and that, I hope, has guided my relationships with women ever since. I plead the best of intentions. But most of all, I plead fidelity to the story as it actually transpired. What happened in the next few seconds early that Sunday transcended usual earthly mores and morals. I give here, to the best of my limited literary talents, an unbiased, detached, dispassionate description of what played out among the warm buns of Worthington's early that morning. I strive to strictly reproduce the objective reality of the scene. The chips of the sexual politics fall where they may—this is my completely honest memory of the encounter at the counter.

The woman who was walking confidently toward me measured ten feet in height. Though the legs that graced her forward measured at least six of that stature, it still took a parade of four and one-half centuries, with all their glories, splendors, and dignities, for her to pace off the last five yards that separated us.

With her first step, time shifted on some pivotal hinge to become thoroughly Einsteinian, measuring itself by quanti of the soul, simultaneities of grandeur, strobing spacetimes of longing and fulfillment, stringed multiverses of beauty and joy.

With the second pace, the drab and outworn physics of life disappeared entirely, no longer able to hold firm matter's center as humankind had lived it in until this very moment of time. Molecules of the body electric pulsed across flesh and blood with energies that dwarfed the kinetics of the sun, that made petty the throbbing forces of a cosmos of fiery stars. Neutrons, protons, and electrons spun faster than the calculations of all the world's colliders. Bosuns higged, bounced, and arched with a purpose and vital nature beyond the paltry imaginings of the endless rows of professors bowed over their instruments. Neutrinos gladly abandoned their petty neutralities for vast expanses of decisive affirmation, delighting to be charged positively for the first instant since the Big Bang. For the only time since the original defeat of Nothingness, energy was indeed both created and destroyed, many times over, in spinning bursts of mad creation and happiness. The earth's axis shifted, and then shifted again.

With her third step, light intensified beyond any rainbow's spectrum, and all the dark matter in all the universes surrendered its attraction to the shadows and began flooding creation with luminous clarity and scintillant luster. She wore upon her feet, I noticed as she took this last gracious step, golden sandals, purchased from Macys and worthy of Aphrodite. The nails of her liminal toes were brightly glossed with the color of the rosy dawn.

Looking on these perfections, I saw and felt—in person, right there beside US Route 206 in the state of New Jersey—the very force that through the green fuse drives the flower. It would be impossible to believe, in fact, that all of us—the man with his *Times*, the older couples with their ham, the babies in Africa, the dads in Antarctica, and all the moms in the Middle East—did not feel that force ignite and release all the potential necessary to construct a new world of infinite potential and bliss.

That, in short, is what happened in the seconds it took for this woman to close the distance between us, look at me with tenderness, and begin to move her lips in human speech.

"I don't mean to be rude. I hope I'm not bothering you."

"Not at all." My voice, I noticed, had somehow adopted just the right touch of Liverpool.

"My friends and I have been watching you since you came out of the woods and…" She paused, cheeks coloring and maybe for the first time ever in her life confronting a break in her self-confidence. She was, I noticed with a touch of interest, having some trouble going through with this. A little shy, I supposed.

I moved several inches forward to help move us past this hint of hesitation. "I noticed. It's OK. I'm flattered."

She looked a little confused for just a nanosecond. Looks of support from the table by the window urged her to move forward.

"No. I don't…" She blushed, regrouped and started again. "My friends and I are nurses, LPNs. Well, Hermonia and I are nurses; Dione is a heart specialist." Another pause. I nodded encouragement, cocking my head just fetchingly enough so she could see she had my full attention. She moved the index and middle fingers (also tipped with the rosy dawn) of her right hand thoughtfully around her lips. Her left hand and arm came up in a very attractive version of the police officer's "stop" pose. And she then continued, the words coming out not in a burst but in a deliberate, studied clip, spaced carefully so that I could absorb them.

"We think," pointing to her table of friends, "that you look just awful. Horrible, actually. We think," pointing again, "that you are probably very sick. Do you have any idea how bad?"

I stepped back against the counter.

"Really, you look incredibly bad. Our guess is digestive tract, serious and probably not transient. But Dione thinks it could be something more desperate. Are you seeing anyone?"

I tried to shuffle further back, but the counter stopped me, forcing a slight feint to the right instead.

"Well, a Special Forces guy up in New York gave me some Lotomil."

"Good. Excellent! Lotomil. That's a good start. But, really, you look way too bad for just that, just awful. I doubt it's enough."

She turned back to her table.

"Lotomil so far." The two women smiled enthusiastically and solemnly signaled their approval in tandem nods.

"You need treatment with something much stronger. Is the diarrhea bad? Totally liquid or at least somewhat firm?" And before I could frame an answer, "Is that throwup on your shirt?"

The spot, which I had noticed this morning but had decided to ignore, was actually some cheese wiped from last night's macaroni. But now didn't seem like the time for quibbles.

"The standard treatment is antibiotics. Unless there's blood. Are your stools bloody?"

I looked at her.

"Do you see blood when you number two?"

One of the women at the ham sandwich table had paused her ginger ale in midair and was now leaning forward to tune in to the conversation. The counterman exhaled forcefully and waved the next customer forward.

"I'm fine, really."

"No you're not. That sort of thinking is probably how you got in this sorry condition. You look like death. I bet you're dehydrated too. From the runs. Your skin has the classic, clammy look." She pinched a pucker up on my forearm. The red drained quickly away, leaving a mass of flesh that looked like the lips on a beached trout. "This isn't just going to go away."

I wasn't sure what "this" was supposed to be, but again it didn't seem like the right time to pursue clarification.

"And probably the last thing that your stomach needs now is all that sugar and fat." She pointed toward a tray of donuts, one I had earlier looked at with total delight.

"Thank you for everything." I shifted hard to the left and, without much hope for success, tried to make for the door.

A movement of her hips, and she countered my escape.

"Really, I know we're being rude. We're sorry for staring and are embarrassed by the need to intervene. But we really did notice just how bad you looked from at least fifty yards away. The way you were dragging yourself across the road all bent and old looking was pitiful."

She looked to her friends and raised her arms in resignation. Dione pointed in the air and made a gesture like she was writing something.

"We're not going to let you go until you promise to see a doctor. Dione's from Connecticut and can't prescribe here. And everything's closed on Sunday in town anyway. But you have to promise. You need a prescription, and you need medicating. Do you promise?" She smiled a lovely smile.

What could I do? All was lost. I made the necessary pledges, twice before she finally stepped aside and left the exit unguarded. With her look of saintly concern at my back, I slipped out the door, heading back for the woods, trying as I left to walk as upright as possible.

This time it was me doing the watching, peering through the leaves a few feet down the trail until they got into their Volkswagen—all laughter, cheer, and summer dresses—and drove away. Her warning still pinching my ears, I snuck shiftily back into Worthingtion's and settled for only three still-hot jelly donuts and a strawberry milkshake. My appetite wasn't what it once was.

Ten minutes and half a mile later down the trail, I paid the price. With only three seconds notice, I barely got two feet off the path and partly out of my prized Dartmouth College gym shorts before the foul tsunami thundered in. I was bent stiffly over, holding my spent, shivering chalk-white flesh up by a small tree, when the first of the Girl Scouts walked by.

The long parade of young girls reacted quite kindly, on the whole. Most passed without comment, pretending not to look. But at least one gagged.

I decided I definitely needed some professional help.

PENNSYLVANIA

Paying the right price for the dull and the ugly

Walk among the naked and the brutal and surely your parts will fail

It occurred to me that he might be looking for his twelve gauge, just to make sure the situation could be controlled should I bust out all violent and crazy.

Most of this story takes place on the last few miles of the AT in New Jersey. But since it does climax just south of the state line with outbursts of harsh sun and hatefulness in the middle of Interstate 80, a case could be made that it really should be a Pennsylvania tale. That's what I've decided anyway. I'm going to choose to place it in the geography where the Appalachian Trail ground me up the most, where the state of the pathway and the state of my own mind conspired to squeeze the joy out of the hike.

During my time on the trail, Pennsylvania, in fact, became less an American commonwealth than a grand, sad metaphor for how things can mount the saddle and completely ride you into the ground. And this once proud, original colony didn't provide, as you'll see, the glorious grinding and grounding of New England's difficult but starkly majestic mountains. Instead, the state rutted me into a spiritual crisis the way that the "middle of the journey of our life" once potholed Dante on his own stumbling path to Paradise.

Somewhere in the middle of Pennsylvania, depending on the additions and subtractions that happen constantly to the trail's length with each year's reroutes, thru-hikers do indeed walk through the exact geographic center of their journey. But the problem with Pennsylvania wasn't a problem of geography, though geology and topology did play their parts.

For me Pennsylvania was a grating two-hundred-mile dark wood where all that is wonderful seemed lost and where all that is soulless and without an ounce of the divine seemed ever present and inevitable. Pennsylvania is where the AT became a full-time job for me. And not just an ordinary Connecticut-like job with its ordinary and acceptable highs and lows. Nope. Think of the worst job you ever had. The one where boredom crushed with an interminable countdown of hours and minutes and seconds. Where the boss was a dullish bully and your cube mates were all overripe melons of self-absorption. Where the days and weeks added up to no great accomplishments, just days and weeks all spent and gone. That's the job that the Appalachian Trail became for me in Pennsylvania.

I was in New Jersey, just north of the Pennsylvania state line, on a long-abandoned woods road making incredible time, four miles an hour at least, well on target to cross the Delaware River that afternoon, get a cheap room in the Pennsylvania village of Delaware Water Gap for the night, and make a wonderful supper out of the blueberry pie in the trail-famous restaurant just across the bridge into town. Tomorrow I'd find a doctor to treat my stomach.

But even my gut wasn't bothering me at that exact moment, all of yesterday's cares as irrelevant as a few air bumps to a Shuttle commander hurtling through the last of the clouds with the Kennedy runway in view out the cockpit window. I'm sure that if some sports reporter looking for the capstone moment in her documentary celebration of peak triumphs in hiking achievement had filmed me in slow motion at just this minute, she would have been amazed to capture the first footage of a human attaining perfect form, both feet simultaneously leaving Earth on each stride, trotting the ground away, motile Derby poetry in motion streaming off my superheated, fire-glowing boots.

It was a total surprise then when I found my nose and chin plowing away in the crumbled gravel and moldering leaves that a second before had been flowing at light speed below my churning leather Tyroleans. No stumble. No trip, catch, stumble, then fall. Just instantaneous transition from upright and forward to sliding log of grating flesh and skin. I jumped up as quickly as I fell, oblivious to pack weight, amnesic to the laws of gravity, like the Civil War soldier who absorbs the shell but keeps advancing a few yards before incontrovertible anatomy confirms that a foot was carried away by the blast. I crumpled, turtled over to dump the pack, and stood again. And again, I lurched to the side, spun a half arc, and fell back to the gravel.

The doctor I saw two days later had no more explanation for what had happened than I did at the time of impact.

"It's like your ankle went suddenly on labor strike, Chicago, 1888, Haymarket Square."

I stared at him.

"Been reading some history. But back to your ankle. You've pressured it for months of long hours without adequate breaks, and it's tired of the vocational abuse. It needed a vacation. Decided to go to the beach for a week. Maybe it's visiting relatives in Hawaii? Checked out with no forwarding address. Didn't pay the bill, flush the toilet, make the bed, or deposit the key either; just shut the door and walked away."

A pause.

"'Walked away'—pretty good, huh? I'm one funny guy for a doctor, eh?

"Nothing wrong on X-rays," he concluded. "Looks fine. Problem seems to be that you just can't stand on it."

I was finding the visit less than helpful.

"I'm no orthopedist and can't talk to the physiology of your strange wobble. So don't take this as settled science or grounds for legal complaint. But I'd say it's like you have about six ankle and foot bones that just turned into congealed church salad, all Jell-O and spongy marshmallows. Nothing I can give you. Nothing really either of us can do. I'd guess it would be best to stay off it for awhile and see what happens."

It turned out that he was right. A few days off the ankle in Delaware Water Gap and it mostly held for the rest of the walk.

I, as yet, knew none of this lying on the ground on some deserted woods road in New Jersey, seven miles or so from the nearest town, but I don't think it would have helped much.

At the advice of everyone heading north, I had just started carrying a seven foot oak staff, both because it looked all Moses/pilgrim cool and because a half dozen NOBOs had told me (they were right) that I'd need it to constantly be pitching rattlesnakes out of the way as I tripped between the millions of rocks that bred the reptiles so prodigiously in Pennsylvania. I now climbed it hand over hand to a shaky stability, and for the next few miles used it to pole-vault clumsily and slowly in the direction of the Delaware River.

A hopping and creeping mile later, the trail took a hard right and began to weave along the shores of Sunfish Pond, usually billed as the world's largest spring-fed lake and near the top on just about everybody's list of the most perfect places between Maine and Georgia. For everyone else, that is. I found my lucky self instead entering what could have passed for some bizarre Italian experimental movie, one sporting a somber cast of hundreds of stoned camper zombies.

I had no hint of the embittered legal maneuverings that set the stage for the scene I walked into, but you'll need a little background to understand how it led the next day to my own Custer massacre at the hands of a mob of irritable cowboys wearing the uniform of the Pennsylvania Highway Patrol.

Sunfish Pond is forty acres of tiny treasure, an unexpected jewel of perfection dug out, filed with the clearest of cold waters, and left untended high above the Delaware River some twenty million years ago when the last great arctic glaciers retreated back up North America towards Canada.

More recently, several Jersey power companies tried to move in, ready in the 1960s to scrape the pond under, backfill it with dirt, and create a very small cog in a titanic scheme to dam the Delaware River and provide water, energy, and flood control for the cities of the northeastern seaboard, a scheme that began to be squeezed to death later in the decade by the flexing muscles of the fledgling environmental movement. It's a tangled story, but for our tale the important plot twist is that by 1973 the legal battles were so muddied that no government agency felt it had the unobstructed authority to enforce camping rules around the lake without being sued by either the environmentalists monitoring the scene or the power companies themselves.

Into that void rushed—heads all nodding to the Grateful Dead—tons of idealistic, disaffected, visionary, and bleary eyed stragglers from the bitter-end ranks of the hippy youth of Philadelphia, New York, and Boston, ready to experience Nature in all its expansive glories. A new Woodstock, in the real woods this time, though without much music since there's no electricity for amps up at Sunfish Pond.

And when they got there, they each and everyone—man, woman, and child—took off all their clothes.

And that's when I limped by.

I was total concentration, mastering the complicated plant, lever, step-right, swing-left maneuver I was using to wallaby forward on one foot. So the first skin-filled clump or two didn't really register. Finally though a particularly large naked guy stepped out of the bushes and got my attention.

"Hey dude, that's a fancy dance you're doing. American Bandstand, my man." He hopped around in imitation of my gait. "Nice work. A ten for the rhythm."

On top, he had a leather Australian bush hat. On his feet, orange Sears work boots, no socks, no laces. In between, a few pimples, mosquito swells, bruisey purplish splotches, some curly hairs, but nothing else.

I tried to keep my focus locked no lower than his eyes. They were bloodshot. Standing beside him were a young girl, maybe fifteen, and two slightly older women, all of them as naked as an ambitious right-wing politician's unfettered greed for power and money.

"I hurt my foot. Know how far it is down to the road from here?"

"Bummer. We don't do roads, though. Don't need your cities and all the rest of that corrupt, worn out capitalist crap."

"Wanna toke? Might help." This from one of the older women. She wore a wool British motoring cap and a very large shark's tooth hung on a long leather string around her neck. At regular intervals, the tooth rotated past her belly button as she moved out of the trees and jiggled up an arm to hand me the joint that was passing around.

"Might not be that good for my balance right now. But thanks."

I like naked people and respect non-conformity. Always have and hope I always will. But the next half-mile did not particularly recommend the lifestyle. Thunderstorms had channeled up through the basin of the Delaware River the last several afternoons, and each of the several dozen campsites I shuffled past was decorated with randomly intertwined masses of soggy cotton sleeping bags hung hopelessly to dry out on pine branches, a hobo's Christmas tree. The rain had also taken every last wave out of the stringy hair that everyone kept fingering back off their foreheads in the iconic gesture that might well have become the national salute had the promised Revolution ever happened. Cigarette butts were everywhere.

A couple of enterprising proto-engineers had used large black plastic trash bags to mark out sidewalks between some of the tribes. But these had long been stomped and torn into masses of wet, ripped garbage. As I passed the last camp before the next trail junction, a couple was sliding back and forth on one of the more intact bags, making slippery, squeaky love as two pubescent girls played nearby with a naked toddler. The kid hailed me with an open, soggy bag of potato chips as I hobbled by, and a few folks here and there gave me half-hearted peace signs. But most just ignored me. The place had all the joy of European trench warfare.

At the southern end of the lake, I stopped for a quick rest and map read at the wooden sign that marked the AT's change of direction down towards the river.

"You enjoy the circus?"

Two teenaged boys, both wearing Phillies caps, were sitting in front of an impossibly old but well-pitched canvas Scout tent in the small clearing where the AT met several other trails that circled around the pond. A *Mad* magazine lay between them on an air mattress, and Creedence Clearwater's "Willie and the Poor Boys" was blossoming from a transistor radio in front of the tent, producing a rush of nerve-deep happiness that kept me, at least temporarily, from forthwith declaring this very day, August 5, 1973, the official death of the Sixties, the precise end of a generation's youthful hope and vigor. I hadn't realized just how much I had missed music for the last two and a half months.

"Wait till it gets dark. That's when the real whooping and hollering begins."

"How far are you hiking?"

"Started up in Maine, trying to go to Georgia. Hoping for Delaware Water Gap tonight."

"You hop like that the whole way?" This said with a smile that wiggled around his aspirational bush of a Mark Twain mustache, the kind that young boys lucky enough to be ahead of the hormone curve always try to cultivate the first time they escape parental oversight.

"Yeah. I'm in the early rounds of an Olympic trial, actually. An official wilderness challenge sanctioned by the International Committee. Kept secret so far to increase its impact when it's finally announced. The money comes from the Australian government. A salute to the kangaroo. I get a big trophy if I hop it the whole way on one foot."

"Nice. A great way to promote pouch packing. New sport. Very natural. Should appeal to these guys." He pointed toward a burst of laughter coming from behind a clump of trees down by the lake.

"No kidding though. It's getting late and you're going to have a hard time on the trail down to the river with your foot like that. It gets gnarly in spots. You ought to stay here the night."

"A ranger shows up in his jeep first thing every morning. We've been here three days now and he's pulled in every sunrise about 6:30. Nice guy. Tries to talk everyone into leaving or at least doing some basic 'leave no trace' camping. They ignore him. I'm sure he'd be glad to get you down to a doctor."

That would complicate things; I'd have to hike back up at some point to cover the trail I'd miss, not a move I wanted to make. This needed some thought. I sat down, back to a large oak, to consider next steps (or lack thereof) over a bag of Chips Ahoy! the boys pulled out of the tent and passed my way.

"We are planning on canned beef stew for supper. Have extra if you'd like to share."

That clinched the plan.

After supper I tried to stand to hang my food bag, but the ankle had gone completely mush again.

"No need," said one of the kids. "We haven't seen a single animal since we got here." On cue, there was another loud burst of hooting from near the lake. "Four legs good, two legs bad," he finished.

So they dug out my sleeping bag and pad, arranged it beside their tent, propped my pack against the oak, filled my canteens, and we watched the night sky and ate more cookies as we fell asleep under perfect skies and the sounds of fratish hippy parties ricocheting around the glacial contours of ancient Sunfish Pond.

Given the unappealing nature of the pathway for the next 150 miles, one that no one who wasn't doing a thru-hike or some other ill-advised, sophomoric dare would be interested in, it would be one of the last times I camped with anyone until I reached southern Pennsylvania, where the dieback of the worst of the rocks and poison ivy and the walk through beautiful high country once stained by the most savage fighting of the Civil War brought hikers back out on the trail.

The boys were spectacularly wrong about the animals. I fought off a dozen Pickett's charges of marauding raccoons all night. And in the irritable light of the next morning, the ankle was still checked out. By ten, it was obvious that no ranger intended to show for the day. So after unsettling my stomach with yet another breakfast of dried milk and cold cereal, I headed out under my own shaky power.

The kids hadn't prepared me for the beauty of the trail down to the river—it tumbled, hustled, and locked stepped beside an incredible stream most of the way. But they were exactly right about how hard it would be. Five miles of pivoting on a walking stick around boulders scattered by millennia of flow, ice, and time was exhausting. And the exhaustion, spirited along by the supper of gristly stew and too many chocolate chip cookies, ripped my intestines into nasty revolt. By the time I stepped onto the Interstate 80 bridge across the Delaware River, I was thinking that some downtime in a clean, attentive, well-lit emergency room might make more sense than a rented room in a decaying small mountain village.

In case you've not yet to have the pleasure of hiking an interstate on a sunny August day, I cannot recommend it. I urge you to find a less punishing form of recreation.

The Delaware Water Gap is one of the most dramatic scenes on the east coast, up to a quarter of a million cubic feet of water busting its way every second through a thin narrows with thousands of feet of shale and quartzite rising almost straight up from the river. It's not quite Half Dome seen gloriously from the line of cars on a Yosemite road, but it's probably the best view you can get from any interstate on the east coast, with the possible exception of I-40 through the Smokies.

Too tired and nauseous to appreciate any of it, I was all tunnel vision, eyes only focusing on the heat waves accelerating out of the asphalt. By my reckoning, the sun had baked the bridge up to, say, 500 degrees, and my bowels were sneering out something like, "Buddy, you know there's no cover out there. Should I choose to make one of my bold moves, you are totally exposed to the excited eyes of the motoring public for the next thousand feet; and I'm kinda thinking that the scene of you squatting on the road might be amusing. Believe me, I am not your friend today."

I made it a little more than halfway before the patrol car did a classic *Bullitt* slide /U-turn and pulled alongside me with lights and siren doing their absolute best to raise all the devils in hell.

A Pennsylvania state trooper bounced his driver's side door half off the hinges (I can't explain why he didn't just dive out the window, *Dukes of Hazzard* style—I'm sure in a perfect world it would have been his chosen predilection), jumped the concrete protection barriers that kept cars away from hikers, and head-down-sprint hurdled his way up to my face.

"What the fuckin' hell you think you're doing walking down the middle of the goddam interstate, you pricky little dickweed. You think you're king of fuckin' China?"

I blinked, my solar-fried mind not agile enough to have the slightest clue what was happening.

He jumped back a foot or so. "Drop that gahdam stick, shithole, unless you want me to smoke your ugly, ragged ass. Do it now, right now."

Still not fully tuned in, my brain darted back to the smoking preferences of the folks back up on the mountain. I couldn't quite make the connection work for me.

He stepped forward, slapped my walking pole a dozen feet down the roadway, and dropped a hand to rest near his service weapon. I started lurching over towards my dangling foot, but quickly squirmed to equilibrium on the good one once I saw how panicked my movement seemed to make my inquisitor.

My intestines wrenched and bucked. My head cleared a bit.

"Jesus, have you crapped your fuckin' stupid pants? Asshole. Fuckin' shit."

I hadn't, but I felt I had no guarantees anymore.

"Officer, I'm hiking the Appalachian Trail."

"And I'm Mario Andretti, and this is the friggin' Indianapolis 500." A few seconds of quiet as he looked around and considered his next move. In quick succession, two other patrol cars, all lights and sirens, pulled in behind his vehicle.

"We're sick and tired of you hippies runnin' this town. Think you rich-ass own the damn place. Now you're draggin' your pootin' butts right down the interstate."

A second officer, much younger, much calmer, walked up while the third, not bothering to shut his door as he moved to the rear of his car, started rummaging around in the trunk. It occurred to me that he might be looking for his twelve gauge, just to make sure the situation could be controlled should I bust out all violent and crazy. Cars were slowing to watch. One drove at slow cruising speed directly into the bumper of the car in front of it, a sharp blam without even a warning screech.

"Finally got one, Captain. Just walking here down the middle of the freaken' road like it's his friggin' living room."

"Tyson, try to watch your mouth a little." I could see him looking over my pack, checking out my boots and equipment, assessing the scene.

"Officer, I'm just walking the Appalachian Trail. I'm sick, and I need to get to Delaware Water Gap to see a doctor."

"Well, son, there are no doctors at the Gap. So that's not going to work for you. And I've hiked the trail up in New York, lots of times. This doesn't look like a footpath through the wilderness to me."

"But it is—there's the blazes." I pointed to the white paint marks on the bridge banister. "We've got to cross the rivers somehow, and the interstate is the only way."

"Yeah, friggen' Mr. Daniel Boone himself blazed that paint with his own trusty friggen' Indian ax."

"Tyson, I think we decided you need to button up."

"I can show you the route in the guidebook if that would help."

"Tyson, I don't think he's one of our squatters. Good vigilance though. By the book. You did the right thing to check things out.

"But now I'm thinking it's best if we let him go on his way before he puddles up here on us. Son, you have a good hike. Best of luck to you." He tapped Tyson on the shoulder, and they headed over to deal with the accident we'd caused. As I passed the patrol cars, the third officer was stowing an ugly pump shotgun back in his trunk.

I was left unmolested out in the sun, fanned weakly by the stream of cars pulling around the wreck and accelerating back up to interstate velocity. Right foot completely limp and stomach slapping and shrieking like a cheap tire unraveling on an eighteen-wheeler, I hopped toward the southern end of the bridge, where an official state sign stoutly proclaimed "Welcome to Pennsylvania."

When I tried to order blueberry pie at the diner just across the river, the proprietor refused to cash my traveler's cheque.

Not to belittle actual assaults, but it's usually boredom that finally beats us down

No matter how much you love the woods, no matter how much your eye delights in capturing inestimable beauty and solace. No matter how much you delight in the freedom of the open road, the sun in your face and the wind at your back. After enough weeks, there's going to come a day when you become tired of this shit—flesh, bone, and soul.

It was still hellfire hot, and once again I dealt with it by easing quietly into another of those hiker-brain saunas that let miles—and rattlesnakes surely—gurgle by without any thought that even tries to penetrate outwards beyond the solid boundaries of the skull.

This is easy in Pennsylvania. If you look at a topo map of the trail there, you'll see a distinct pattern, repeated and repeated to the fullest, most level end of oblivion. First, drop a thousand feet into a gap, where you cross a road or a river. Then, climb a thousand feet on the other side. Next, march forward twenty miles on a ridge that never elevates or drops any more than the height of the teased hair on an earlier generation's First Lady. And usually in more or less a straight line. Pause for a night of rest, then hit the replay button for a groundhog day of the same.

But then it got even hotter. And then hotter still. Until I had to grudgingly creak open the spa doors of consciousness just the slightest, a mental inch or less, blink at the light of the outside world, and shift merely the tiniest bit of attention to external realities.

It took a few seconds to register, but there it was. The trees were gone. All of them. Not a one in sight. At least not any one more than three feet tall. Not that Pennsylvania had an abundance of majestic giants of the forest to begin with. Mostly the first 150 miles of the trail in the state offered a tramp through areas that appeared to have been clear cut, mined, or otherwise blasted enough in the past that the woods always seemed a little bulimic, characteristically thin and worn, like someone's morose granddad who stopped taking care of himself the second or third time the kids hadn't brought the grandchildren down for Thanksgiving.

The rocks were still there though. They are always there in Pennsylvania, the plague of the AT in the state, as many as there are stars in the universe, sands on the shore, beer bottles abandoned in Florida. Pointed, unstable, wobbling seas of rocks, broken, razor-beaked, heaved by ages of water tricking into the cracks of the foundations of the land, freezing with implacable strength, and dumbly ripping bedrock into recremental rivers of opportunities to break the human ankle.

After an eight-day week of walking in the state, I was used to the Pennsylvania stones, used to cursing along a pathway that offered much the same trail experience you'd get walking mile upon mile across the bombed out remains of concrete buildings. But only if the concrete buildings had originally been carpeted with the planet's healthiest muddle of poison ivy and had just completed a spectacularly successful marketing campaign that promised free rent and riotously fun house parties for every snake looking for a place to get down, slither around, and have his first shot or two at tender hiker calf.

Given the obviously unnatural state of the treedom around me, I probably should have considered my next move more carefully. Especially given what I learned later.

But I was hot. And hungry. It was well past two, the morning's granola having long roared its way around a curve in the calorie highway. And the moonscape of barren rock and pygmy trees lengthened on down the trail as far as I could see (which was pretty much to the earth's horizon, given the obscene flatness of the walk).

So I energetically slashed my Moses staff around under the lowest branches of a nearby waist-high bush, hoping to convince any rattling friend it was time to party elsewhere. Hearing nothing, seeing nothing, I dropped the pack and slithered on my grumbling belly down into the shade, curving and bending as necessary to find as much chilled accommodation as possible with the nasty dust and tangles of stubborn rock. I, believe me, had not any more desire at that moment than you do right now to assume this troubled position in the Pennsylvania dirt. But remember, as far as you can see to the ends of the world, it's a thousand degrees every place in the known universe except in that little circle of starved, beaten shade. So I did it.

In that single meal alone, I'm sure I ate a sizable portion of my proverbial peck of dirt. Try this. Go ahead; it will give you a chance to stretch a bit before you continue the book. At the very least, please at least try it in your imagination. Here goes.

First, lie on your belly with a combative corps of razor branches four inches above the back of your head, stabbing away each time you move too clumsily. Then, still in this awkward pose, beg the blade out of your Swiss Army knife using only the same hand that holds the tool, the other being trapped on the wrong side of your opposite leg and held solidly in place by either a storm-curved bush root or a particularly large, stable rattlesnake, you can't see which. Then spasm your plastic bear bottle of honey from somewhere down near your boots and nag it into position above the cheese and eventually as near as possible to your mouth, your head all the while angled with the full strength and agility possessed by your neck, up and backwards into a baby-bird-crying-to-mom-for-the-worm pose. Here's the important part. Do all this while wallowing in small clouds of moon grime that puff and whiff and draft all about your tonsils and nose each time you move.

Then find out, as I did several years later, that all gooped up in that dust is a toxic mixture of wonderful things like lead, zinc, and cadmium. That, in fact, the trees are all gone because since before World War I the local vegetation has been continually assaulted by prevailing winds blowing in from a zinc smelting operation down in the nearby Lehigh Valley. Find out that a few years later after your hike that area will become the center of a huge EPA Superfund effort that has to scrape the soil, drag the mess off, and push the reset button on the mountain's vegetation, including planting over 13,000 new trees in 2013 alone. Find out that forty years after 1973 is the EPA only now beginning to work on restoring the purity of the area's water supply—creeks, streams, and ground water that spent decades being filtered through the thirty-three million tons of slag still sitting in place near the smelting site, all piled in a hundred-foot-high mountain of toxic cinders, two to three football fields wide, extending well over two miles through the Pennsylvania countryside.

Forty-five years ago, I had no clue about all of this.

Wriggling out of the bush, I wiped off the sticky, crumbly remains of cheese, honey, and heavy metals with my bandana and summoned up just enough enthusiasm to start heading south again.

It was a march of death, the small bushes becoming smaller until they disappeared altogether, the tiny grasses between the rocks becoming thinner and thinner until they melted away completely. Apparently the full blunt force of the pollution had fallen on the rock at the end of this particular mountain, the south face that fronted the Lehigh River. Almost a thousand feet straight down, it had—if my lead-infested memory serves me at all—not a single plant, not a living thing, just coffin sized rocks piled upon each other from the lip of the plateau down to the short stretch of riverine land at the bottom. In another place, it could have been the sort of rock scramble that hikers dream about jungle gyming through, the sort of vertically-oriented "trail" that makes Katahdin, or Mahoosuc Notch, or the White Mountains such monkey-bar delights. But in a relatively temperate zone, at an altitude only slightly higher than humankind's most ambitious skyscrapers, all this exposed rock just seemed wrong, bizarrely unnatural. On pitch after pitch, fully uncovered to a sun that clearly hated me and baked to a temperature just short of the surface of Venus, I picked my way down to the river. At the bottom, I was in a funk that not even two Cokes and a plastic-wrapped brownie from the Atlantic Service Station near the bridge could touch.

The next half of the afternoon was worse.

The chain of simple shelters strung down Appalachian Trail at half-day intervals is one of its most perfect treasures. The mostly primitive lean-tos are primarily meant to be a place out of the rain and snow, a respite from wet tents and cold, muddy ground. And they provide these creature comforts perfectly. But that's not their real brilliance. They are also perfect examples of beneficent social engineering, perfectly executed, working like super magnets every afternoon to draw most of the hikers from miles around to a single spot where they can have the pleasurable adventure of getting to know a group of total strangers. At the end of each day, the shelters become the superglue that cements the social experience of the trail, melting pots that have cooked up thousands of instant and deep friendships, some lasting a night, some for much longer.

That's the theory, and it's mostly the practice. But later in the walk one of these shelters in Pennsylvania almost ended my hike.

However, let me first lead you down to the AT camp at the bottom of this Pennsylvania climb, the Outerbridge Shelter, less than a mile south of the Lehigh River. This short detour will begin to explain a lot, both about why your average AT shelter is more Motel 6 than Hilton Waikiki and why so many potential AT thru-hikers just decide to go home someplace along the way, often long after they have shown the physical mettle to complete the walk.

The incredibly hardworking, mostly unpaid, and totally admirable exemplars of selfless public spirit who build and maintain AT trail shelters always begin, of course, by choosing a perfect setting from a Sierra Club calendar, a majestic perch of alpine splendor created eons ago specifically to capture sunsets and sunrises worthy of your most succulent honeymoon fantasy.

Then the calls of creature necessities kick in, and the shelter planners must go looking for the water that could make the scene a viable campsite. And usually they don't find it. Streams and springs only rarely choose to exist on top of the mountains, a place where gravity does not love them.

So, looking for water, the builders and maintainers pull out the maps, regroup, restudy, replan, and move downhill a couple of hundred yards to somewhere rich in aqua, if no longer on a much desired summit. Perhaps by a lovely stream or in the middle of a glade that might be used for, say, the photo for the July Nature Conservancy spread, some shady, branches-filled-with-cardinals, trail-immersed-in-blooming-red-and pink-rhododendron glen.

Maybe just the tiniest bit disappointed but still satisfied withal, the trail designers put away the compasses, hitch up their pants, give the thumbs up all round, and pull out the maps to begin construction planning in earnest. Then the harshness of backwoods physics thumps in, the kick of some bitterly misused horse you keep forgetting that you can never turn your back on. At the very least, decent materials for an average shelter weigh in at tons of lumber, cement, roofing shingles, stain, plywood, and nails. And every pound of it will have to be stumbled miles on someone's back up a backcountry path over months of awkward tugging and pulling.

So it's not all that surprising that you sometimes just look around a little shiftily, sigh, and reluctantly make a bargain with the AT shelter devils. Somebody remembers that beautiful spot just a tenth of a mile up the trail from the parking pullout on the highway, the nice, flat, open space where everyone stops to fill water bottles in that healthy stream at the beginning of the hike. Or maybe the place just off that old gravel road that the Forest Service keeps open to move in firefighting equipment and to give hunters access in the fall. Both of these spots are mighty nice—and a few pickups can make short work of dumping all the raw materials within a sane tote to the site. Done. Let's start building!

Here's how it all shakes out. I'm making a somewhat educated guess about the numbers, but I think they are at least in the ballpark. Maybe fifty of the 250 AT shelters sit by some glorious lake or roost up on a perfect bald on top of the world, places where in all your dreams you somehow get transported from the senior prom just in time to share your first slurpy kiss with your first wonderful flame. Another hundred or so are placed in that enchanted glen you'd be happy to dream about on a more routine but still perfect night. Seventy-five of the rest provide a nice enough place to get out of the weather, cook up your ramen, and rest in a neighborly way with whoever else has just spent a long day on the trail and wants to share stories and tea.

The remaining twenty-five or so, however, always feel like they might just get you murdered. Especially after the first time you've found yourself at one when it's too dark to hike out and a group of drunken yahoos stumbles the hundred yards from the nearby road, all hostile, loud, and out of sight of pretty much any nosy authorities. Those easy-to-access sites may have looked appealing to trail architects, back when they were all safe in their big, pleasant, congenial group sharing a root beer around the planning table. But I've never spent a night in a shelter within a mile of a road without expecting the Manson family to show up ready to party and tempted to make a part of that celebration some sort of horrible sport with one or two of my more beloved body parts. Sad but true, backwoods massacring seems to be a sedentary occupation, with most of the assaults and killings on the AT clustering where the offenders don't have to lug themselves and their macabre tools of torture very far to fester in their mayhem.

So I wasn't pleased over my Cokes and brownie to read in the guidebook that the Outerbridge Shelter sat a mere .7 of a mile from PA. 873. At the very least I could well imagine an unpleasant Saturday night with a bunch of local yokels hooting it up and throwing empties at each other. Thirty minutes later, I wasn't at all surprised to see the parking lot at the trailhead filled to its weedy edges with cobbled together teen cars sporting window stickers pledging allegiance to the local high school. But the half dozen police vehicles and two ambulances wedged in among the Camaros and Dusters did bring me up short.

I started meeting them 200 yards into the woods. First a boy and a girl, both in madras shorts and tennis shoes, holding hands, she crying quietly, he not responding to my "Hi!" Then a cluster of five guys, walking fast, heads down, snaking around me as I waited for them to file by, no one saying a word. Then two girls, leaning on each other, shuffling along whispering thoughtfully in low voices. And finally a policeman, one arm in consolation around a weeping young woman, followed closely by two paramedics carrying an unused EMT stretcher, both taking deep draws from their cigarettes as they struggled with the awkward and apparently unnecessary apparatus. No one acknowledged me as they passed.

The thirty people in the shelter clearing when I arrived were bunched as far away as possible from the shelter itself, where four policemen were talking earnestly with two boys sitting on the sleeping deck, one with a very noticeable smashed eye, the other with a considerable amount of blood out his nose and splashed across his undershirt. Several other officers were circulating the area, pushing sleeping bags over to check underneath, picking up an occasional grocery bag, pulling out its contents, and taking notes on small pads they then tucked back into shirt pockets. A female officer was talking angrily with two girls, their shirts tagged "Seniors Rock!" with magic marker.

Before I had a chance to get my bearings, four student types headed over my way and started in:

"He actually did it. I can't believe it."

"Well, *she* 'says' he did her. But we know what a big mouth she has. Drama all the time."

"If you can't handle the stuff you shouldn't be drinking it."

"Or smoking it."

"You saw how she was acting all afternoon. Asking for it."

"Bullshit."

"Needs the shit beaten out of him."

"Amen."

"Think he's probably in enough trouble as it is."

"Looks like this party is dead. That's the truth, and all the truth."

"There's not shit to do in this town. I'm sick of it."

In North Vietnam, U.S. sailors were pulling the last of the American mines out of Haiphong harbor. In Washington, Richard Nixon was formulating bold health insurance reform anchored on a strong employer mandate. Henry Kissinger had just been to Stockholm to pick up his Nobel Peace Prize. In the U.S. and Britain, all the Beatles were still writing and playing. In Florida and Texas, NASA had just placed the Skylab space station into permanent orbit. The American Psychiatric Association had just declared that homosexuality was not a mental illness. Two seniors in a California high school, Paul Allen and Bill Gates, were busy trying to market a traffic counter they had made themselves from off-the-shelf Intel 808 processors. The Peace Corps was still accepting applications. Fender Telecasters were selling new for less than $150, and the town these kids lived in was poisoning their families with a carcinogenic fog of heavy metals. But they couldn't find anything to do.

A police officer stepped away from the shelter, waved everyone over, and rumbled, "You kids need to go home now. The bandstand's all out of tunes for today. When you get home, I think it'd be smart if you thought real hard for a day or two about what happened here this afternoon. Those of you who will need to testify will hear from one of my deputies in the next week or so. Have your parents call if they have questions."

He did a big circle with his right arm and hand, ending the motion by pointing his index finger at the trail back out to the road. Gathering some of the bags, parcels, and other stuff—but leaving abandoned knots of clothes and equipment here and there—the kids fell in with their own privy circles and headed in small clumps up the path.

It was too late in the day to move on, so I parked my pack in the shelter and began working to shrug off the ugliness I'd just seen.

To my complete astonishment, I soon had company though. The kids started filing back in an hour later, first a small group of bruisers that must have been the linebackers from the football squad, next a faction with matching headbands, then apparently every other teen in town with the wherewithal to crank a case of Miller on his or her shoulder and slog the half mile in.

An hour later, ears just beginning to trickle blood from a hundred alternating plays of "Bad, Bad Leroy Brown" and "You are the Sunshine of My Life," I pulled my things together, found a flat spot a hundred yards south, put my Ensolite down in the dirt, and spent a long and ugly night sweating into my down bag. I left as the sun came up, somebody's radio playing "Killing Me Softly with His Song" loud enough for me to hear it for another five minutes down the trail.

But this wasn't rock bottom. That came at another Pennsylvania shelter a week later.

Try this thought experiment. Go get a copy of your favorite short story. Or click up the greatest YouTube video you've ever seen. Or just cue up anything at all that you love to read, watch, or hear. You could even choose your favorite chapter from this book if you like. The only criteria are that it be something relatively brief and something that completely lights your awe. Now enjoy it. Bathe totally in the pleasure. Float around in it. Feels perfect, right? Makes you totally alive, tingling with significance, breathing fully in the groove of all that is vital and real and invigorating.

Then watch, read, or listen to it again. Still nice! Well of course it is. In fact, you probably liked it even more this time, dug a little deeper, found some tingling nuance that didn't tickle in before.

Then watch, read, or listen yet once again. And don't stop when you're done. Watch, read, or listen three hundred more times. Do it all day, doing nothing else. Dig totally and completely in, and watch, read, or listen to it for a week, for a month, for several months in a row.

Is your favorite, by this time, beginning to feel like a life sentence, some sort of self-imposed, bizarre solitary confinement, a fun time only in the eyes, maybe, of Franz Kafka?

At some point, that's what thru-hiking the Appalachian Trail inevitably becomes. For everyone at some point. No exceptions. No matter how much you love the woods, no matter how much your eye delights in capturing inestimable beauty and solace not just in row upon row of majestic mountains but in the abstract form of tree upon tree, sky upon branch, blossom draped across leaf bejeweled with the sparkling dews of the mountains. No matter how much you delight in the freedom of the open road, the sun in your face and the wind at your back. After enough weeks, there's going to come a day when you become tired of this shit—flesh, bone, and soul.

Enough trees, enough hills, enough noodles, day after endless day, each made up of hour after endless hour, minute after minute, second after second, listening only to your own labored breathing and the sound of your boots pushing again against the ground. At some point jaundice spreads across your eyes and bile into your brain. You can't help but start to notice that backpacking the entire Appalachian Trail is finally just choosing to bring an intense and passionate focus on an inherently meaningless task. Why Maine to Georgia? Why not Maine to Florida? Why not Cape Gaspe to Atlanta? Why bob right or turn left just because a white blaze tells you to? It's hard, and it's ridiculous.

You might think that it's bound to help that you're halfway done as you pound the rocks through Pennsylvania. You've already walked a thousand miles; you only have just that same amount of distance to left go.

But it doesn't help at all. You know how hard those first thousand were; you know in your knees and your feet and your sweating back. "Just another thousand miles" sounds like the cruel sentence an angry judge might intone from high on the bench, you cowering in your torn and nasty rags, aware that the crime doesn't fit the punishment, that you can't stand another night in silent, solitary, hopeless captivity.

That's the way it felt, sitting at the end of another day in one of the final shelters in Pennsylvania. I was alone of course, hadn't talked with anyone in days.

At one time, the hiss of my great Svea hiker stove had been a comfort, a hymn to self-reliance, a brave psalm to the ingenious ways my fellow humans could cleverly engineer a few ounces of dumb metal into a miracle to meet the elemental need to enjoy hot food. Now, it sounded like the clanking of a cell door somewhere down a long, paint-chipped hall. My sleeping bag stunk over in the corner, and the zipper to the central compartment of my pack hung lopsided out of its channel, the victim of last night's Vandal hoard of foraging mice.

This particular hill of Gethsemane faced a mountain stream, it's true. But it was late in a very hot summer, and the water was mostly gone. Mosquitoes congregated over the few pools remaining in its trickle. The view as I cooked was of a muddy bank of twisted, bashed, ugly roots, the mud hardened into the least interesting colors of brown and grey in the palette of creation. Over where I couldn't possibly rescue it, a ripped and greying plastic grocery bag hung on the last branch of a small, dying tree pushing out of the creek bank. The air was still broiling at seven in the evening. But I doubt if it would have helped if the shelter sat on the most beautiful site atop Matterhorn, with the sun setting full and beautiful across the Alps. I was lonely, and I wanted to go home. I was tired of walking. I went to sleep in the darkest of moods.

In the morning though, I put everything back into pack just like I'd done for seventy-nine days in a row, walked back up the blue blazed trail a hundred yards, turned left onto the AT, and headed south again.

I don't want to overdo the moral here. It's a tortured analogy at the very least. And I'm well aware that the most meaningful comparison I could make to this night in Pennsylvania probably would not be to the world of employment, to the careers we all end up adopting once we settle down a bit. It's certainly not where Dante would go with the story.

But the analogy is not one that I've been able to escape. That shelter in Pennsylvania has always been the symbolic place where I sit down when whatever job I'm doing has become intolerable, as almost all of them finally do when you've done them enough. At some point, you become competent, you've met the challenges, you've figured it out. And you are just slogging. It's no longer meaningful. But it's still hard. And there are often more than a few snakes in the weedy grass of the cubes around you. Even worse, you might be so bored that you don't notice or care when you begin thinking about poisoning your neighbors or assaulting your friends.

Here's how I handled it. When I reached what felt like the dead end of one of these metaphoric Pennsylvanias, I usually just ended up acknowledging that it was a place I had to be for a bit in order to get someplace else. It isn't very pretty, and I guess it's pretty obvious. But it's still true. You have to go through the state to do the rest of the trail.

If toxic winter comes, can spring poo be far behind?

I skip backwards across the shelter clearing, on the fly slipping into the unwinding spin of the discus thrower, all the while keeping my eyes firmly on the surface level of the water in the pot, ready to abandon my grip should the container's hazard become emboldened and try a leap for freedom.

The next night I seemed destined to have to stay at the notoriously depressing Darlington Shelter. Early on in Maine, I'd camped with a gentlemanly retired naval officer who'd annotated my *AT Mileage Fact Sheet* with pretty much all he'd learned from two thru-hikes—everything from the state of water supplies at iffy campsites, to rural fire stations that might welcome an overnight visitor on a rainy night, to which waitress in some small Virginia town was likely to bring a free scoop of ice cream with your dessert order. His handwritten comment beside the Darlington Shelter was short and—as it turned out in my particular case—entirely prophetic. "Shitty" was his comment in total. He was right in ways he possibly hadn't considered.

The shelter was a rough-board disaster most likely originally created in the ninth century as a pre-execution holding pen for abjectly poor and totally broken peasants who had seriously irritated the Spanish nobility. Though I haven't done the research to substantiate my conclusions, I'm reasonably sure it was then transported, with not much care for its structural integrity, across the stormy Atlantic in 1531 to house the original shipment of domestic pigs brought to the New World by brutish Spanish conquistadors, a group not especially known for their love of beauty for beauty's sake. Lost in the dim back halls of history is the chain of baseborn decisions that somehow deemed appropriate its repurposing as a ignoble place of rest for noble AT hikers.

It was, of course, sited only ten feet away from a well-used jeep road, ensuring, among other unpleasantries, that its landscaping could be seamlessly crowdsourced to the party community in the area. They had chosen well and carefully, to wit: a charming array of smashed bourbon bottles, an ocean of crumbled, rotting aluminum foil, a carpet of cigarette butts, dozens of expended shotgun shells, and a partially burned, totally savaged Art Deco love seat, its leather bottom now shredded by generations of riotous possums. Or more likely by many a posse of restless Pennsylvania teens, given the dozen or so small caliber bullet holes it now displayed.

But the Darlington Shelter also sat just above and north of the dreaded Cumberland Valley road walk, and, in spite of my best planning, I reached it in the very late afternoon. So an uneasy night there seemed inevitable. At least it wasn't a weekend. Maybe the hoot-it-up-crowd would stay at home watching *Gilligan's Island* until Friday rolled around and they could resume their big times vomiting it up in the lonely, derelict pines.

Two decades later, after a thorny series of negotiations with local residents, many of whom wanted to keep hikers on the asphalt rather than risk them traipsing through the burgeoning suburban growth and thriving farms in the area, the trail was moved to a perfect route up on a ridge through the valley. Everyone now agrees that it's a great walk and that the AT hikers who use it have mostly proven to be respectful, welcomed neighbors.

But in 1973, the walk across the Cumberland, under Interstate 81 and the Pennsylvania Turnpike, and on towards Maryland promised ten miles of hot, shadeless pavement pounding, mostly on rural two lanes. Everyone coming north warned me, unless I aspired to be as well done as the Christmas turkey, to do the valley crossing early in the morning, before the sun was completely awake and ready to start its daily baking. I planned to take their good advice, even if it meant another night in a roadside slum where one might acquire a slit throat if just the right adventurer decided to jeep in for a night of bloodshed and carnage.

So I laid the sleeping bag out to air, dipped my cook pot into the spring for supper water, and idled away fifteen minutes filling up a trash bag with shelter garbage while my mac and cheese gooped along on its journey to reconstitution.

Maybe some tea might be nice with the Kraft, I belatedly thought.

So back to the spring for another quart of water to finish off the cooking.

Unlike the shelter, the spring was a beauty. Only a hundred feet away, it was a two-foot diameter of superb mountain refreshment, expertly stoned in at some point by some thoughtful craftsperson of taste and charm, with a nice surrounding deck of matching stone so that no careless boots could ever carelessly kick even the smallest amount of mud into its crystal treasures. It was perfect.

Well, perfect except for the large human turd bobbing with carefree, jaunty vitality at the spring's very center, a treasure I'd somehow not discovered on my earlier water-scooping mission. I'm pretty sure it was human. I did no forensics, took no DNA. But it certainly looked human, appearing much like all the other human dumps I've ever seen. Too large and linear to be deer, too lumpy to be bear, too horrible to imagine in its all-too-clear relation with the water happily boiling up my supper just yards away.

I don't know how I could have missed it on my original trip to fill the pot the first time around. The water was perfectly clear; no weeds encroached the small area of the pool; no mountain mists swirled around to limit views. I desperately sought rational explanations. Perhaps I had discovered a rare submarine-diving poop, with high-tech powers to confound hikers by sliding soundlessly down among the depths at the times when it chose to lurk unsighted? Maybe an invisible, quiet, uncharacteristically bloated Naiad with digestion issues had slipped in unnoticed while I was doing my cleaning tasks? These are, with proper and long consideration, the only logical reasons—other than trail weariness and the usual all-consuming joy at taking off the pack at the end of the day—for how I could have not noticed a poop the size of a police officer's flashlight as I bent over an area barely larger than an average hat.

In less than a minute, my sleeping gear was corded back on the pack, the pack was restuffed with everything that had come out of it, my partially cooked macaroni and excrement was spread down the mountainside, my cook pot was wrapped in my entire, complete collection of available plastic bags and tied to the outside of my pack frame, and I was off down the trail toward the Cumberland Valley, trying to outpace the radioactive miasma that I knew had to be streaming off my aluminum kitchen utensils.

Fifty yards down the path, a burst of belated awareness—equal part disgust and conscience—pivoted me around and back toward the shelter.

I read a novel when I was a kid about Benedict Arnold's disastrous 1775 march up through the forbidding Maine forest to try to take Quebec from the British. On about the same route across the Kennebec River and through untrodden wilderness that I had taken two months before, his troops got hopelessly lost and quickly ran out of food. As the unforgiving Maine winter closed around them, some of the soldiers felt the unfortunate need to resort to cannibalism to keep together body and what was left of their souls. One minor character was particularly attractive and vivid to the gross-out sensibilities of my teen self. I was remembering him hard and steady as I approached Darlington for the second time.

The character's best buddy, as it turned out, died early on as the wilderness closed in, and, being dead, no longer had much need of his head and its rich stores of protein. So for chapters, my favorite character, by now completely insane with hunger, would look carefully around, pull the decaying and increasingly slimy skull from his duffel, and secretly dig in for a little tasty, precious brain snack. In the climactic scene, where all is finally set right, his saner mates discover this grotesque heart-of-darkness cafeteria and move with alacrity to place the hideous head underground.

Headed back up toward the Darlington Shelter and its hideous fresh-water spring, I now fully understood their horror. A proper burial of my own nonfictional abomination had become my first priority. The turd must be safely entombed. And, I never, ever, planned to eat from my cherished, lightweight, indestructible Sigg cookware again. Never. It must be buried too, soon and deeply, in the nearest clearing I can find far enough away from the shelter never to offend the sanctity of human decency. Off came the pack, down I go on the knees, frantically goes the walking stick into Pennsylvania earth. But, alas, mostly into Pennsylvania rocks. Ten minutes later, all sweat and cursing, I have a ragged hole, pot-wide but less than two inches deep. Defeat is acknowledged.

Off the knees, I grasp the pot with a plastic bag and step toward the spring again, perusing it from the safe distance that one might scope out a cave that one suspects might harbor a sleeping dragon. The turd still floats placidly on the surface, rocking and surfing short, graceful waves stirred by the prevailing winds.

I scoop the poo and skip backwards across the shelter clearing, on the fly slipping into the unwinding spin of the discus thrower, all the while keeping my eyes firmly on the surface level of the water in the Sigg, ready to abandon my grip should the container's hazard become emboldened and try a leap for freedom, perhaps starting by a lunging liquid assault up against my hand.

At the edge of the clearing, I stop, pivot, and uncoil in an impressively fluid motion, hurling a quart of water and five ounces of gleaming waste into the Pennsylvania wasteland, where no human, I hope, will ever encounter it again. With a dozen or so equally desperate movements, I empty the spring, step back to watch it slowly refill, empty it again, and then tag a warning note of explanation to a nearby tree: "Please, Dear Friends, don't drink from this spring for three centuries. Ask not why. Trust me." Then I engulf the violated pot back into its plastic bag, slide several more bags around the heap, tie it again back to the bottom of the pack frame, and head back down toward the hellish road walk I expect from the Cumberland Valley.

But the road walk turned out not to be hellish. In fact, perhaps as cosmic pension for my good poo deed, the next few miles were some of the most pleasant of the hike. With the sun now behind the trees, I spent the next two and a half hours walking largely deserted, rural roads, with tall, proud, healthy corn dipping and waving on both sides, the universe practically breaking into song with harmonious verses from "This Land Is Your Land" ringing out across the valley. In fact, the guy who drives slowly by, the left hand resting on his outsized towing mirror breaking free to give me a friendly salute with his index finger, looks all the world like Woody Guthrie. Two kids playing in a sprinkler look up, stop, run to the road, and ask me where I'm heading. An apple tree fragrantly close to the road is tempting, but I keep walking. The air is heavily instilled with the smell of hay, though I see no stacks in the fields I walk through. A teen rumbles up from behind on a mint 1950's-era tractor, gives me a huge smile as she passes, turns partially around to shout out a "Keep on truckin'," and moves past into her bright future. A middle-aged couple sitting on a porch nods a "hello." As the remaining light revolves toward dark, the distance streams out beneath my boots like unbroken time itself, and I find myself continually breaking into a rousing but tuneless whistle of "Zip-a-Dee-Doo-Dah," a welcome hymnic change from the Beatles' "Long and Winding Road," my ear bore for the last month or so. The Pennsylvania malaise was gone. It never returned the rest of the hike.

Seven miles in and the sun completely gone, I stride into the huge, halogenic flatlands of a mega truck stop on U.S. 11 and immediately make for the cafeteria at the glowing center of its diesel-muscled empire. Like any smallish, colleged, un-tattooed middle class guy who didn't play high school football, I approach this sanctuary of manly motor culture with humility and not a little concern. I'm not where I belong, and I know it. So I plan to enter quietly, under all radars.

Everything goes wrong almost immediately.

First, there's the struggle with the front door, apparently too much for my atrophying arms now unaccustomed to any physicality more challenging than lifting handfuls of peanuts to the mouth. As I finally get the creaking right panel moving, the top of my pack awkwards around some unseen jut on the left, ricocheting my toxic pot against the tympanic safety glass in the door. The pot vs. glass confrontation is loud enough, I assume, to offend even the Teamster ears of Jimmy Hoffa, way off in some concrete or deep water sanctuary. Several wobbly-bearded men looked up from their coffees, and the hostess slam-gums her way over.

"That wasn't all that smooth. Sorry. Nothing broken though."

She looks at me, head just slightly tilted, Double Bubble doing steady, studied cycles.

"I was just checking to see how late you stay open. Wanted to see if I had time to check into the motel and clean up before I came back to eat."

She smiles the way a mother might smile at her six year old's first attempt to change the new baby, the one where the diaper somehow wraps up at least one hand and a foot along with the targeted bottom.

"This is a truck stop, Sugar. These guys don't sleep much. They drive against the clock. We stay open all night, every night. Christmas, Easter, the Pope's vasectomy, my birthday— we're gonna be right here, eager to serve."

The four men in the closest booth look at her, look at me, look at each other and laugh.

She says all this kindly enough that I am encouraged to get right down to what I have in mind, my secret plan, concocted across the last seven miles. I can see the kitchen steaming away through a set of swinging doors just behind her hostess stand.

"Is there any chance you'd be willing to put my pot in your dishwasher while I'm checking in?"

Just for the slightest second, this calm and capable woman seemed a bit confused.

"You brought dope in here and you want me to do what with it?"

"No, no. It's for cooking. An aluminum pot. Well, I'm pretty sure it's aluminum. Legal. I promise. Nothing illegal about it. All straight. Just an aluminum bowl."

I paused, trying to save the situation, trying to conjure a most compelling, strong, and lawful case for my request.

"It's dirty."

She senses the foul, right off the bat.

"Just how dirty? And how'd it get that way?"

I don't immediately answer.

"We don't have a fancy machine. Our dishwasher's named Randy. Don't want to lose him."

I feel a supreme test of personal integrity coming on.

"I just didn't wash it fast enough. That's all. A raccoon dragged it around. Didn't appear to have rabies or anything." I paused, plotting desperate ways to strengthen my case. "Seemed like a healthy raccoon."

She looks at me steadily.

"I just don't want to take any chances. Needs really hot water.

Along with an unusually long soak."

She continues to look at me. I step a half step backward.

"I can put it in the shower, I guess. No need to bring Randy into this."

"Hardly anybody ever succeeds when they try to put one over on a smart lady in a truck stop. Pumpkins don't fall off the trucks around here. You know that, right? Doesn't happen, Honey. Not part of the story."

She doesn't move her eyes off me. "No clue what you're up to. You're strange, not to mention a little dirty yourself. But we'd be glad to wash your pot. Just give your waitress a fair tip when you come in to eat. And don't tell everyone out there that it's part of our usual service. Don't want to be washing a ton of hobo pots."

I came back an hour later, completely proud that I'd bargained the motel down from ten to eight dollars, a generous concession to my late arrival.

Over the next few hours, as the mystery poop continued to molder up on South Mountain, I had a country-fried steak dinner, complete with butter beans and mashed potatoes, talked until late about my hike with a table of drivers from Florida, Minnesota, and Chicago and did, indeed, leave a good tip. The waitress came back with my pot when she brought the check. It was as gleaming as I'd seen it since it left the outfitters in its original box. It was still warm when she put it on the table—not a ghostly after-presence of the poop, I had to tell myself. Just freshly washed, professionally.

Still, I had the hardest time picking it up without wrapping a napkin around it first.

When the company I worked with for over twenty years blew up at the turn of the 21st century, we went from 120,000 employees down to less than a third of that in one year. It was shitty for all involved. The mornings I knew there were going to be layoffs were particularly brutal.

I sincerely hope that you never have to hoist this particular load. But if your turn comes, you'll discover it is hard to push back the covers, brush your teeth, get dressed, and drive into work knowing that, say, you're going to have to tell someone whose husband is dying of pancreatic cancer that in two weeks she'll have no income and that they are both going to lose their health insurance.

If I had been the main character in one of the novels I liked to read as a teenager, I would have dug deep into my collected life experiences and invoked the Darlington story to find solace on mornings like this, knowing that even the nastiest beginnings can somehow transform later into a perfect day.

And, in fact, the story sometimes helped me a little when I remembered it. But never even close to enough. I always still felt like a desolate hollow on some denuded mountain every single time I sat there in the conference room with my employee, the HR person, and the ream of layoff papers that had to be signed before we could all go home and start the next part of the journey.

MARYLAND AND WEST VIRGINIA

Learning to decide what to stomach

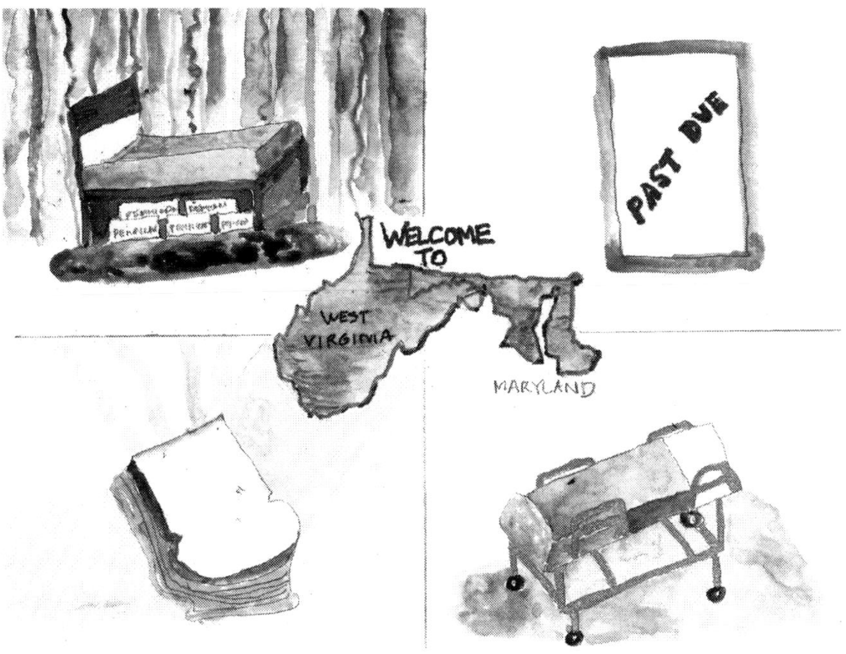

Always know just how much crap you're willing to eat

Engaging in promiscuous eating, I would be sharing this treat with the gum and teeth biome of at least one stranger who came before me. But I was willing to compromise, to go along to get along.

This chapter is a bald and unapologetic allegory, a story that uses, as they say, concrete images or actions to represent abstract or spiritual or political meanings, making a lesson that otherwise might be hard to grasp become easily clear. Rather than bury the meaning the way some savory stews hide their sausage, a good allegory has its fun by dishing out the truth so plainly that it becomes as obvious as a series of six-inch white blazes painted on trees and rocks from Maine to Georgia. It's hard to get lost in a well-marked allegory.

The moral of this story—though not announced in a well-crafted, memorable paragraph at the end—has to do with either the creepy, bossy boss, the exceptionally whiny employee, or the sadly overbearing friend or lover in your life. You choose. The universal principle for dealing with these types: that's what this parable is all about. There is no scary trigger alert here. You may, without harm, read this fable to children.

Early in Maryland I came upon a clump of pemmican in the middle of the trail, only partially wrapped its original package. One large bite was gone.

Pemmican, as your elders will know, is usually associated with Native Americans, a concentrated lump of fruits and berries, dried meat, and whatever high-calorie fat is available when it's all mixed together into its brick-like form. Compacting a huge shot of high energy into a very small bundle, it's the perfect hiker food: light, indestructible, and delivering a taste treat just this side of the ill-washed blanket under an aging, partially incontinent sled dog. Once the standard fare of everyone from the way-off-the-grid pelt traders who opened up North American forests for commercial exploitation, to Arctic explorers, to U.S. Special Forces, it's no longer much in use, having been leveraged out of serious competition once M&Ms began stuffing today's delicious gorp with sufficient butterball content.

Towards the end of the Vietnam War, my father—a shrewd and unscrupulous wheeler-dealer working in the early days of the computer business—bested a Green Beret logistics sergeant at Fort Bragg in what he always considered one of the most masterful of the signature off-the-books dealings that kept the Hiscoe family solidly in the middle class, even though my father had no college degree and very little actual knowledge of computers. In this particular transaction, he entered the sergeant's office with an ancient used Olivetti portable typewriter another client had paid him to take away; he left with fifty pounds of U.S. Army pemmican, which was soon stashed under my bed and often in my knapsack. At the time, I assumed that his aim was to thriftily further my climbing and hiking endeavors. Much later though, in a deathbed confession, he admitted that his real goal was to thrash some sense into my head by way of my stomach. At about my age, he'd lived a few rough years on Army C-rations himself and assumed that my romantic attachment to roughing it would soon be squished by a good dose of reality in the form of some truly odious food paste. "I thought that a good set of the runs," he reasoned, "might be just the thing to get you to put your college education into an expensive suit and a real job."

His larger strategy was unsuccessful. But he was right about the inevitable intestinal distress. After a few meals of pemmican, I launched the rest of the boxes into a dumpster and clanged the door shut, I hoped forever. By the time I hiked the AT, this timeworn culinary disaster held no glamour in my outdoors fantasies, as deeply held and sturdy as they otherwise proved to be (just the tiniest whiff of a mixture of Kendal Mint Cake and underarm stink can, for instance, still dredge up my younger self's utopian joy at the romance of sleeping on the ground).

The piece of pemmican I found on the trail in 1973 was especially repugnant. According to its ripped, soggy paper wrapping, this particular knot of belly jelly was at one time in the ownership of the U.S. Coast Guard. The date on the packaging was 1944. Almost thirty years old when it transferred to my ownership, it was covered in ants, at least a hundred of them, working slobbery mouthed away all over the fatty lump of ancient Uncle Sam. The ants did so at some risk to themselves too, weaving between two plump spiders sharing the feast and having to navigate to the buggy delicacy through the mucky mud-slime in which the pemmican rested. But once they were on board, it was probably easy to penetrate deeply into the pemmican center, given the drippy disintegration the piece had undergone during the couple of days it had apparently sat gunking away in the sun and rain of the Maryland summer.

And remember, there was at least one bite already gone before I arrived. This was not an untouched piece of virgin candy. Engaging in promiscuous eating, I would be sharing this treat with the gum, teeth, and tongue biome of at least one stranger who came before me.

But I acted with no hesitation. None. I was hungry. The pemmican would not kill me. It would probably not make me sick. Might not even further upset my already quaky stomach. I needed the calories. So I was willing to compromise, to go along to get along. Still walking, I scooped up the treat, brushed off most of the dirt and some of the ants, placed the glutinous mire into my mouth, and ate it.

That's the end of the first part of this parable.

Now enter symbolic character number two. You may call him Major Baloney Sandwich.

Major Sandwich was in the firepit of the next shelter, bathed in a mystical cylinder of sunlight that found its way through the foliage and focused eerily on the brown lunch bag in the middle of the detritus of aluminum foil and singed sticks that remained of someone's abandoned fire. Leaving my own 11 a.m. snack of stamp-sized chocolate abandoned on the picnic table, I dug the bag out with trembling fingers. This could be my lucky day, twice.

The bag was lightly charred over the side that rested in the cold coals of the fire, obviously thrown in by some brainless trog who assumed it would quickly catch fire, wholly disappear, and not somehow burn down acres of the forest in which he or she left it. Instead, the bag apparently had just smoldered a bit, given up, and resumed moldering at a natural pace in the Maryland sun.

In the bag I found a Baby Ruth wrapper (and its heavenly smell), an orange peel (an aroma that even now makes my mouth begin to lubricate), an empty Doritos bag, and a carefully cellophaned, completely unmolested baloney sandwich, totally intact, not a single bite gone.

I looked it over carefully; I studied it with care.

This was not a dilettante's luncheon, not some *italienische Mortadella* bologna decorated with a carefully arranged array of fresh Batavian lettuces and sun-ripened miniature Campari tomatoes, dabbed artfully with an artisanal ginger and cucumber sauce and placed between two hand-tossed Staffordshire buttered crumpets. Instead, Major Baloney was a proud piece of workingman's craft, a meal meant to grow chest hair, a majestically gluttonous, larded salute to the straightforward need to eat fast and eat simple. And then be done with a burp of satisfaction. Two pieces of white Wonder Bread (one a heel from the end of the loaf), seven (oh yes, I counted them with greedy anticipation) slices of baloney, and a thick blanket of mayonnaise, the only nod to healthy eating or gourmet ornament a halfhearted rip of black-edged iceberg no bigger than two hypodermic needles.

My stomach cheered; my heart soared.

But my brain balked. If this was indeed meant to be someone's lunch, it had sat out on the ground, warm mayonnaise and lettuce curating bacterial delights, for somewhere around twenty-four hours—a day's worth of diligent growth for any lurking and ambitious e-coli, listeria, and salmonella.

This could make me very sick. This could kill me. Major Sandwich could end my journey, both the trail and the mortal one.

Reader, I didn't eat it. I buried it (rather easy to do in the rich Maryland soil). Then I ate my chocolate in chaste, grateful silence and headed on my way.

When you invite someone to your meeting, try to listen to what they say

If she had been around to be a Facebook founder, she would have been the one to come up with the idea of "liking" a comment on your page. She knew how to make you beam.

The Colonel was everything a colonel should be: tall, strapping, movie-star handsome, confident, courtly, and darn sure used to having others attend to his pronouncements. I tried. But it was hard.

One of the perks of thru-hiking the AT in 1973, back when the crowds were still manageable, was the honor of getting to have a personal meeting with the executive director of what was then called the Appalachian Trail Conference. Anticipating the larger role that it would play as the 1968 National Trails Act moved toward implementation, the ATC had just opened a new headquarters in Harpers Ferry, West Virginia, housing itself temporarily just off the trail down in the historic part of town, the part administered by the National Park Service to commemorate the key role the area played in our murderous Civil War.

As far as I can tell, the ATC had a grand total of two employees at the time. One of them was Jean Caslin. Every time I hear someone say that the existence of a completed, maintained, and protected AT is one of the greatest wonders of the do-gooder world, I think of Ms. Caslin. Though the trail is now managed in part by the Park Service and the US Forest Service, its fundamental strength is still and always has been in the volunteers who largely built it and who now largely keep it wonderful. And it stays wonderful in great part because the ATC has always done a masterful job of making its volunteers know they are important and special. For the two and a half decades after she hired on in 1972 as the ATC's second employee, Jean Caslin was the chief cook and bottle washer who kept those relationships all fed and shiny.

The morning I checked by the ATC headquarters, she treated me like Abraham Lincoln himself had just strolled in for a briefing. I reminded her that we'd talked on the phone several times as I had planned my trip, and she said, of course, she remembered. And gave me no reason to believe that she didn't. Ten minutes of answering her questions, drinking her tea, and telling her my stories, and I was ready to give up every cent I had to the cause. Unfortunately, I was down to my last several traveler's cheques. But I vowed to be a lifetime supporter of the trail once I found my fortune, and I've kept that vow, even though the fortune has never completely materialized. She was wonderful. If she had been around to be a Facebook founder, she would have been the one to come up with the idea of "liking" a comment on your page. She knew how to make you beam.

"Make sure you come back at 1:30," she reminded me as we shook hands at the door. "The Colonel wants to meet you too." The Colonel was the ATC's first employee and its current leader. "He considers you end-to-enders the absolute best source of intelligence about the trail. Boots on the ground. He'll be really interested in how you've found it, especially just north of here, where we've had some bad reports. Be here."

I came, but it wasn't a good meeting.

I admit right upfront that I returned that afternoon in a sour mood. First, there was that certified letter from the Wake County sheriff that I picked up along with my supply drop and other mail at the post office. It said—in the language that is at once both so heartlessly bland and completely threatening that is a hallmark of legal rhetoric—that I'd better have my ragged bottom in Raleigh, North Carolina, sitting in a chair in the accounting office at Rex Hospital by end of day, September 15, 1973, or a warrant would be issued for my arrest. I'll tell you the whole story in the interlude that follows this chapter. But it's enough to know at this point that I'd crept quietly out of town to hike the AT while owing a large sum of money to a large corporation and several powerful, well-connected citizens of my hometown. And they were now tired of waiting to be paid. I might be off well-hidden in the thickets of what's left of the howling North American wilderness, but the powers that be in

North Carolina somehow knew exactly where I was and how to get my attention.

Feeling as dark and stuck as the floor in a dollar movie theater, I phoned friends in Raleigh. They agreed to pick me up ten days later, 150 miles down the trail in Waynesboro, Virginia.

My hike was over, at least for now.

So my mood was already a mess as I walked around the historical exhibits in Harpers Ferry waiting for my 1:30 meeting.

And then I got mad.

Ahead of everybody else by a year and a half, John Brown decided in late 1859 that it was time to stop the talking and get to work making the gore and blood start to flow. If everybody else was content to make vain appeals to reason, to bluster, to threaten, or to complain, he was dead ready to move down the trail and deliver on the civil war that angry voices both North and South seemed to be demanding. With twenty-one insurrectionists—black and white, including three of his own sons and two of his daughters, one only fifteen years old—he seized Harpers Ferry the night of October 16, planning to distribute rifles from its huge U.S. arsenal to enslaved comrades in the area. He would soon, he was sure, be joined by hoards of brave men and women from throughout this country and Canada, slaves and citizens alike, all rallying to his holy cause. Equipped with the means to fight for freedom, this guerrilla army would then escape into the Appalachians, where they would begin a campaign of raids to terrorize slaveholders in the surrounding valleys and hurry the nation into an apocalyptic war that would cleanse the land of human bondage.

As it turned out, almost nobody came to help.

Things did start well though. In an inspired public relations coup, Brown's first move was to send a small squad upriver to capture the plantation of Colonel Lewis Washington, free his slaves, and bring this esteemed gentleman back as their first prisoner. As George Washington's great-grandnephew and closest living male relative, Lewis had inherited, among other things, his great uncle's ceremonial sword and a pistol our first commander in chief carried through the Revolution. With a fine sense of allegorical justice, Brown was determined that when the government sent in soldiers to try to stop his raid, the troops would be confronting a powerfully symbolic interchange with history: the original sidearms of our first president and executive owner of human beings would be in the hands of slaves fighting for their liberty.

This was the last tactic to go right for Brown.

In one of the sadder ironies of our history, the first person to die in the raid was Mr. Heyward Shepherd, a free black man and landowner who often ran the local office of the B&O Railroad at night. As he moved down the rails to try to determine why the trains had stopped running, he either didn't hear or chose to ignore the calls to halt from Brown's men, many of whom had scant military training or experience. Shepherd was shot in the back as he tried to retreat in the dark to his office.

Within a day, federal forces led by Robert E. Lee, a West Point grad and in 1959 still a colonel in the Army of the United States of America, easily overwhelmed the guerillas. Brown and most of his surviving compatriots were jailed, brought to court, convicted, and quickly hanged. The bodies of many of the rebels, including one of Brown's sons, were donated to a local college, with the understanding that they be promptly dissected by the school's medical students.

General Lee was, of course, never executed for the rebellious treason that he signed up for a year later. Nor for his central role in the deaths of the almost 750,000 Northerners and Southerners who died during our civil war. The outsized scale of his crimes is worth considering for a second. If the same percentage to today's U.S. population were to be killed, we'd have seven million dead Americans to bury.

Instead of being hung by the neck and sliced up at doctor school, General Lee quietly offered to hand over his sword after his defeat and was graciously allowed to retire from the field, sword still at his side, to become president of a southern college and allow himself to be transformed into much beloved rallying point for the century of racial hatred that was to come. When he died in old age, he was buried with great ceremony in the Lee Chapel at Washington and

Lee University. The chapel and the university, of course, are named in his honor.

Though the conclusion of this sordid story should be enough to get any fair thinking person a bit upset, it's not really what most heated me up on that hot afternoon in Harper's Ferry.

Just before I headed back to the ATC headquarters, I happened to run across a plaque conspicuously affixed to the wall of a Park Service building in the center of town. Placed there in 1931 through the combined efforts of the Sons of the Confederate Veterans and the United Daughters of the Confederacy, it proudly proclaimed in bronze that Mr. Shepherd deserved his own set of honors for:

> exemplifying the character and faithfulness of thousands of negroes who under many temptations throughout subsequent years of war, so conducted themselves that no stain was left upon a record which is the peculiar heritage of the American People, and an everlasting tribute to the best in both races.

I don't know much about Heyward Shepherd; there's not much left to find about him in the actual historical record. Maybe he really was a faithful SuperTom, a compliant servant who gave his life so he could become an eternal tool of the sort of the deliberately ignorant, pigheadedly obstinate bunch I'd spent way too much time around growing up in North Carolina. Not the big-mouthed, poor, angry ones who you might excuse a little because they had been fed a mess of half-truths and hate since they were babies. Those folks didn't write up or pay for the plaque. This had all the marks of the teapot, school tie, and country club bunch who used their good educations and eloquent newspapers to pull the strings of racial foolishness from their law offices and verandas. In my experience at least, they were the ones who loved nothing better than to praise up one of their "faithful negroes," one who would never even consider staining himself with the temptation of doing anything to end the slavery of his people or our own peculiar heritage of racial nastiness.

Maybe the Confederate boys and girls had accurately described the essence of Mr. Shepherd's contribution to the peculiar heritage of the

American people. But one likes to think that the kind of man who had somehow clawed out a place for himself as a property owner and a manager in a hostile community might have instead become one of those who later slipped away in the night, joined the 54th Massachusetts, and put a bayonet in the neck of the legal practice of owning men and women in the United States.

Shot in the back, indeed, his dignity still being stolen in public over a century after his death.

That was my mood when I headed back up the hill to the ATC offices, disgusted that somehow the Park Service had given official sanction to one of those twisted, self-satisfied nonsense stories that for centuries had been used to justify the cancer at the center of my community. If my retelling of my meeting with the Colonel seems too sour, let's chalk it up to the bad attitude I carried into it. As the first authority figure I met after choking on this lumpy bit of self-serving pseudo-history, he probably never had a chance to outrun my own prickly irritability. By all accounts, he was an exceptional gentleman and officer, a loyal lifetime supporter of the Scouts, and a very effective administrator for the Appalachian Trail. I give my apologies in advance.

At the door to the ATC headquarters, I met up with Jack, who I'd invited along for the meeting. For the last five days I'd been hiking with this extraordinary young man. Like John Brown's daughter, Jack was just fifteen, a high school student who had bargained permission to leave school early in the spring semester and spend three months hiking alone on the AT. Though he was in full and undisguised terror at spending a night by himself in the woods, he had sucked up his courage and made it from Georgia to central Virginia before getting a flu that sent him home to New Jersey for a week of chicken soup. The first night I was recuperating in Delaware Water Gap with my ankle and stomach problems, his parents dropped him off at the boarding house where I was staying. We talked briefly that night, and in the morning he disappeared, beginning the walk back south to Roanoke where he'd earlier had to bail. If all went well, he'd have hiked over half the trail before he went back to school in September. Though I was half again his age, we teamed up when I caught him in southern Pennsylvania and walked on and off together, he getting the advantage of having someone around when the scary things came out at night, me getting long, interesting lectures on Appalachian plant life, a topic on which he'd somehow made himself an expert.

Mrs. Caslin was in the Colonel's office briefing him, the door open, when we let ourselves into the main room of the ATC headquarters.

"They'll be two of them. David is the older, skinnier one with longer hair. A very nice young man though [I grinned, feeling a little of the sourness dissipate]. He's a graduate of North Carolina State University, doing the trail before graduate school. He started in Maine in June.

If you can believe it, the younger, cute one is only fifteen. Walked up from Georgia this summer. Out by himself before he's even old enough to drive. I can't believe his mother would allow it [Jack grinned]. He's headed south from New Jersey to complete the Georgia to Delaware Water Gap section. His school is giving him academic credit for the walk."

"Thanks, Jean. Please show them in when they arrive."

A quick series of firm, manly handshakes [Jack grinned], and we were seated in two chairs across a broad desk from the Colonel. He shut the door, pivoted back, and sat, hands folded in front of him. Back straight, head raised, chin out, eyes locked: "I've been hearing a lot about you two boys. Creating quite a stir on the trail network." A pause for effect, letting us bask in our celebrity. "Everybody's impressed that you figured out how to get out of school early."

He was looking at me.

"Shows initiative. Very promising. Good work."

He smiled.

I decided to let it go and nodded.

He didn't though. Hung right in there.

Again to me: "Very impressive that you've taken on an adventure like this before you're even old enough to drive. Your mother must be very proud."

I could see Jack grinning again.

"I'm sorry, sir. I think you have us confused. Jack's the one you should be congratulating. I'm twenty-three." I could have left it there, but the sourness was inflating inside me again.

"My mother died when I was twelve. Breast cancer that spread to her lungs and backbone."

The Colonel looked quickly down at the notes on the table.

"I see. I'm sorry for your loss, son."

Head back up, chin out again:

"Jack, I hear that you are getting high school credit for work you're doing on your walk. What's your project?"

Things got momentarily better as Jack described the essays he was writing and the list of plant species he was keeping.

"Very impressive. Excellent work." The Colonel unclasped his hands, raised them to face level, and clapped lightly several times. "Were you able to document any fiddlehead ferns on the trail in New England? I hear from the head of the Maine club that they are excellent eating." He paused, looked across the room at the door, looked down at the desk top, moved a pen to the left an inch, and continued. "The Canadians cook them with butter, lemon, and a little garlic, cover them with hollandaise. Steam them. Fiddleheads! Because they look like the business end of a violin." Another look at the door. "There's a small village up in New Brunswick that bills itself the fiddlehead capital of the world." He looked at Jack.

"I haven't been to Maine yet, sir. Will finish New Jersey to Georgia this year. Hope to complete the trail next summer."

The Colonel looked down again at his notes, moved them a little to the right, then moved them back to their original location.

"I understand from Jean that you both walked in from Maryland yesterday, right?"

"Yes, sir."

"Just had a crew up there last week, clearing brush, building waterbars. Trail's getting into top shape. You boys see anything that needs work?"

Jack looked at me. Age before beauty on this one. Before he'd agreed to go with me to the meeting, he'd insisted that I be the designated truth-to-power. I looked down at the scratches on my legs, the network of rips across my forearms and hands, but decided to go diplomatic.

"The trail itself is in great shape, sir, particularly the nice rockwork on the climb down to the Potomac. Well marked too."

The Colonel sat straighter in his chair, pushing back his notes toward the edge of the desk.

I made it my point not to look toward Jack. I could feel his eyes though, watching me the way people of refined sensibility and good conscience might look at an adult slinking past a group of bullies as they tortured a kitten.

Jack sighed quietly.

We had spent a good ten miles in Maryland elbowing through stinging nettles, shoving brambles of seedy blackberry bushes out of the path, poking through poison ivy, and wrestling over a couple of large downed tree limbs that barricaded the way forward. Over lunch the day before, Jack had insisted that we hold a mock trial for the trail crew responsible for maintenance on this section. Being older, wiser, and more inclined to mercy, I had held out for a life sentence at hard labor, all the while shackled to a series of large, decaying dead cows. Jack had insisted on slow disembowelment for the lot. No mercy, no surrender. Using the scissors from his scout knife to trim off a piece of briar-sliced skin from behind his knee, he had volunteered to carry out the sentence himself.

Jack barked a fake cough into his palm.

I tried to rise to my responsibilities. "We did see a whole lot of overgrowth though, sir. Not way too much. Not awful. But some. Ten miles of it, about twenty miles north of here. It would probably be good to have a team go up and do a fall clearing."

The Colonel was looking intently at me now, so I tried to backfill a little: "When they have a chance. Maybe next time they are up that way."

"Son, I guess I'm a little confused by your comments. I talked with Don just the other day. I have a report from him right here." He stabbed at a stack of papers in front of him with his index finger, hard enough that I wondered if it hurt. "My men say the trail is clear and clean, tiptop." He looked around the desk, moved a few papers, and looked back at me.

"They could have been talking about another section."

The slush of air slowly coming out between Jack's lips was most likely the sound of his illusions of adult steadfastness sliding steeply into a lifetime of disillusion.

"Really, sir, ten miles of the trail north of here are just a mess. I don't think they've been cleared in months."

"Years." Jack spoke for the first time in a bit.

The Colonel looked again toward the door, moved his notes directly in front of him, picked up his pen, and studied it for a second. Back straight, head raised, chin out, eyes locked.

"If that were true, I think I would have heard about it. I haven't had a single complaint this year."

"Most thru-hikers are headed north, sir. Maybe we're the first who stopped in here coming south."

The Colonel looked again at the door.

I held up my right arm, Martian in its red, welty mesh of fresh briar canals, trying to think of what to say next.

A knock on the door and Mrs. Caslin stuck her head in. "You have a call from the Park Service. Can you take it?"

The Colonel stood quickly. "Well, boys. Thanks so much for stopping by. Your information has been invaluable. I cannot thank you enough." He reached out, pulled a note off his desk, and put it in the trashcan beside him. "Good luck with the school year. And be sure to send us a card when you reach Maine and climb Katahdin. What a great mountain! Eat some of those fiddleheads for me."

Another round of firm handshakes, a good-bye to Jean Caslin, and we were off.

The last time I saw Jack he was sitting in a lawn chair in front of the slimy motel room we rented in Waynesboro the night before my friends picked me up for the trip home to Raleigh. He was having a great time, sharing a Dixie cup of Pepsi and vodka with an ancient, toothless man in a dirty tank top. The old gentleman borrowed a few dollars from him, taught him how to properly shuffle a deck of cards, and poured out tale after tale from his younger days. He had once, as he told it, toured Scandinavia playing bass guitar with B.B. King's band.

A LOWLAND INTERLUDE

Paying for dumb on the installment plan

It's always too expensive not to insure your success

Why on this rich man's earth would a healthy young man, zombying through dozy-eyed, long days thirty feet in the air on shaky scaffolding juggling a half dozen sharp, gyrating electric saws ever need medical care?

Up to this point, you and I have been travelling along through West Virginia in the heat of late summer. But suddenly in a few pages you'll find yourself just a hundred or so miles further down the trail, camping out in a sleet storm with the temperature well below zero. This will seem odd.

Here's the explanation.

I originally planned to hike the AT south to north, starting in March and following sweet, mellow spring up the trail like nine out of ten thru-hikers have always done. Just before I was about to leave though, a nasty accident at work sent me to the hospital for a round of expensive trimming and sewing. And, of course, I had no private health insurance. By the time I had healed and worked through (I thought) the Workers Compensation process to pay for the operation, it was too late to start in the South. The northern end of the trail at Katahdin would be totally iced in and open only to technical winter climbing before I could ever hope to reach it. That's how my hike became a Maine to Georgia walk—and how that harsh letter from my local sheriff derailed the trip just south of the

Shenandoah National Park on Labor Day, 1973, sending me home on threat of arrest until I could satisfy a medical bill more weighty than any pack I'd ever before or since hoisted.

The summons I received in Harpers Ferry was, in fact, the final straw in a whole Halloween hayride of bad decisions dating back to my early planning for the hike. Once I had gotten serious about the walk, I needed to save a considerable pile money to fund the trip. So I grabbed the best paying job available for recent English majors in the middle of the recession we faced as the frantic spending on Vietnam evaporated at the end of the American war. For something like twice the minimum wage, I put my back to work, doing carpentry twelve hours a day, seven days a week, often with very little sleep. The night was always young, and the world was filled with interesting movies, books, and companions, occasionally even females when some desperate one of them would deign to talk with a college grad doing manual labor.

Since I needed to save as much money as possible, health insurance was surely a luxury not worth considering. Not needed. Think reasonably about this for a minute: why on this rich man's earth would a healthy young man, zombying through dozy-eyed, long days thirty feet in the air on shaky scaffolding while he juggled a half dozen sharp, gyrating electric saws—usually with their safety features cleverly disabled to maximize manly efficiency—ever need medical care? Especially a healthy young man who rode a motorcycle on busy roads every heavy-eyed morning and every body-dead, exhausted trip home. A restless guy who then hopped off whenever he could find a few free hours for a frantic bout of prudent backwoods motocrossing or a completely safe binge of sloppy mountaineering or whitewater canoeing, which he undertook without instruction, decent equipment, or judicious and experienced companions. What, as they always say, could possibly go wrong?

In my case what went badly was a long tumble down a muddy hill, both legs clumsily mated with a hundred pounds of cement-covered plywood. Which produced two inguinal hernias that quickly pushed out of my groin like a herd of ambitious grapefruits diligently campaigning for the presidency.

Then more bad decisions, starting with hobbling around tearing the muscle more completely through a couple of painful days before I dragged my increasingly panicked self to a physician. And finally, driven by the need to get the operation done and the healing finished in time to get on the trail as early as possible, the choice to check into the hospital and have the surgery with only an unofficial nod from a low-level Workers Compensation official that the State of North Carolina's insurance fund would certainly pay for it.

Two months after the injury, three hours before I was supposed to board the plane for Maine, I got a call from a clerk with the insurance board. "This is an official conversation," he started. "We'd like to ask you a few questions about your claim. And I'd like to record your answers, with your permission, of course." Because of an interesting case of mistaken identity, my telephone line was, at the time, already tapped by the North Carolina State Bureau of Investigation (a story for another book), so I was quite used to having my conversations monitored.

"No problem," I naively consented.

Two hours and a hundred or so detailed questions later, I learned from my exacting inquisitor that during the first minutes of its birthing an inguinal hernia should "burn" rather than "ache and feel unnaturally warm." With this verbal misstep, I had failed the test, my claim was denied, and I was now officially responsible for paying all bills myself.

The guy at the other end of the line then turned off the recording mechanism and completed our conversation: "Look, I didn't tell you this, okay?" We had learned during a rest stop in the interrogation that he had graduated with an English degree a year before me at the same college. "The first time around we always turn down people with hernias. I'm not even a doctor, but even I know that a hernia is almost always caused by a hereditary weakness in the tissue, almost never by a single fall." I didn't know this.

"You get an automatic appeal though. Sometimes we change our minds if your physician will come and testify."

"How long does the appeal take?"

"Half a year, maybe longer."

"What happens with my doctor bills during the wait?"

"I honestly don't know. I don't work that side of the house."

I called the hospital and then my surgeon's practice, but never got through to anyone who seemed to know what to do next. So, I left messages at each office explaining the situation and got on the plane for Bangor, gambling that I'd be home before push came to shove. And then I forgot about it for the next three months.

The letter from the sheriff made it clear I had lost the gamble. From a phone booth across the street from where J.E.B. Stuart captured John Brown in the center of Harpers Ferry, I called the hospital: "I'm sorry, sir. You are already four months delinquent. You need to immediately send us at least half of the balance you owe. And we'll have to meet with you in person if we're going to work out a payment plan for the rest."

Next a very brief conversation with the sheriff's office: "Nice story, Bud. But if you hadn't satisfied the bill by the date on your documents, we're gonna have to do our best to arrest you, no matter where you are. We're pretty good at it, too."

So, I went home, made the rounds of my creditors, negotiated payment schedules, and worked ninety-hour weeks over the winter to make things as right as possible (though all the debts were not fully retired for three more long years of painful payouts). And April 1st, I returned—winter still in full swing in the mountains of northern Virginia—to finish the hike.

The Appalachian Trail Conservancy sometimes generously defines a "thru-hike" as an end-to-end walk of the AT in one year, 365 days. I ended up finishing my 351 days after I started it. I've been officially dubbed a thru-hiker.

But for most of the rest of us, a real thru-hike is a walk of the entire trail in one trip, as continuous as humanly possible. I had a considerable vacation in the middle of mine, albeit not one of my own choosing. It is a turn of events that I'm sick about to this day.

Insure that this doesn't happen to you.

VIRGINIA

Feeling the gravity of the human voice

Find your balance where you find it

Well after dark, a northbound thru-hiker powered in, shaking hard, ice on the ends of her braids, but okay.

The trail crossing of the Hudson, the moose-filled Maine lakes, the view across the Cumberland Valley from the McAfee Knob—part of the AT's pull is its iconic beauties, and I still carry them, some in old photographs, many more in grey matter.

But the one I carry in my soul is from a haggard lean-to in the middle of the Jefferson National Forest. It was the first really bitter night of the trip, twenty degrees when I finished my noodles, much colder when I drifted off watching Orion's Belt disappear into heavy, wet cloud.

Well after dark, a NOBO powered in, shaking hard, ice on the ends of her braids, but okay. We spoke for a few minutes over tea; then I rolled down warmly into my sleeping bag, watching her candle reflect on the log wall with the snow piling up outside.

I don't have the words to fully explain it, but suspect I don't have to. If you've stuck with this book this long, you probably already pack around your own version—some few minutes of unexpected joy, beauty, and companionship on the trail. In the middle of tomorrow's petty work squabble or coming up behind a numbskull texting away in the left lane at twenty miles below the speed limit, I'll dig out this moment to keep myself on track.

Put them under the right weight and they become buoyant

"He has flags on his legs!!" A thin girl, blond hair in a ponytail, about nine, but much taller than she had any right to be. "He looks like a parade." An even thinner boy, Beatles haircut, about seven, shorter than he probably would have liked.

I'm pretty sure that when they first saw me I didn't look like the sort of young man you'd want to take home to your mother.

I'd been back on the trail for six days after six months at home sorting out my medical bills, and I was still smacked and staggered by how cold it was in the northern Virginia mountains in early April.

It wasn't anywhere close to spring up here at 4,000 feet, not the tiniest green leaf in sight. Clouds grayed the sky and scoured the summits almost every day; snow and sleet blankets dropped in regularly to cover the brown of everything. When the sun was out, it paled down with all the warmth of a frosty headed receptionist demanding full payment before she'd let the nurse give your flu shot. And you know the needle is going to be dull. The night before was the first that the temperature hadn't bombed down close to zero.

The inevitable result was that none of the few of us up in the mountains, even those of us who were still very proud of our brand new haircuts, were likely to be recruited as smiley-fresh models for the next REI catalog. Sleeping every night in all of your clothes tended to ruin even your most fashionable look, and interest in even the most basic personal cleanliness had thudded down along with the mercury levels. Most nights it was too cold to walk down and break up the ice in the stream, and it was way too cold to deliberately place handfuls of that stream on your bluish skin. So you didn't wash. And you looked it.

But that isn't what the two kids first noticed when I walked into the shelter that Sunday about lunchtime.

"He has flags on his legs!!" A thin girl, blond hair in a ponytail, about nine, but much taller than she had any right to be.

"He looks like a parade." An even thinner boy, Beatles haircut, about seven, shorter than he probably would have liked.

"Our very own Easter parade, right here in the woods!!" From the girl.

That hadn't been the effect I was aiming for, but their observations were accurate.

Three mornings earlier I had woken to snow yet once again. By the time I was ready to walk, it was above freezing though, so shorts seemed like the right choice. A half mile sloshing down the trail and the daggers started in on my right knee, the pain hobbling me to whatever gait you naturally fall into when you can't get one of your legs out of locked straight position without incurring gape-mouth agony.

"Most likely you've got iliotibial band syndrome," concluded the pharmacist in the only drugstore we could find open in Roanoke, Virginia, that Easter afternoon. "Most likely you aren't warming up enough before you put weight on it."

I thought about mornings stomping around in the slush without pants on. "What can I do about it?"

"Aspirin will help a little." I thought about what a steady diet of those would do to my frothy, giardized stomach.

"But your best bet is to see an orthopedist, preferably one who specializes in sports medicine."

"Could you recommend one who might see me on Easter?"

She looked at me the way Billy Graham might peruse a belligerent heathen who offered him a Big Gulp of gin and Tru-Aide.

"The absolute nearest practice is in Charlottesville. That's two hours away. And it'll take you a month to get an appointment. Those folks have a football team to keep on the field.

If you went ahead and broke the whole leg though, they'd right off take you in the ER at University of Virginia hospital. Required to by law."

"Anything else I might consider?"

"A good elastic brace should keep the pain in check. Won't do any healing, but should get you back on the trail. We have a rack of them over there next to the old-people canes."

I had been one step ahead of her brace idea all along with the handkerchiefs wrapped tightly around the pain. And that's exactly why I looked like a parade.

Cursing along in the snow earlier in the week I had learned through multiple trials and many errors that if I took my nasty, sweaty red-bandana headband off and ratcheted it around the bottom of the knee and then knotted my mucous-stained blue one tightly just above the joint, the pain would mush down considerably and eventually merge into the usual background agonies of lugging a pack all day. The pharmacist's prescription was dead-on too. The Ace bandage looked less clownly, returned my sweat and nostril maintenance devices to their original uses, and let me lame and limp the last 750 miles to Georgia in relative comfort.

"Why do you have handkerchiefs all over your knee?"

The two kids—sharing a chilly picnic with their mother and father across the clearing—had watched me from a distance as long as they could stand it. There had been a brief period of parent nagging, some clandestine but not overly rude parental observation, a somewhat reluctant granting of permissions, and the boy and girl were at the shelter all over me with questions.

"Maybe his leg is runny."

"Nice one." The girl shook her brother's hand.

"Well, if it's snot that, must be some other perfectly good reason." She shook his hand again.

"Maybe his legs are just getting over a cold. It's pretty chilly out here."

"Don't be a drip."

They suddenly went shy, looking at me a little sheepishly to see how I was dealing with their clumsy but enthusiastic booger humor.

"You guys are pretty nosey about my outfit."

Eruptive and totally undeserved laughs, even a little happy dance from the boy.

I explained the medical reasons for the handkerchief placements.

"Why are you so dirty?"

I explained about the cold temperatures and about not washing.

"Why is your nose all black and peeling? It's gross." The girl stepped on the boy's foot and whispered something to him, trying to be stern but breaking into a grin that she obviously couldn't control.

"It somehow snuck out of my sleeping bag one night and got frostbitten."

"Will it get better?"

"I hope so. I'll never get a girlfriend looking like this."

"How long have you been hiking?"

An instinctive lean-in from both of them as their eyes popped with exactly the proper response from any rational human when he or she first learns that 25,000 years after the species wandered into North America and seventy-five years after Henry Ford started building automobiles it was still possible for a normal person to walk 2100 miles through the mountains. A big stereo "Wow," and they were gone, all elbows and tennis shoes, chirping back over to their parents, torquing, spinning electrons returning to the nucleus. The mom and dad, I noticed, were holding hands.

In a few minutes the father walked over.

"Hi, I'm Walter." He reached out a hand. "Thanks for being so nice to Pat and Barbara. They're pretty excited." It was sounding like halftime at the Super Bowl across the clearing. "They tell me you're hiking the Appalachian Trail."

I told him a little about my story, including an explanation for the colorful medical apparati on my leg and my plan to spend the night in Roanoke so I could pick up a resupply box in town on Monday.

He nodded.

"Listen, we've been talking. We'd love it if you'd join us for Easter supper and stay the night with us. My mother is back in Roanoke cooking. She lives with us, and she likes nothing better than company. You'd make her day, and the kids would be ecstatic." He looked over toward the squeals. "With great effort, we might be able to calm them down to that level. We could try to hunt down a better solution for your knee, and one of us could bring you back to the trail in the morning."

I, of course, accepted the invitation. The night in a warm bed, the room all decorated with pictures of horses and boy bands; a fabulous meal with a glass of wine; the company of a loving family; the charm and grace of the wonderful grandmother—all these were a welcomed sabbatical from an arctic AT.

But they aren't the part of that day that I remember most clearly, that still envelopes that afternoon with a glow that rivals anything I've experienced since, with the possible exception of everything that includes new little babies.

There was one more convocation across the clearing, marked by bouncing children and grinning adults. The mother then walked over.

We chatted a bit while the rest of the family cleaned up from the picnic. It was fairly clear I was being looked over and parent tested once again. Then came the question:

"You can completely say 'no' to this without penalty. And please don't agree if you're not comfortable with it. The kids desperately want to walk with you—and just you—down to the gap. Would you mind? Our car's in the parking lot. If you like, you can drop your pack in the trunk and head on to Route 11. We could pick you up there—it's another two miles. The kids can stay in the car if they are driving you nuts by the time you get to the gap."

I didn't have children of my own then, but still I had just the slightest idea what honor was being given to me.

Five minutes later as Pat, Barb, and I headed into the woods, I noticed that Mary and her husband were holding hands again. As I looked back for a last time, they were hugging and she was kissing the side of his neck.

The kids never stopped talking the three miles down the mountain—about their friends, about my trip, about animals they'd seen on family hikes, about their grandmother and how she needed a boyfriend, about the absolute necessity that I find a girlfriend once my nose wasn't so ugly, about leaves, about aphids. They were, without even the tiniest doubt, the best company I had on the Appalachian Trail.

But the real magic switched on when they reached the car and I started to dump the pack into the trunk.

"Please, don't leave that here. Please!" From the girl.

Thus far, I'd carried the pack every inch from Maine. And

unfortunately, after this day I'd carry it every inch to the end of the trail. We were still a decade away from the holy ceremonies of slackpacking, the inspired practice of convincing good-hearted trail angels to deliver your pack to you at some distant road crossing, bestowing foot-healing miles without the turtle weight.

I was dumbfounded by their irrational request.

"Please, please, please, we want to wear it some. Please." From the boy.

It had been a week since my last resupply, so the pack load was already down seven or so pounds. I emptied the canteen, snuck the stove, cook kit, fuel bottle, and tent into the trunk unseen, and we flipped a coin.

Barb carried the Kelty the first mile, with a huge smile, without complaint, without slowing down even a little. Then Pat, weighing in at little more than twice the twenty-five pounds on his back, carried it the rest of the way. I walked close beside each of them when they first put on the pack. But pretty soon it was obvious they weren't going to need my help.

Unless you count my wife and me on the day of our son's birth, I have never seen any other two people quite so proud, quite so happy, quite so surefooted on the path.

When glory comes, allow it to carry the day

At the moment I first noticed the man, he was doing this work in a circle of light exactly as it might have been created for a painting, the sun having just pressed apart the clouds and placed the acre he was plowing momentarily in the center of its focus. From the distance, the rows of newly turned brown took on the feel of some mysterious writing, of abstract promises of significance, of an outsized alphabet with a message about something fundamental.

The cold had retreated a little, still freezing the boot prints around shelters at night but the full sun thawing them later in the day. There wasn't as yet a single leaf on any of the thousands of tree poles I passed every mile, but by noon it was often nice enough that I could walk comfortably again without a shirt. Right on cue though, a new army of unhappiness tried to stream in to seize the ground abandoned by ice and chill. More deeply than ever before on the AT, I found myself cheek to jowl with the mute forces of iron-bar-beating loneliness.

I hadn't seen anyone in three days when I topped the sunny pass in late afternoon and started to cross the empty two-lane that lazed through the wide, flat notch in the mountains. But I didn't cross, just gradually walked slower and slower as I looked over the asphalt toward the darkened opening where the trail resumed through the trees. Without meaning to or really even thinking about it, I stopped in the gravel pullout on the north side of the road, dropped the pack, and stood there, not reading my maps, not reaching for a snack or for water, not pulling out a sweater, not even particularly luxuriating in the warmth reflected off the twenty feet of black tar in front of me. I just stood there, distracted, shifting my weight from one foot to the other, looking.

I initially told myself I was stopping because the gap was the perfect place to be noticed by a passing car. They'd pull over; I'd finally have someone to talk with, if only for just a minute; and maybe if the planets aligned they'd invite me home for a hot meal and further conversation.

Not a single car came over the hill, though. And, in truth, the hope for an easy ride to comfort wasn't even close to the real reason I put roots there for a good twenty minutes, long after the sun's progress warned that I was going to have to really hoof it to make the next shelter before dark and cold ruled again.

From where I stood, I had an unobstructed mile-long view down the quietly descending route that the road took as it moved toward the valley and the humans, houses, and commerce it was built to serve. I was looking at a scene drawn right out of some modern-day Brueghel. A half of a mile away, the road took a placid curve to the right and arced around a large and substantial field, fallow, still stubbled with the remains of last year's corn, a landscape of yellows and greens and browns as old as life on earth. At the far side of the field, a man under a large hat piloted an aged, earth-red tractor up and down the rows he was steadily engraving on the ground.

At the moment in time I first noticed the man, he was doing this work in a circle of light exactly as it might have been created for a painting, the sun having just pressed apart the clouds and placed the acre he was plowing momentarily in the center of its focus. From the distance, the rows of newly turned brown took on the feel of some mysterious writing, of abstract promises of significance, of an outsized alphabet with a message about something fundamental and beautiful.

From where I stood, far enough away to smooth out erratic movements and to cradle away all noise from its engine, the tractor seemed to move with studied deliberation, with measured cycles as regular as bow to cello. By any common-sense laws of physics, its regular cycles must, at some level, be oscillating forth rhythms of music to fill the valley with slow and deep harmonies. At that particular time and place, in the mood that held me, I would not have been surprised to have heard rich, full chords channeling up from the painting below.

I stood at this mountain pass feeling the loneliness of the past few days with an intensity that was making me far too poetic for anyone's good, certainly not anyone doomed to a less than mystical dinner of boxed macaroni and cheese. Clinging weakly to the sensible, my first impulse was to scurry a detour down to talk with the man on the tractor. But the first wasn't the strongest impulse. And it's not what I did.

The sound of a human voice would have been a huge relief. The farmer and I would have, I'm sure, talked about his corn, his machinery, the beginnings of spring, my hike, maybe our families. Perhaps we liked the same college basketball teams. Maybe this rural man in Appalachia was a big fan of Doc Watson, who lived just a few valleys over from where he was plowing. I had never in the past had any trouble getting a gab going about Doc Watson's music. The conversation, any conversation, would have wrested me out the longest silence of my life. I had never before been three days without a word with anyone.

But instead of walking down to chat, I crossed the road back onto the chilled path.

I was still two days from Damascus, Virginia. It was mid-week—most of the world's people were in the usual places, doing their work. I suspected that it was unlikely I would see anyone during the next forty-eight hours.

But as I pulled the pack back on, I was beginning to understand the ecology of loneliness on the Appalachian Trail. I wanted to see how that process might treat me if I continued to follow it a few days longer.

Back in Maine, I was often frightened when I was alone, afraid of the woods, the heights, the weather, and the creatures that toothed and clawed about in them. Later, in the middle of the walk, loneliness no longer frightened me. Just the opposite. It sucked all emotion away and wed itself to boredom, the steep, soul-punishing price paid for familiar and plodding routine.

Now, long solitary hours had put me in an entirely different emotional landscape as I passed day after wordless day through Virginia. An elastic sky continually painted anew up through the leafless trees. The potent glory of mountains hung with ice reconfigured the big, rounded hills into old-planet beasts of earth and rock, rounding out to the far horizon like uncounted numbers of placid, enormous mammals. With these glories all around every second of every day, loneliness pared away normal distractions. It demanded strict attention to what was around me. It encouraged me to marvel at the scene that the man, the sun, and the clouds were carving out along the road in the silent valley.

As it turned out, I did not see anyone else for the next two days.

In compensation though, I did view one more beauty that has never been pushed from my inner vision, even by the ugliest things I've seen, the tedium of commuting for hours past nail salons and dry cleaners, the grey-faced, breath-choking agonies on the sweated pillows of dying friends.

For hours, the trail just north of Damascus, Virginia, had been following the bed of a long abandoned rail line, with a stampeding creek below and acres of sun-coned firs above. This part of the trail is now a section of the wildly popular Virginia Creeper Trail—a bike, hiking, and horse route, filled with families on most days during nice weather. But in 1973 this AT section was notable for its quiet, its scenery, and for the break it gave hikers from the rough terrain north and south of the area.

Almost completely level and smooth enough to have once safely handled locomotives, it provided blessed relief from the eternal curse of having to obsessively watch your own boots for the most of the day. Stumble-free, relieved of rock and root, you could safely look up, look down, look in any direction you wanted.

Like most humans though, my capacity for beauty apparently had an internal clock, one that had timed out a mile or so back. Moving a pleasant three miles an hour towards Damascus, my brain abandoned me for another full-blown hiker reverie.

No light of grace fell on me in exactly the way it fell on Saul/Paul on his trip to his own Damascus. No deity parted the sky and spoke. But I was glory-slapped, full-stopped, dead-halted nonetheless.

Fully engrossed and entirely happy in my head bubble, I didn't even realize what I walked among for at least a good fifty yards.

Trees, creek, momentary view of valley, more trees, a pine, an oak, rocks, sky, creek, more rocks, a color-burst of thousands of miniature flowers in full bloom, trees, rocks. What?? Thousands—maybe hundreds of thousands—of flowers. A whole slice of the mountain up the slope, now somehow bare of trees. Maybe the scene of some long ago fire? Maybe stripped clear and exposed to full sun by some recent hurricane or ice storm? I don't know how it happened. But for a tenth of a mile the hillside, as far as you could see before the roll of the mountain stopped the eye, every rich-dirt inch blossomed a dwarf iris, a bright two-inch pennant of yellow snugged in the middle of indigo and violet.

Just one would have been something to lie down beside and admire, Whitman with his leaf of grass, the brown of earth transformed into a bright flag of rainbow. I haven't often used words like *transcendental* in this book. But seeing thousands of the these irises at once, all unbidden, all a surprise and gift, a tide of color and grace where few people ever walked, all there quietly on their own, me a stranger who just wandered by—it felt, well, transcendental.

In Greek mythology, Iris is the goddess of the rainbow and the mother of Eros, of love. Her chief role is to receive the messages of the gods and bring them to humans. For a few minutes on the mountains above Damascus, I felt like the message was very tangible. The world—and my walk in it—was nothing less than transcendent.

In spite of all the "leave only footprints" ethics that I like to practice in the backcountry, I picked two of the flowers and pressed them in the back of my trail guidebook. At the next post office I sent one, a peace offering, in a letter to a young woman who I felt had wronged me. I never heard back from her.

When I finished my hike, I remember transferring the other to mark a favorite page in some book of poetry I especially loved. Forty years and a dozen houses later, I've recently gone through the thousands of books on my shelves. I did not find the dwarf iris in any of them.

I ate a very late lunch on a large rock, sunning among the flowers for a long time. I took a nap, and had another snack. Then for another hour or so, I would make moves to leave, fumbling things around in the pack, arranging this and that, reclipping gear and tying again, checking map contours, but always deciding to stay longer.

Finally, from someplace down in the Great Appalachian Valley, a far-off, deep horn announced the end of the workday in some factory in or around Damascus. I pulled myself back into the world of the waking and returned to the walk down to where I could talk with people again.

TENNESSEE AND NORTH CAROLINA

Learning some humility, even after epic accomplishment

Who's to say who's a hog?

I don't think that I've ever spent a day walking the wilderness without at least once contemplating dying out in the middle of nowhere, my cries and screams choked to silence by the surrounding endless miles of trees and dirt dumbly going about Nature's business. I doubt that you have either. And now it was apparently my turn.

At some point along the way, you get almost totally comfortable with the woods. Most things that snout about after dark no longer wake you up, at least not completely. You accept that bears are bored with you unless you're sloppy with your food. You step calmly around the snakes, if you see them. When you trip over a root and whack something on a rock, you lurch yourself up and keep walking.

Then there are the days of paranoia. Sometimes justified, sometimes just paranoid.

Act I

1,700 miles into the walk on a perfectly fine morning when the sun was shining, the birds were busy, and I was only hours away from a resupply respite in Erwin, Tennessee, I'm not sure why I became absolutely certain some hugger mugger was dodging along a hundred yards or so behind me, bent on a prolonged, nasty session of woodsy abuse. Maybe it was because I hadn't seen anyone else in the last two days of rumbling forward, talking to myself. Maybe some tree shadow spooked me without breaking through into my comfortable brain daze. Perhaps it was a vitamin deficiency that a stalk of fresh celery or a nice Brussels sprout might easily have cured.

Or perhaps walking through spookily named Indian Grave Gap at the start of the 3000-foot drop toward the Nolichucky River quietly triggered the scare. Read any of the national origin narratives left to us by our Puritan forbearers and it's always there: the woods as Satan's favorite home and abode, filled with his tribes of bloody-minded kin waiting to violate the unwary. A myth that, of course, has filled many a grave and fueled 300 years of ugly history. Apparently from the very beginnings, many of us have always entered the trees carrying a solid load of unease and dread.

Take a minute and go Google "murder on the Appalachian Trail," however, if you want to get a reassuring sense of the extent of the actual danger. Almost every item starts off confidently declaiming that the car ride to the trailhead is more likely to kill you than some stalking maniac. All the articles then soothingly point out that the AT has provided the leafy setting for less than a dozen killings in the forty years since I had my own particular day of paranoia. Let's assume an average of three million people are on the trail each year (as does the Appalachian Trail Conservancy), then let's multiply that by 40 years and deftly divide by 12 (one more killing than I can find on Google, but we'll round up to be more than fair).

There it is: on the back of an envelope, you have only a one in ten million chance of being a victim of deadly crime on the AT. Not bad odds, considering that recent FBI stats show that, say, Cincinnati at its 2013 rate of mayhem would have created 28,000 bodies in the same period if the same number of folks were wandering its streets as were trekking the Appalachian Trail.

But before we let ourselves get totally comfortable, let's push a little further, a little more deeply. Pick any Google item from your search list of AT murders and jump in to a full reading. Savor the details. I guarantee that by paragraph two all your statistical reassurance will have melted away. Each victim, you will see, dies alone (or worse, just before or just after someone they love and were out with sharing a pleasant walk with), tortured, stabbed, shot, beaten, all out of earshot of any possible help. I dare you to read any of the accounts without a sympathetic shudder at one of our greatest primeval fears. I don't think that I've ever spent a day walking the wilderness without at least once contemplating dying in the middle of nowhere, my cries and screams choked to silence by endless miles of trees and dirt dumbly going about Nature's business. I doubt that you have either.

And now it was apparently my turn.

For over a mile, each time I turned my head quickly enough on one of the trail's gently looping switchbacks, I could just catch sight of a hand or shoulder as the future tormentor dodged behind a tree. Never a clear view (he was too practiced in the ways of the stalk for that sort of mistake, I was sure). But he was always there, a hundred yards or so back. Menacing me, the pitiful mouse to his proverbial cat. A sadistic killer who would leave me in a shallow pit just off the trail. I'd probably not even be honored by having a gap eventually named to memorialize my grisly end. I could feel the crosshairs; I sweated.

And finally I'd had enough. Even I could be pushed just so far. It was time to act. Showdown at the AT corral.

At a sharp right angle in the trail, I slipped behind a large hemlock, drew the blade on my Swiss Army knife (later I noticed that I'd pulled out the screwdriver/can opener instead of the mighty two-inch carver), cocked my walking stick, and waited. One minute (he was probably being cautious in his approach, having lost sight of me). Two minutes (no, that sound was a squirrel in the dead leaves). Five minutes—off came the pack, and I headed back up the trail to have it out. Five more minutes and a quarter of mile of backtracking—no sign of anyone.

My bold offense surely scared him off, the only explanation that made any sense to me at the time, the only explanation that makes sense now.

Act II

I surfed on the receding tide of adrenaline for the next few miles, awash in the satisfactions of my courage. The trail then bottomed out into the flat valley of the Nolichucky River, and I began gathering the excitement that long distance hikers collect as they near a road crossing, with its restaurants, showers, and safe beds. A $10 night in the area's finest hotel (a YMCA, it turns out) was in the cards, and I was more than ready to lose my landfill odor in an hour-long shower.

The birds were again singing, and as I walked through the abandoned remains of the apple orchard of some long departed farming family, around and through rock walls tumbled across time,

I was more in the land of *The Waltons* than the fields of murderous intent.

Then came a storyteller's perfect gift, a ready-made event I instantly realized I could use to frame this day in the many retellings of it that were certainly to come.

Fifty yards in front emerged another sign of civilization as sure as the apple trees around me: an oversized pig, nose down pushing around in the forest detritus, certainly close to home and thus probably close to the road. "This will make a fine finish to the tale of today," I quickly grasped (and probably said out loud, uncensored talking to oneself being another inevitable mainstay during long walks alone). "Foolish man earlier thinks he's in mortal danger—instead, (I'll tell it with a touch of self deprecation) he later finds that he's really in some rural Eden palling around with the most comic and unthreatening of domesticated farm animals." A photo must be had to accent the irony and get the chuckles going.

So off came the pack again, out came the camera, and I strolled up for the shot. No need for quiet; your average portly pig doesn't scare that easily.

At twenty yards, its head comes up and our eyes meet—mine wide and popped as I see the brutish tusks; its eyes as fixed, uninterested, stupid, and unfriendly as a shark's. Just today I read with mixed feelings in *Wikipedia* that "actual wild boar attacks on humans are rare, but can be serious, resulting in multiple penetrating injuries to the lower part of the body." And today I rejoice that I knew nothing then of the "serious wounds to lower part of the body" possibilities. At the time, my degree of panic was substantial enough, thank you very much. As a young boy I had seen what the wild boar does to the canine hero in the climactic confrontation at the end of Disney's classic *Old Yeller*. It wasn't pretty.

I have no memory of how I mounted the nearest apple tree, but there I was, fifteen feet up, spending the next ten minutes or so watching the substantial beast aggressively root up a patch of dirt the size of a suburban front yard and then swagger off, never bothering to look in my direction again.

I climbed down, fumbled clumsily with weight of the pack, and headed off again toward Erwin.

Act III

In a few hundred yards, the trail teed into the Nolichucky River, took a right angle, and began a quiet amble a half-mile alongside the water, aiming toward the highway bridge across the river and into town.

The only slightly unnatural mar to the scene was the jacked up WWII-era Jeep—done up in extravagant camouflage paint—parked in two feet of water out towards the middle of the river, the current breaking across its rear bumper and wave-cresting down its sides. The driver spotted me about the time I spotted him, sparked up the brute with a cauldron of spumes from submerged mufflers, and bumped and crashed toward me with none of the swinish grace and tact that Mr. Boar had shown just minutes before.

Crank up your imagination a second and help flesh out the driver's appearance for me. Start with the movie *Deliverance*, of course. No shirt, but a grimy vest fashioned from a denim jacket by cutting off the sleeves, apparently with a knife that had long since seen sharper days. Lots of chest hair. A handful of teeth, spaced here and there, the one in the front shaped like Mt. Everest. A slurp of tobacco juice dried down one side of the face accenting a sizable scar that tore through the ragged beard down the chin and across the neck. A full array of tattoos, long before these reached kids in the suburbs. And, of course, an ax in the back seat and a glint sparkling from the floor on the passenger's side, created, I was sure, by a half-hidden handgun.

"Whairyuh goin', boy."

"Well, I'm heading down to the road and then into Erwin."

"Git in—I'll gitcha thair," said with what I took to be somewhat of a leer.

"Thanks, but I'm hiking the Appalachian Trail and have to do all the walking myself."

A long, long pause and the studied look you might give your bathroom sink if it started babbling metaphysics in Algonquin.

"Git in—I'll drop yuh down at the brige."

"Thanks. But really, I have to do the walking on my own."

"Wher'd yuh walk from."

"Maine."

Another long, long pause and a scratch down below the belt.

"Well, okay then. Yuh have yerself a nice walk, boy."

The Jeep bumped backwards, hit its stride midstream, and lurched away around a bend in the Nolichucky.

I breathed out, wet a dry throat with a swig from the canteen, and made it a couple of hundred yards down the trail before he powered up beside me again, cutting the engine out in the river so I could hear him clearly.

"I'll be waitin' down to the brige."

A defining difference between most of us and your usual action hero in the movies is that when the rubber meets the road and the danger gathers, we don't come up with a clever plan, daring in its courage, cunning, and execution. We might, in fact, not come up with any plan at all.

So I obediently walked to the bridge, where, just as he promised, he was waiting, chewing on an apple.

"Yuh don't havta walk to town, right? The rules let yuh take a ride with me on the road, I'm guessin'."

"Yes sir," and I climbed in like the sheep I was, noting the evil-looking revolver stuffed between his seat and the gearshift. I put my pack in the back with the ax—and a chain saw that I noticed for the first time. The Jeep's clutch was set up for river riding and just the sort of massive bear legs he sported, so the ride started with a hearty leap and tire burn. And we were off down the paved but ragged two-lane, toward Erwin. At least that was my fondest hope.

"I been hearing about that trail since I was a kid. Didn't know it ran down thair though. Always intristed me. Always wanted maybe to do it myself sometime." He ripped into the art of conversation like he'd never tried talking before. "You like it? You think I could do it? Really glad I ran into you and glad to give you a ride. Maybe you can drop me a post card when you finish? Where're you wanna be dropped off?"

That's how it ended. He obeyed all traffic laws for all four miles to town, asked a dozen more questions about my opinion of his suitability for a future thru-hike, and fifteen minutes later placed me in front of the YMCA doors.

"My name's Rudy—you need a ride back to the trail tomorrow, just ask round town and somebiddy'll hunt me down." He reached out and shook my hand. "Have a good one, and, no kidding, let me know when you finish. Just send the card to the police station. They know where to find me." A hard snap of the clutch and he was gone.

Epilogue

For thirty years, I made my living doing communications and public relations work. You've seen *The Good Wife* and *Mad Men.* I wasn't at all like that, but you get the general idea.

You know that the essence of the job is to quickly size up a situation, get to the nut of the motivations of the humans involved, map out the dangers, and stake out a plan to mitigate them, seizing the opportunities quickly when they present themselves.

In my day of paranoia, I learned I had no talents for doing any of these. I'm an idiot.

This knowledge is a good thing.

I learned I'd better approach every situation at my work with the phantom killer, the boar, and Rudy hanging around my neck like a hospital gown on a cold day. I knew it wouldn't take all that much to make my bottom visible to all. I second-guessed every impulse; I rethought every situation from every angle I could imagine. I was paranoid the whole time. The humility hung well on my shoulders and kept my disasters to a minimum.

Always take a look backwards when you leave

My maps were five miles downhill, on the shelf with the toilet paper.

The tiny Baptist church in the woods just off the trail in Tennessee had the smell long distance hikers admire above all things not hamburger—the fine odor of a working outhouse, an actual seat promising crouch-less serenity. So I slipped around back and scoped out the next few miles in the guidebook as I made my comfortable peace with too many macaroni dinners.

An hour or so later up the trail, I was again in the Zen state you reach when you are left every day with only your own thoughts and the horrid rhythm of five million boot steps—your mind, as Bill Bryson has said, like a balloon that bounces along behind you on a string. I may have heard the motorcycle coming, but the sound didn't register. The flailing elbow of the helmetless fellow piloting it did though, as he saw me, reacted badly, lost control of the bike, and whacked the side of my pack. From a position across a juvenile Douglas fir, I saw his rear wheel grind out one hundred years of leaves turning into mulch, mulch firming into soil, and trail maintainers creating a careful path through it all. Spitting a couple of bushels of eroded granite out of the trail bed, he yahooed his way upwards, powered by the liquefied remains of dinosaurs.

Martin Luther King, Jr. famously reminded us that the arc of the moral universe might be long but always bends toward justice. And so it did a week later in North Carolina. This time when a stripped down Yamaha came plowing its way through the fragile mountain bald, I was walking with four large guys from the wrestling team of a southern land-grant university out for spring break. With joy in our hearts, we waved down the gentleman (blocked his way, to be honest) and took the lead wire off the motorcycle's distributor. Without a working distributor, the motorcycle could not be started. With the distributor wire in one of our pockets, we clapped the young cyclist a few times heartily on the back and left him to wrangle

250 pounds of steel, rubber, and plastic down to the road, hurrying along ourselves, lest we still be in the area when he returned with a posse of cousins.

But back to my original oily-headed yahoo.

Disengaging myself from the fir, I pulled off the pack to simmer down and dig out maps to figure the distance left for the day. The horrible realization was immediate and crushing. My maps were five miles downhill, on the shelf with the toilet paper. In 10,000 miles of walking I've never backtracked five miles. Never. In 10,000 miles of hiking, I have left behind only two things: a tent footprint that wasn't worth the weight and a prized red bandanna lost to Vermont's Long Trail after a satisfying nap that lured me into forgetting a prime directive of happy backpacking. Always, always—when you leave a place—stop, turn around and take a long, hard look back to make sure you are not carelessly abandoning something valuable.

I started working through the usual curses, but they were sonically erased by the whine of a stressed motorcycle engine. And soon the original young lad was resting cockily by my side, listening most politely to me plead for deliverance. The smiling boy soon agreed to do his good deed for the week (he charged five dollars), and in minutes the maps were back in my grateful hands.

Forty-five years later, the shame is still with me, the heavy weight you risk carrying forever when you move on too quickly without taking a careful inventory of what you might be leaving behind. Tempted to shortcut a bit on your taxes, listen to that hothead with easy fixes for illegal immigration, say something snarky to your spouse in an argument—it's worth a quick second look before you go too far down the path.

If it doesn't ride on your back, it's just air guitar

"You ever seen a squirrel all hunched over,
stumbling along all day, busting his nuts on a Kelty backpack, big,
heavy boots on his feet, all hot in a rubber rain suit?"
"No, don't believe I have. Pretty sure I haven't."
He stroked his Lenin beard, pondering mysteries.

Never has any human-built construction been more aptly named.

The truth, however, is that I can't actually remember its full, complete, official name—or even exactly where it was located. The day had been a long one, and I suppose too many brain cells were too iced up to file away specific details. The important things are that this particular building was somewhere in the northern Great Smoky Mountains National Park and that I had been walking in an ocean of cold downpour for ten hours when I reached it. Even in early May, when the rest of the South is all happy with spring, the Smokies are good at concocting a special kind of miserable rain, the kind that you can only get when you are at altitude and not lucky enough for the temperature to drop another couple of degrees and give you nice, firm snow to bounce off your clothes like fluffy little bunnies.

Instead, you are visited by obsessed, devil-beast packets of icy wetness crafted in deepest Hell to torment humans out walking where they don't belong. Animated by fury-begat, demonic malice, the spring rains in the Smokies pay any price and bear any burden until they have infiltrated even the most perfectly designed rain gear and made you curse your life on earth.

I was wet, and I was way past cold, and two hours earlier I had foolishly passed up a perfectly good AT lean-to because it was crowded with Scouts far gone into party time, fifteen-year-old style. No alcohol, no drugs, but also no jokes that didn't involve gay people, delusional sexual conquests, or pork and beans, the effects thereof. I could, I decided, always tent out if I needed to, ignoring the fact that it was mostly illegal to camp on the AT in the Smokies and that I perfectly well knew that the worn, beaten, cheap piece of junk tent I was carrying was no longer up to the task of keeping me warm or dry in a long night of storm at 6,000 feet.

At this point of the hike, I had spent almost a hundred nights in Appalachian Trail lean-tos. So I guess I have to admit to being a little slow on mental processing at this particular moment. Maybe I was a little hypothermic.

When I sloshed around the last curve in the trail, muddy to my knees and wet down to the undies, there it was, sitting in a clearing in all its stone and wood solidity, water streaming off its tin roof into crazed, boiling streams flowing down its sides, but dry inside, leaking only laughter from the dozen hikers already packed into it. Another Civilian Conservation Corp masterpiece, dragged by strong human backs and legs into place piece by substantial piece and assembled in the 1930s, still standing strong, still a sight for sore feet.

I pulled up at the edge of the clearing.

"Damn." I was a little surprised to hear my own voice. I liked the sound of it so much I continued to talk to myself for the next few minutes.

I walked a few more yards.

"Never thought of that before. But that's it, that's why they chose it. I get it."

I took another few steps, pulling back the hood of the rain jacket and pushing up the brim of my cap to get a better look, to study the situation a bit more carefully, with greatest acuity.

"It was just brilliant. Perfect really."

A little knowing laugh, like I'd been the first to understand the centrality of chattel slavery to the American experience or to fully fathom the universe-splitting implications of $E = MC^2$.

"That's why they call them *shelters*. That's it. They are where you go when you need to find *shelter*. Perfect. "

A guy in a wool onesie and flip-flops pushed open the chain door, locked at dusk to keep out the bears. I thanked him, bumped his extended fist, and started pulling off my rain gear. Over my shoulder,

I explained my hard won insight to him with a fierce hammer of excited conviction:

"It's a *shelter* because it gives us *shelter*. Wonder who came up with that? Good stuff! I think it's just brilliant."

There was a moment's pause in the shelter chatter, some serious looks in my direction, and then everyone went back to their cooking or loafing.

My plan—one I'd been savoring for the whole of the long, freezing, soggy afternoon—was to shed the clothes, grab some chocolate, and steam myself in the bag until I baked back up to 98.6.

But then I saw the guitar, and all plans immediately changed. It was a huge acoustic jumbo, old-fashioned looking, Elvis-style, being whacked around not very tunefully by a very large guy over in the corner.

I love guitars, love the feel of them, love the look of them, love the way the thirty or so I now have in my house look neatly lined up and gleaming in my climate-controlled, humidity-managed office/guitar shrine, the joy fruits of my wage-earning, bonus-reaping middle age. They are, I am the first to admit, as vivid a demonstration as you will ever see of how the lusts of materialistic acquisition can far outpace both need and talent.

Even when I was a dirt-poor guy hiking the AT though, when the best I could afford was the cat-peed Japanese acoustic cheapie waiting for me at home, I would have known there was something fundamentally wrong in dragging such a nice instrument out on the trail. Guitars hate water, and this was a fine piece of craft, a super-expensive Gibson. I was sure even then that if we all stopped our noisy shelter chores and listened carefully enough, we could hear its glues ungluing, its fretboard popping out metal frets and bowing, its neck twisting and writhing. Across the player's sleeping bag were draped the two still-dripping garbage bags the guitar was apparently being toted in, a far cry from the maximum 45% humidity the manufacturer painstakingly insists on in its Montana factory and sternly dictates in the warranty that is tucked into the case of each new guitar. This guy might as well have been strapping a Stradivarius across his back and sloshing into the waves for a sloppy run on his surfboard.

Moral bile burned in my righteous throat. I headed over to give him a good scolding, stopping only because finger pointing and high-minded hectoring, by unwritten agreement across the mountaineering world, aren't considered practical ethics in a small tent or a crowded trail shelter. Besides, at somewhere north of 250 pounds, the guitarist was twice my size—and his mastodon-thigh arms were fully and aggressively decorated with about seven thousand skull tattoos, prominently displayed for effect. I figured they were a message, a warning of destination to those who offended. That, and I wanted to play the guitar, would probably have happily picked away at it even if it meant that the strings would have pulled away soggy tuners from the head and the spruce top would have immediately begun waving and bobbing like a downhill ski run.

"Mind if I take a turn when you're finished?"

"Not mine."

A long pause as he rattled through some final chords and sang some lyrics about the time he killed a man in Nevada just to watch him die. I stood there, not sure of my next move, but still wanting to play.

"Not mine. Need to ask the Squirrel."

I stood there.

"The Squirrel. It's his. You need to ask him."

He pointed to a small guy, about my size, looking more hipster than tree-climbing mammal, carefully combing out a Lenin goatee with his fingers as he sat crossed legged on his bag, looking out at the rain, apparently having some pretty deep thoughts.

I walked over.

"You the Squirrel?"

"That's what they call me, have called me since April 1 on Springer Mountain, Georgia."

I did some quick calculations and decided he was scooting, dodging, and weaving north much more slowly than your average squirrel. At his current speed, he'd reach Maine sometime in March of the next year. He'd have to walk through winter. For the moment though, he was content with continuing to stroke the goatee, pondering mysteries.

"Why the Squirrel?"

I had given him the opening he was no doubt waiting for since I walked up. He looked slowly away from the rain, met my eyes for longer than was comfortable, and patted an empty spot on his bag.

"Have a seat. You need some education. I took a good look at your pack when you were dragging yourself in. Jesus, what a load of bloated crap." Actually, my pack weight, stuffed with seven days of food, was down well under thirty pounds, and I was pretty proud of it.

"Hard on your back, right? Hard on the environment too, all that plastic."

I wasn't sure if my pack had any plastic. I didn't remember seeing any, and I'd been pretty close to it for months now. But I took his point.

He looked up pensively at the shelter roof, silent for a couple of seconds, doing more pondering—advanced, graduate-school contemplation from the look of it. A great philosopher gnawing on a meaty problem. "Too much world, too much civilization. Too much shit. Too much resistance to the fundamental laws of The Path."

I'd heard way more than enough smoked-up dope talk during college. I wanted to leave. But even more I wanted to play the Squirrel's beautiful dreadnought guitar.

He reached behind his back and pulled out what I initially thought was a particularly nasty pair of pants.

"Here's my pack." He paused long enough for me to have a good look. "Cost me nothing. No waste, no manufacturing, no over-educated engineers. Just me and the squirrels. Designed it myself." He gave a pet to the pants with one hand, stroked his fuzzy chin with the other.

I waited.

I knew there was more coming.

"You ever seen a squirrel all hunched over, stumbling along all day, busting his nuts on a Kelty backpack, big, heavy boots on his feet, all hot in a rubber rain suit?"

"No, don't believe I have. Pretty sure I haven't."

I could tell he was picking up on the sarcasm. I did a frantic squirrel-scold to myself to watch my mouth. I wanted to play the guitar, wanted it even more than I wanted to be cleverly judgmental.

"Squirrels are too smart for that. Little fuzzy heads, but lots of brain. Don't ever burden themselves with trips to the Big Box." It was true; I'd never seen a squirrel in a Kmart. "Don't carry around two tons of unnecessary stuff." Then he decisively went to the clincher, the thesis he'd been craftily building toward all along. "Squirrels—they just eat their nuts, bed down in a leaf pile, and live in harmony."

Most squirrels I'd ever seen were spastically bullying each other up trees, biting one another in the back ends in ways that I took to be abusively, maybe even criminally, sexual in nature. But I held my zoological observations close to my down vest, under my breath. I knew there was more coming.

"I made this myself." He held up the jumble of denim.

I tried to look sufficiently impressed, but still wasn't at all sure what I was looking at.

"Well, my sister actually made it, not me, not by my own hands exactly. But I told her what to do. Keep it simple." He looked again toward the rain. "I went to the woods because I wanted to live simply. That's what Mark Twain once said."

I think he was thinking about Thoreau, but again decided to keep the school-marm correction to myself.

"'Just cut me off the leg of one of your jeans, I told her.' She's bigger than I am. Both my mom and my sister are pretty overweight." He realized he was forking down an ill-conceived detour and pulled the bus back onto the main road. "'Sew one end up,' I told her. 'Put a button on the other so I can open that end up and slide my nuts and things in there. Then cut both ends off a belt and attach one end to each side.'" A pause and a goatee stroke. "And then what do you have?"

I tried to appear the eager pupil, the sort of student you'd be happy to reward later with a little guitar time.

"You then have yourself a squirrel pouch. Patent applied for, stamp of approval by the master Man-Squirrel himself."

He slid off the shelter's bed platform and modeled it for me, a cylinder of Levi leg with a buckle sewn nicely to one end and hole-end of the belt on the other. It wrapped comfortably around his waist like the sweaters that Ivy League boys used to drape around their tummies in glamorous pose of devil-may-care casual.

I had to admit that it looked like a pretty good idea, an interesting concept nicely executed.

"That's really great. Guess it leaves your back free to carry the guitar."

He looked a little puzzled for a second, then just a little annoyed.

"I never carry the guitar. Way too heavy. You ever see a squirrel dragging a large, bulky musical instrument through the woods?"

"But it's yours?"

"Yes."

"You play?"

"Every day. Mostly jazz, some progressive rock. Hard stuff, real difficult to master, needs real skills. Need to keep the spirit alive in these fingers even when I'm out here in my woods. Every day. Practice. You may not have heard my work yet, but I'm close to landing a contract. Pretty big-time actually. Going into the studio when I finish with Maine. Probably Muscle Shoals."

"So… how does the guitar get from shelter to shelter?"

"Thomas volunteers." He nodded toward the skulls guy, now picking out an occasional random sequence from a string of outlaw country songs. "Loves to carry it. He's a lot bigger than I am. Hardly notices the extra weight. Bigger shoulders. Fits easier."

"What do you carry in the Squirrel Pouch?"

He gave me the look the elementary teacher gives the kid who asks to go to the potty for the third time in the last hour.

"Nuts and berries, of course. Squirrel food. Humans do fine on that stuff. Did for millions of years. All you need, Georgia to Maine." He patted his belly, which was surprisingly bulky on an otherwise skinny guy, perhaps a genetic burden shared with Mom and Sis.

"How about sleeping equipment? Doesn't look like room enough for that in The Pouch." I pointed to the nice down bag and air mattress he was sitting on.

"Don't need one really. Keep it simple. Just pull up a pile of leaves and climb in. You got yourself a Squirrel bed."

This was too much for me, both of us sitting here in a masterwork of backwoods National Park Service construction, paid for with the generous taxes of U.S citizens who at the time it was built were themselves battling their way through the middle of a brutal depression.

"Really? You sleep in the leaves?"

"Could. Easily. But haven't needed to so far. Got all these nice shelters. And if it gets too cold, Tim loans me a bag. This one's his. I think he usually carries two." He pointed to a guy about his size resting nearby on top of a damp plastic poncho.

"Water?"

"Drink from streams, just like the furry guys."

I realized I'd never seen a squirrel sip at a creek. Maybe I just wasn't watching closely enough.

"Anyway, on dry stretches, somebody's always got plenty of extra H_2O. Water's cheap, and people out here are rich in generosity. Money can't buy friends like these." He did an extravagant wave to encircle most of the people in the shelter: "share, baby."

"Rain gear?"

"Don't walk in the rain. You ever seen a squirrel shaking his precious tail up a trail in a downpour?"

"You'll never reach Katahdin if you don't walk in the rain."

"Got the Squirrel logic all down on that one. If I get behind, my sister says she'll shuffle me around some of the dull spots, maybe Pennsylvania and New Jersey. Not much there. Rocks and hills. Trade the white blazes on trees for the white ones in the middle of the road. We'll figure it out. I'll make it. This squirrel is seriously northbound."

He dipped his paws into The Pouch, pulled out some gorp, and munched away as I thanked him and walked off.

Later, with the Gibson cradled at last in my hands, I watched, struck dumb, as one of the younger boys in the shelter moved over beside the Squirrel, carrying a battered, well-used Svea 123 stove. The young guy expertly cranked it up, poured a full package of Mountain House beef stew into an oversized cook kit, and stirred the freeze-dried for a few minutes. When the steam from the pot eased off a bit, the Squirrel pulled a tablespoon from the Levi leg and dug in, stopping every now and then to trace the outline of his facial fur with a deep look of pleased serenity.

Three decades later, I ran into the Squirrel again. Not the same exact individual. I don't think so, anyhow. It's hard to tell sometimes. These squirrelly types all look the same unless you really study them up close. But getting close can be dangerous. They sometimes bite. They don't carry rabies, but you can sure pick up serious infection from their busy little teeth.

This second squirrel was only thirty-five years old in 2002, so the numbers didn't add up. He was definitely related, however. Of the same rodentian species. I was glad to have had my AT meeting with the original to make it easier to spot the second, one who was a lot more sophisticated in the ways of gathering nuts into his feathered nest.

In 2002, the company I worked with was flourishing by selling revolutionary fiber-optic gear that made the Internet much faster, letting our customers make their mark on commerce by delivering video, distance medicine, multi-player on-line games, faster downloads of photographs of people with their clothes off, and the like. At the time, our engineers and physicists made up one of the only groups in the world who could help communications companies make the transition to the new technologies. So we were profiting hand over fist—right up until it became clear that many of our newer customers weren't actually even turning on the equipment we sold them. Some of the multi-million dollar gear never actually made it out of the boxes we'd packed and shipped it in. This group of customers was way too clever to actually sell communications abilities to people who wanted those services. Instead, they'd brag to Wall Street that they had a cool network, show a few reporters our gleaming new gear, get some good press, watch their stock rise, and then sell themselves to a conglomerate, making themselves and their investors rich enough to buy Greek islands and a senator or two.

When the government finally noticed that the emperors' bottoms were bigger than their Levis, huge numbers of our customers, even the honest ones, bubbled and burst overnight, and our earnings disappeared. Our management handled the catastrophe the way corporate managers usually do.

Here's how it goes, in case you ever have to handle one of these yourself.

First, create a huge distraction by laying off 65,000 loyal, hardworking employees. In the middle of the ensuing chaos—the noise of the gut-turning weeping from large numbers of your friends facing unemployment, sleepless nights, and home foreclosures—sneak around to where you've buried all the nuts (you'll know), dig up all you can carry, cash in your stock options, take early retirement (say you want to spend more time with your family), and scurry off to your island with your pouches filled with money.

I was lucky enough to still be employed to help with the cleanup. The first step is to try to reestablish credibility with customers, who are naturally wondering if you can still get the job done when two thirds of your employees are scattered to the wind and the rest are mumbling around in sackcloth and ashes.

So that's how I found myself one afternoon reviewing a presentation with one of our top executives, a new guy just recruited to help set things straight. He was scheduled to present the Powerpoints to a huge meeting of some of the most savvy network builders on the planet. It was his first time out, and it needed to go well.

This new guy, as these things happen, became a key person in a hundred year-old company for many of the usual reasons: he was handsome, he'd played football in college, and he had an MBA from a good business school.

"Wait—that's not enough," you might naively say—even before you knew that he had recently gotten himself into the newspapers when he pushed to the pavement an older lady who didn't get out of the way quickly enough as he moved his kids up the line for a Disney

World ride. Just by lucky happenstance though, he was best friends with our brand new CEO, who was also handsome and had attended an even better business school. Unfortunately for us and for our customers, neither of them seemed to know very much about fiber optic telecommunications gear.

The day before the big meeting, we sat down to go over his presentation. I was nervous, but things started off fine. The third slide declared we were the only company in business with the skills our customers would need when they were ready to transform their old-fashioned central offices into the data centers that could make them Internet giants. It had a really nice graphic with lots of colors.

"Good chart," he said. "Dead on." I liked the way this was going. "But what's this *central office* that you keep referring to? It was back on the second chart too."

I don't want to bore you with technical details, but follow me here just for a paragraph. It's important for the story, I promise.

A telephone central office is the place where, for a century, old-fashioned telephone companies kept all the old-fashioned gear that was used to make old-fashioned calls before cell phones and the Internet came along. There's probably one still in operation down the street from you, cranking out calls for people who still use landline telephones. It's easy to spot—it's the big bombproof concrete building with the AT&T logo and absolutely no windows. Central offices are the first things you learn about when you become a telecommunications engineer.

I looked closely to see if he was kidding. He wasn't. "Central office" was a new concept for him.

You need a gut-level understanding of just how frightening this lack of basic knowledge was. Try this analogy:

The Rolling Stones finally figure out that Keith Richards has indeed been dead for many years. They decide that they need a new guitar player. They've heard about you, and to your delight, they call you in for an audition. You look perfect for the job, all ragged but kind of glamorously dangerous at the same time. It goes well at first, a great interview. Mick loves you. You remind Charlie Watts of his best friend in second grade, and he enthusiastically says so. Ronnie takes control of the conversation, wants to close the deal, and asks you to play a few bars of *Satisfaction* with him, just to keep the whole process on the up and up.

But sadly for you and for your future induction into the Rock and Roll Hall of Fame, here's where things begin to come unglued. Unfortunately, it seems that you never actually went to the trouble to learn all those hard chords; you can't even tune a guitar, if the truth be known. You eventually have to admit that you can't play at all. "I can sing good, though," you counter. "I do a great version of *Layla.* You'll love it."

So only three slides into the presentation and I see my future dimming, the frightening ignorance of our new Senior Executive Global President for New Product Introduction sucking all light from the company's new day.

It's not a good career move to embarrass someone higher on the ladder than you. I try to be tactful.

"Sir," I start, "this audience will likely expect you to talk about our transition plan from old-fashioned central offices to advanced fiber-enabled data centers. Let me give you the backstory on central offices."

People in business almost always love it when you say "backstory."

He gave me the look you give the puppy when you tire of playing tug with his slobbery old rope. "You don't need to do that. I've got another meeting in ten. Don't have the time to sit through the gory details." Given his perch in the highest heavens of the company, it wasn't always necessary for him to be polite.

"But, sir, they'll want to talk with you in detail about the CO plans."

He leaned in and made manly eye contact. "I carry a lot of weight around here, David. If I'm gonna be successful, I've gotta keep the load up here as light as possible." He pointed to his temple with his index finger. "Just the important stuff. You know what I'm talking about? Just the Big Picture." He leaned back, thought a minute, and then leaned back in with a plan.

"I've got offices full of engineers, experts all of them, smart people. I've got hundreds of technical staff who love getting down in the weeds, eat that weedy stuff up, chew it over all day long." He waved around at the dozens of computer-filled cubicles that stretched miles down the hall outside his glass-walled suite. "Talk to my admin and make sure she gets the word out on those central offices. Make sure the folks with their names on those fancy badges around their necks are cued up to handle the idea."

His well-groomed, extravagantly bushy tail snapped up in a long arc up and across the back of his blazer, quivering in wild whips and snaps. "Now let's get down to business and finish this chart deck. I've got a long flight this afternoon."

Another rodent wanting to go the distance without hauling his share of the weight.

I scurried out of his office and started my search for a new job.

Consider leaving when they start playing with sticks

The older, skinnier kid stood the younger boy back against a pine tree and placed the apple on his head. It was a large apple. They grinned at each other. The older boy then turned, marched out fifty feet through the pine needles, and handed the hefty cowboy revolver to his sister. She appeared to be about ten. "Don't miss," he ordered, looking over his shoulder at me.

I had come down three thousand feet out of the sleet and rain of the Smokies, and it was much warmer now. Well into May, spring had finally come to the southern AT, at least at the lower altitudes. But despite the nice weather, it was mid-week, everyone else was at work, and it looked like I'd be alone again for the night.

So even though it was only five in the afternoon, I cooked a quick supper, wandered across the site's clearing, put down my sleeping pad, and laid across it for a drowsy rest amid the perfume of pine needles. Above me thousands of new baby-green leaf buds were unfolding from the branches of ash, hickory, and oaks. In that uncanny transition between normal waking alertness and the drift of sleep, I found my eyes had become keen enough that I could see the new leaves actually birth-dancing out in slow motion, like one of those time-lapse movies they play on nature shows. Or maybe I was already asleep. At the very least, I was happily meandering towards a really fine nap.

The panel truck put an end to all that. Banging and bouncing in cacophonies of rust and a crayola of owner-applied paint, it pushed through the bushes on the other side of the clearing and pulled up in front of the shelter, door creaking ajar and scattering an assorted clown-car of family, the whole spectrum from barefoot toddlers to kerchief-headed grandmas.

No one seemed to notice me as they ant-busied a charcoal grill, piles of bedding, and bags of food out around the shelter. But once a couple of the family teens spotted my gear in the lean-to and started rooting around in my pack, I stood up, coughed to signal my presence, cranked myself up on spasmed knees, and started over to reclaim my belongings.

The grandmother nodded a snaky-necked welcome as I passed the picnic table where she was spreading out dinner. But it was all-eyes-everyplace-else-except-at-the-hiker from everyone else at the campsite. Except from the two older kids, one decades-of-mountain-poverty skinny, the other too-much-pig-and-fried-everything large. They evil-watched full on as I approached, heads swiveling back and forth from me to each other, grins going through orbital velocity. It was absolutely for sure that trouble was coming, so I began quietly loading my gear back into the Kelty, my heart starting to run the rapids through the macaroni still sloshing around in my stomach.

And trouble did quickly unfold. But not exactly how I expected.

The two boys made a quick stop to grab something out of the truck, a flyby of the picnic table, an elbow tug on a much younger sister, and then led a group swagger out to the spot where I'd been dreamily watching the rites of spring. Every step or so, they'd look over in my direction again and do a happy little snicker dance.

The older, skinnier kid—the one whose ribs showed clearly once he'd taken off his t-shirt and gotten down to business—stood his slightly younger brother back against a convenient pine tree and placed an apple on his head. It was a large apple. They grinned at each other. They knew I'd seen this movie before.

The older boy then turned, marched out fifty feet through the pine needles, and popped out the cylinder of the heavy cowboy revolver he'd picked up from the truck. A quick spin or two of the chamber was made in theatrical nod to every horse hero who ever checked to ensure his weapon was loaded, the skinny boy's eyes spot-lighting into mine whenever I forgot for a second to feign indifference and looked his way.

The boy handed the gun, barrel first, to his little sister. She appeared to be about ten. But she too was skinny; she might have actually been a year or two older. "Don't miss," he ordered, looking over his shoulder at me.

I hadn't seen the father since he twisted out from behind the wheel and disappeared into the woods the microsecond the panel truck first came to a stop. But he was there now, all 300 ragged-beard pounds of him, zipper still two-thirds open and eyes pulsing as he stepped in front of his daughter, grabbed the pistol around the front sights, and jerked it away, hammer cocked and her finger hooking the trigger. I fully expected the inevitable sharp pop and the slowly spreading hand of blood sprouting red on his trousers. It was a conclusion that every cinematic version of this scene would surely deliver, one that any fair version of universal justice would demand. But nothing happened.

I also didn't expect what came out of his mouth as he tucked the pistol up under his armpit like a riding crop and John-Wayne-gaited his way back over to the truck. No hillbilly outbursts, no crude bumpkin curses. Instead, from this giant of a slob streamed the snooty British-nostalgia accent you sometimes hear from a teacher (probably of Latin) if you spend much time at one of Charleston or Richmond's finest private schools, found most often well into some boozy afternoon of mint juleps and cold medicine.

"My errant broood, meyh lost beybies. Meyh sad, sad lusahs."

A few steps.

"And specially a stay-it of dullness from my fust bohne."

A quick stop and a look of disdain back toward the older boy.

"No respect for ahwuh long traditions, no strivin for the bettuh."

A moment of rooting around in the back of the truck among a mess of spare tires and cat carriers and he was back, carrying a homemade bow—knotted bailing twine spanning across a five foot draw stick still marked here and there with pieces of bark. One arrow, missing a third feather, was tipped with the classic, blunt aluminum point found in children's target sets; the other with a razor-steel broadhead fully ready for wooly mastodon.

No one was looking at me anymore, all eyes on the little sister as Father handed Daughter the tools of medieval chivalry. She slotted an arrow—the lethal one—and raised the bow to aim, lowered it to sweep her hair behind her ears, and then raised it again. Both boys were looking at me, and it seemed like a good time to leave.

And so I did, an evil whiz and thunk behind me, slinging on the pack and heading up the trail long before I took any time to tighten up the waistband or fiddle with any of the normal adjustments to the shoulder straps.

I stopped when the sunlight ran out, in a gently ascending, tall-grass meadow on the upslope of a mountain several ups and downs to the south.

By this point in the hike, I had a thoroughly practiced routine for the nights when I trusted the volatile Appalachian weather enough to sleep out in the open. I carefully staked out my cheap, ragged tent and tied, but didn't tighten, the single rope that was used to pull it upright around a nearby tree. It was the best of both worlds, stars above me if all went well but a quick pull of the rope and instant shelter if I woke up unexpectedly in an errant storm. Boots under the pack and both under my head so that no animal could pull them away while I slept, I lay in my bed of feathers on top of the tent, watching the Big Dipper rotate slowly and counting shooting stars in a sky that the words "vast" and "beautiful" are far too impotent to capture.

Although I had to scramble up and into the tent sometime in the night as a shower blew through, it was, all in all, a perfect evening.

In town several days later, I read the local newspapers obsessively but found nothing about any recent archery mishaps on the Appalachian Trail. I assume that all went reasonably well after my departure.

And, for better or worse, I've ever since found that standing up and leaving is not a bad strategy for avoiding most childish theatricals. I've had to stay, of course, for an occasional fight that really mattered: when the country went to war, when a thoughtless or twisted teacher did something awful to my child, when some new competitor or half-baked new direction in my company threatened my livelihood or the people I worked with.

But almost always, especially in the corporate world, when people pulled out their crude but beloved weapons and made ready to entertain themselves and their colleagues with a little outburst of mayhem, I've usually opted to go someplace more quiet. Sometimes someone noticed. Most of the time though, nobody much cared that I'd left.

It's never too late to rub things the wrong way

By late 1973 my virginal feet were widely considered nothing less than a universal hymn to the human capacity—after a thousand generations of learning nothing from war, slavery, aggression, rabid savaging of the planet, romantic breakups via Internet apps—to profit at last from experience, a fleshy tribute to humankind's sacred ability to redeem our past and at last grow wise.

I was just north of the Georgia border, less than one hundred miles to go, and I hadn't suffered a single blister the whole walk, not really even the hint of one.

Celebrating this miracle, I would religiously practice a ritual thanksgiving every night, peeling and scraping off my toxic socks and gratefully basking in the relative health of my feet. Toe by sanctified toe, I would reverently clean them in the same spirit that a priest might give to his evening genuflection before his order's most prized relic, the hallowed knucklebone of St. Christopher himself.

Then I would lovingly slide the holy feet down into my sleeping bag, now still habitable, though barely so, because its devoted owner had been ever vigilant to defend it against every attack of foot stink for five long and dirty months.

After 2000 miles of slogging through mud and snow, smashing against rock and root, roasting and freezing through all the tempests that mountain weather could muster against them, my feet still remained fully baby bottom in their untroubled purity (except, of course, for their mushy-white coloring). And this triumph I would proclaim each night to the admiring skies and to anyone who could not quickly look away to avoid the showing I would bestow on all at the shelter, as proud as a new father, as joyful as the local Chamber of Commerce when the village favorite is at last crowned the new Miss America.

I had the best of reasons for this pride. This feat of orthopedic preservation was no accident, the farthest thing from just mere luck.

To all those who believe deeply in progress, to those of us who hold against all evidence that the inhabitants of this planet can somehow profit from past missteps or mature in wisdom begat in struggle, my two healthy foundations were, at the very least, a moving testament to careful planning. If you'll step back with me for just a little more cosmic perspective though, we can see that they had earned the right be considered much more—nothing less, in fact, than a choric hymn to the human capacity—after a thousand generations of learning nothing from war, slavery, aggression, rabid savaging of the planet, romantic breakups via Internet apps—to profit at last from experience. My feet, as I understood their significance in May of 1974, were fleshy tribute to humankind's sacred ability to redeem our past and at last grow wise.

Here's why.

For many years when I headed out the door to hike I first laced on a worn pair of plain old Sears work boots. Their elaborately ribbed rubber soles had a trusty grip; they were relatively waterproof if you worked in a big enough goop of Sno Seal (which also mellowed their color from the factory Day-Glo orange to a mature earth brown); they were poor-guy cheap enough to bespeak a working-class chic; and they had never failed me, at least not until I took my first extended trip on the AT.

My original plan was to thru-hike the trail a year earlier, in 1972, back when the list of end-to-enders totaled up to less than fifty eccentrics, oddballs, and other pioneering heroes. But as March approached, I was just out of college and had absolutely zero savings.

So it was an easy decision when a group of guys I'd met in Modern Lit 443 served up an unexpected invite for a road trip across the continent and up the Alaska Highway. "No money, no problem," they insisted. "We'll handle the cash. You just bring your enthusiasm and your feet. And we'll sweeten the deal with all the Baby Ruths you can possibly desire." I had no idea where the candy bar angle came from, but liked its generous spirit. I signed right up.

We all know that there is absolutely no shortage of proverbial warnings against offers too good to be true. But it's also true that no similar proverb ever warns against an offer that is demonstrably too good to turn down. So I soon found myself squeezed into a twenty-five year old Dodge with a ton of camping gear and three other newly minted college grads I hardly knew.

When your parents tell you, as all good parents do, not to accept candy from strangers, I hope you listen more carefully than I did.

Once we were on the road, it quickly became clear that the signature passion of my new friends was to get staggeringly blooped in every bar mentioned in the Jack Kerouac novels we'd soaked up in that modern literature class. If there had been a sign on the side of the Dodge, it would have read something like "Welcome to the Great North American Kerouac Memorial Saloon Tour and Cheap Beer Celebration."

To my comrades' eternal credit though, we did, as promised, stop at dozens of parks and wilderness areas in a broad wandering path through the dingy bars of North America. But as the only light drinker in the bunch, I was generally the only hiker to head up the trails without a crippling head throb. Against all odds, the expedition finally made it as far as San Francisco. But all the real joy of the trip had long since evaporated, pretty much instantly out the window late one night in Denver when one of our latter-day Jacks stumbled over a shin-level hotel casement and arched dived himself into the concrete sidewalk twenty-five feet below. He survived. But the spirit of the trip didn't.

After a few days on the West Coast, we slithered back home, sporting assorted casts, concussions, and sutures, and much wiser, the rest of the troupe poised to find adult jobs, me to plan my 1973 AT hike. But before we threw in the towel and ended the trip, my trusty Sears boots had carried me up Deep Creek in the Smokies, down to the bottom of the Grand Canyon, across the lava flows of Craters of the Moon National Monument, across thirty grizzly-stalked miles in one long day in Yellowstone, through an epic flood in South Dakota, and up the path to Yosemite Falls—all without any serious trauma to the footsies.

Restless back at home, I managed one more trip before I settled in to the eighty-hour weeks that would allow me to pack away dollars for the thru-hike the next year. With a ragged assortment of gear, including my Sears boots, I headed down to the southern terminus of the Appalachian Trail at Amicalola Falls State Park for a week's hike out and back on the first forty miles of the AT and its approach trail.

But it wasn't my pack, sleeping bag, or boots that I was really setting out to test when I planned this test walk.

Like a surprising number of people who finally end up jumping into the deep end, I had become terminally obsessed with the idea of taking on the entire AT long before I had ever taken a solo backpacking trip of any great distance. I was, in fact, most worried about myself, not my gear.

Was I in good enough condition? Would loneliness corrode away at my will to stay out in the woods? Would I actually enjoy being hungry, nasty, scared, and tired for a large lump of time? Would I cry myself to a restless sleep night after pitiful night? Then, beaten and begging for mercy, would I vow to properly comb my hair, put on a white shirt and wingtips, and seek safe employment in the chilled halls of a oak-lined advertising agency?

If you take no other advice from this book, I beg you to consider this piece of wisdom: before you quit your day job and swagger off to tell all your friends about your upcoming thru-hike, go do it for a week or so. You can't try this at home. You can't experience the trail without putting boots on the ground and walking fifty miles in your own shoes. Try it first.

So I went to Georgia. And I learned a lot. I found out, for instance, that a cotton sleeping bag wouldn't keep me warm, even with that special purple reflective lining its tags claimed was the latest in toasty space-age technology. I learned I needed a warm jacket in the damp Appalachians, even in summer. I learned I needed a smaller, lighter flashlight; a smaller, lighter cook set; a smaller, lighter sleeping pad. I learned a pound of carrots was rabbit food, not quick energy nor workable nutrition for a hungry hiker.

And I learned that I absolutely and completely loved long distance hiking, even when doing it alone. In that one week in Georgia I was never more focused, more ready to get up in the morning and do the day's work, more ready at the end of the day to sit wherever I was and be happy with what I'd done since breakfast.

A mile or two north of Springer Mountain, I spent thirty minutes or so dream-walking through a tunnel of rhododendron and mountain laurel, showered by petals as a savory breeze that conjured up off a nearby stream blew them around me. In those few minutes, I saw and felt more beauty than I could have imagined existed on the planet. After my week in Georgia, I found it impossible to envision being ever again satisfied if my life was somehow shoved forward without first immersing myself in more of the pleasure I found on the AT. I was hooked, lined and sinkered.

I was also completely and mercilessly mangled from the ankles down.

On day one, all was fine, at least as fine as things could be in a state of perfect and total exhaustion, an exhaustion that imploded my brain so completely that I somehow missed a well-marked turn, zombied through a huge, slow nine-mile circle, and ended up six hours later within a hundred yards of the beginnings of the approach trail, exactly where I'd camped the night before.

Then the pain started. By the second day, my feet started to swell, as everyone's tend to do under a fifty-pound load on a rough surface for ten hours. Not swell much. Not swell noticeably to the eye. Just a little. But enough. Just enough to start the slow, steady rub of the side of my foot against the welt of my boot, of the front and tops of my feet against the nodules of seams raised by the heavy threads that joined leather to leather across the top and sides of the shoe.

The pain wasn't bad, nothing like the medieval tortures being visited on my thighs and lungs on the long ascents and endless slip-and-slides down the hills I'd just climbed. So it was easy to ignore the foot pain among the other screaming sirens of discomfort.

All the while though, my cotton athletic socks were steadily excelling in their quiet, inexorable work, busy sucking in accumulated hours of foot sweat and then leaching a potion of brine, mineral, and bacteria back to slowly chemistrate my skin into a soft, slimy mush—mush just the color of the slushy, salted, grey layer of snow thrown up on the sidewalk when the streets are scraped for the last time in some ugly place where spring comes late.

The feet continued to swell, and the leather continued to rub, and the wet continued to bask flesh in a petri dish of putrefaction until the pain rose above the background noise enough to register.

So at some point I stopped, pulled off the boots, and audited the damage. "Just a little redness, just a little scrape or two, a few abrasions, some unimportant squeegees of whitish, greenish pus," I told myself. And I put it all in context. An absurdly inexact context, but a context nevertheless.

I remembered an often repeated family story: my father on a troop ship in 1944, crossing the Atlantic on the way to England, on the way to stage up for the invasion of the Continent, bored for weeks in close quarters with hundreds of other bored, edgy young men and boys, all deciding for absolutely no reason that it would be fun to do a group shave of their arm pits, all spending weeks afterwards with wet handkerchiefs stuffed in their underarms to control the burning, the last bit of childish silliness before sixty percent of their battalion became casualties in France and Germany.

Considering this context, my own discomfort was nothing. One day, I thought to myself, I'd hoot it up at my own story, making my kids smile at my goofy foolishness. I plastered on every on of the few Band-Aids I had brought along and kept walking.

In college, a roommate's girlfriend once stopped by unannounced with several pans of fresh-baked lasagna. A nice, loving gesture interrupted when the roommate and another young lady, a friend, exited our apartment door and met the girlfriend on the steps as she brought up the pasta. There were unpleasant words, and somehow the casserole was left outside the door overnight, a warm summer night with several inches of rain.

On the fourth morning of my trip, both of my feet looked sickeningly like the lasagna we found festering on our steps the next morning, a barfing blend of reddish, pinkish sludge, punctuated by small, irregular islands of whitish solidity occasionally summiting out of the goo. The pain could no longer be ignored.

The misery was bad enough when I was fussing around with breakfast and repacking, before any foot made any significant contact with anything solid. But I was now forty miles away from the trailhead, and there was no way to get back to my motorcycle without walking. So regardless of all the avoidance I could muster, the boots had to go on and the day's hiking had to start. Dragging leather across wound, dragging socks and boots across bleeding, oozing feet—it was the agony of a thousand wasp stings, a bad-hop baseball to the inner thigh or stomach, the breath-sucking thunk of a finger in the car door. And when the boots were finally laced and the sweat wiped off pale forehead, the walking had to begin, the first steps dainty, carefully placed half steps in foolish hope that any strategy to lessen the pain could make any difference.

There's more.

The two toenails plastered in the socks at the end of one day. The soakings in streams that brought some short relief but made one wonder what busy germs might be attracted to open sores the way giardia loves the intestines. The growing signs of infection and the absence of antibiotics.

It was a long hobble back to Amicalola Falls, and I swore on all that's good and holy never to play bleeding host to a blister again.

So that's how the health of my feet began to become a widely acknowledged, universally recognizable token of the promise that wise men and women, focused and determined, can stop being stupid. My toes and arches had become nothing less than a latter day Noah's rainbow signifying that humans can climb a bit higher on the chain of wisdom. I'd screwed up in the past, and I'd learned my lesson. Carrying the banner for all humankind, I vowed never to screw up again.

As I waited to leave for Katahdin the next year, I formed a full and careful plan. And as I started south from Maine in 1973, I implemented that plan with faithful rigor and discipline.

First came the new boots, fancy Italian ones that consumed two weeks of salary and overtime, a size larger than my at-home feet, with a smooth, seamless, padded leather liner, all built on top of an unbending steel shank that minimized the twisting and sliding that initiates the rub toward blisters.

Then came the all-powerful majesty of the Holy Order of the Socks. First on always, every day without fail, a thin cocoon of silk, kissing my skin as smoothly as a parent osculates his newborn, coming all the way from China to whisk even the hint of moisture away from vulnerable epidermis. On top of the silk, a thin wool merino for padding and additional wicking. On top of these two, a traditional thick ragg, as bouncy as a goat on a trampoline and always bunched at the ankle as final protection against any slight detritus of dirt or scree hoping to finding its way in to begin sandpapering away at my skin. Then there was the moleskin, just then starting to show up in outfitters and running stores, a breakthrough as potent to skin abscess as penicillin to streptococci. At the slightest, tiniest inkling of irritation, I'd slam the brakes, break out a miracle sheet, craft a piece to fit exactly, and paste the aspiring blister to smooth, velvety oblivion.

But the unparalleled *piece d'resistance*, the veritable Great Wall of Protected Tootsies, was the tanning.

Yes, I tanned my feet. But if you're thinking sun umbrellas, cold beer, flip flops, and romantic splashes in the breakers, you clearly don't have enough experience with the subtle brain workings of young men. My thoughts were not the least focused on a trip to the beach. Think furniture manufacturing instead. Think belt, think saddle, think shoe leather. Without thinking much myself about any possible differences between my living, breathing skin and the brutalized remains of commercially slaughtered animals, I set out enthusiastically to leatherize my legs from the lower shins down.

I can no longer remember exactly where the original inspiration came from. Though today it's not completely uncommon for desperate ultra runners to use various high-tech, carefully formulated compounds to toughen up their feet, I came to this solution at least a decade before I ever met a marathoner. I think—not to brag too much—that I may have come up with this bright idea totally on my own.

But once the die was cast, I had no dearth of advice on how to get my own hide expertly dyed and tanned. A mechanic friend immediately jumped forward with a recipe calling for a five minute immersion in a combo of automobile battery acid and breakfast bran flakes: "My daddy used it all the time during deer season. Worked beautifully on them long as you were careful to handle the hide with those big, black, long rubber gloves. Believe we still have his rubber boots and apron someplace down at the house." This recipe didn't seem especially prudent.

A forestry major acquaintance pushed me in a more fruitful direction: "Christmas trees—that's how you want to go."

I looked at him, one of us clearly being somewhat of a weakly lit holiday bulb.

"*Oh Tannebaum*!" No light came on for me. "It's German." I'd never thought about it, but conceded that he might be right. "*Baum* is *tree*. *Tannen* is *fir*." I still couldn't see a path forward here. "Fir tree!" he flourished out his conclusion, speaking with labored distinctness in the manner that idiots fall into when trying to make themselves understood by other idiots who don't speak their language.

"Learned conclusion, nice parsing, good vocabulary workout. So?"

"A fir tree—a tanning tree. They're the same thing." Still seeing no brain flicker, he clinched his point: "It's a pun in German." Then with some exasperation: "thought you were an English major, Hiscoe. Jesus."

Still no juice to the bulb.

He spelled it out.

"Fir trees are rank in tannic acid. Filled with it. Ooze it. You know that brown stuff we always see floating in slow creeks? Not generally sewage, my friend. The brown is mostly tannic acid leaching in from hemlocks on the banks. We just need to grind up a few Christmas trees and we've gotcha covered."

It was April. Not a holiday tree in sight. And it was almost time for me to leave for Maine.

So I went the more direct, sensible route, asking around at hardware stores, which sent me to gun shops and hunting outfitters, who sent me to my local pharmacist.

"Tannic acid? Sure. It's in lots of products that we carry. Are you dealing with fever blisters, poison ivy, or hemorrhoids?"

"No."

"Diaper rash?"

"My feet."

"Oh." A pause. "I'm not sure I understand."

"I'm getting ready to go on a long hike." She was actually the first outsider that I'd spilled my ambition to. "Maine to Georgia. I want to tan my feet, toughen them up."

"I'm not sure that's a good idea."

I looked at her with my best puppy eyes.

"There's a safety issue. For medicinal purposes, it always comes in solutions of considerably less than one percent. It's pretty caustic stuff."

I strained to make my eyes bigger and to water them with the hint of a tear.

"People put it on their lips, on their babies, on…"—I skidded up to a halt before entering the nether regions—"…on other soft places."

"Yes… but…" She paused, in her head probably doing up some rough balance sheet to calculate the relative worth of my obvious cluelessness, my unlearned determination, the value of her time, and whatever legal and ethical minefield into which she might be treading. She stepped into the back of the pharmacy and returned with a quart of powdered tannic acid. I noticed at least two warning signs on the label.

"Thanks! Do you know how I should use it? Is there a formula?"

A very small sigh, another pause, and another mental formulation.

"There isn't a notice on this. You are way past the farthest reaches of what they teach in pharmacy school. I'd just start very slow. Use common sense." She sighed again, probably at the unlikely chance of that outcome. "Dilute it, and see what your skin can tolerate. Go slow. Be careful."

Thirty minutes later I was at home, my feet in a turkey pan. Two tablespoons. A minute. Nothing. Four more tablespoons. Another minute. No visible effect. But no pain, I noted. The rest of the container all at once, a little more water, ten minutes. Nothing. A total—it would seem—waste of time and money. I poured the mixture into the toilet and went about my business.

The next morning both feet were the yellowish-orange of a new baseball glove, noticeably hot to the touch and sweating like an unfixed bull at a Texas rodeo. And they itched with the force of every hemorrhoid, every diaper rash, every spent-all-Sunday-afternoon-pulling-up-poison ivy-by-hand outbreak ever treated by every pharmacist in every drug store in all of North America.

They continued to itch just that virulently for months, especially when warmed up by layers of socks inside of excessively well-padded, airproof Italian boots. I might just as well have shaved my armpits.

But, all in all, mission accomplished. My feet were now as tough as leather, and remained thus right up to the night just north of the Georgia border.

It was way past one in the morning, and I had to pee, had to go in that horrible way that wakes you up from dreams of raging rivers and torrential rains and compels you, after the long minutes of ineffectual bargaining with your officious, potentate bladder, to zip out of a warm sleeping bag and obey Herr Tinkle's evil will. It was cold, so I wanted the business to go quickly. The shelter was filled with sleepers, all nestled down at blissful peace with their own wholly adequate bowels, all who, if asked, would have wanted me to go as gently as possible into that good night, quietly, at a respectful distance.

Yet the ground around the shelter was muddy, as it always is, and it was well sown with the usual pointy, stabbish rocks.

So I slipped out of the bag and slid into my boots. It was cold, I remind you, and the polite and necessary distance was less than two dozen yards. No need to bother with all those socks, no need to struggle with bothersome laces, I reasoned in my sleepy head. No need to worry about that slight burning on the outside of right big toe when it started making itself known ten stumbling yards out from the shelter.

Three minutes. Business done, back in down, the rest of the night passed in dry and arid peace.

The next morning the blister had, of course, already fully raised its impudent flag of aggression, blood-red blazoned on a field of white suppuration. I covered it with moleskin and walked later that day across the last state border into Georgia.

This is the first time I've ever told anyone about this particular abscess of shame.

In fact, I had shut the blister out of my own consciousness for decades, up until the 2008 U.S. presidential election. Early on in the contest, a candidate from my state had a fair shot at the prize, a prize he had assiduously prepared himself for over a lifetime of carefully cultivated achievement. The son of unrich mill workers, he had made a success of himself through education, hard work, shrewd planning, and an admirable ability to profit mightily while doing the right thing—using his legal skill, for instance, to punish large corporations that repeatedly and knowingly sold swimming pool equipment that had the unfortunate habit of sucking the entrails out of small children.

Having escaped poverty himself, the presidential candidate had a very clear-minded view of what causes it, some good ideas about how to alleviate some of those causes, and a charisma that seemed to bring out admirable, kind, and progressive impulses in his fellow citizens. When his spouse was diagnosed with a fatal cancer, he rallied to her side, a perfect family man, and very handsome, to boot. He was, many thought, on a smooth path toward the White House.

And then, while his wife was fighting for her life, he managed to father a surprise baby with a campaign worker. He denied at first he was the dad, but the worker sued, genes were tested, and the truth was out. I now see him sometimes shopping late at night in my local Target. Fellow shoppers—the neighbors who once enthusiastically voted for him—don't speak to him when he passes.

I once stayed up all night to complete a presentation the CEO of my company was to give the next day in Geneva at a United Nations conference. It was a very good presentation, one that I'd worked on for months with a huge group of really bright people. We'd nailed a really innovative approach to a very complicated telecommunications problem, one that could improve a lot of people's lives and make our company even more successful. The all-night session had solved one last technical problem with a graphic that used thousands of synchronized lights to dynamically show the coast of China lighting up as new Internet servers came on line to support our new solution. After several of us worked till dawn to tweak it, the graphic worked perfectly on my high-end Apple workstation.

None of us ever thought to try it on the more pedestrian machine that our CEO would use at the conference. We sent the file directly to Switzerland and started anticipating our next year's bonuses.

When the CEO came to this slide during his presentation, five thousand of the globe's most influential communications experts watched his computer slow a bit, stutter several times, black off, blink back fully on with a dramatic flash, and then catch fire, shooting flames three to four feet out into the audience.

Happens all the time.

GEORGIA

Acknowledging the loads that are worthy of the pack

Don't lug Blood Mountain down the trail

"Never even broke wind."

Unlike nine-tenths of thru-hikers, I hiked from north to south, dragging a sixty-pound pack in June through Maine's devil black flies and daily seven-thousand-foot altitude changes. By the time I hit Vermont and started meeting north bounders 1500 miles into their trips, my pack was half as heavy and my legs and my lungs were (I'm being honest here instead of humble), Olympian.

Each NOBO shuddered out the same story as we compared trail notes: the slog up Blood Mountain that beat their buns a week into their trip. Straight up 3,000 feet, sleet all the way, trapped by fatigue at the icy top and forced to spend a night that spooked up the Cherokee massacre that armed the hill with its name, they each ominously warned me of the trial waiting down South.

For three months, I carried Blood Mountain with poisoned dread. Then I went up and over it in less than an hour. The only disaster came on the downhill when a dizzyingly attractive northbound University of Georgia student asked how the climb was. "Not bad," I quipped with a veteran's studied casualness. "Never even broke wind all the way up."

The AT taught me to carry the future lightly. That horrible challenge coming up at work, that romantic breakup if things go sour down the road, enough money to live on when I'm seventy-five? I do the preparation, get things in shape, and assume I can make the haul when the time comes.

If you can't get no satisfaction, go do something that's satisfying

Sitting there, just relaxing and feeling happy, not reading a book after dinner for perhaps the first time of the hike, I sensed that if a sparrow did indeed fall from some nearby tree, someone might indeed mark its circumstances and care about its fate.

For a month or so I'd had a definitive plan in mind for my last night of the AT hike. I was headed for that mountain laurel and rhododendron tunnel just north of Springer Mountain that I'd found so perfect on my 1972 test walk. The rhododendron and laurel probably wouldn't be in full bloom on May 24, but there would likely be enough flowers to keep things magical—and I thought it might be nice to tuck myself away in a hushed spot off the trail and have one last night of solitude before heading back to the real world.

That isn't what happened. But my final night in the woods turned out much better than I'd planned.

It had been a rugged twenty-mile day when I came down into a lengthy gap about three miles from my enchanted thicket and hit the one-lane, gravel fire road that the trail piggybacked on for a half mile before heading up the next mountain. I was tired, and the sunlight was starting to mustard away behind the trees. So the nice flat road was a welcome sight, a level runway to build up acceleration for a hurried climb up the last hill of the day. But instead of rocking along at the speed I anticipated, I found myself slowing down, and then slowing down some more, slowing finally to a casual walk, the better to watch the circus going on in the woods to my right.

It turns out my last full day on the trail was the Friday evening that started the Memorial Day weekend. Running parallel to the road was a perfect fishing stream, and everyone with a pickup truck within a hundred miles of Atlanta had picked their spot, backed their vehicle a dozen yards or so into the woods, and struck camp. It was a sight that the Sierra Club in me did not warm to immediately. The bumper stickers weren't the ones I'd be proud to have on my own car. The music coming through the trees was mostly obnoxious, with none of the honesty of real country, little of the urgency of Chuck Berry rock, all of the hokum and jangle being sausaged out in Nashville at the time. The first tent I passed was a disaster from Kmart, a house-sized box of heavy canvas, covered with construction plastic in open admission that the tent would provide exactly no cover if the weather turned bad. The charcoal grill in front of it had two of the metal legs that it came equipped with from the manufacturer, supplemented by a third made from a shovel handle, the king-sized bottle of charcoal lighter beside it declaring the owner's assertive lack of interest in an artfully constructed fire. I expected to feel my feet picking up the speed to move through the Valley of The Weekend Noisers as quickly as possible.

But as I slowed to a casual walk I couldn't help but notice how happy everyone seemed. Kids were tossing around baseballs, teens were sitting by the creek holding hands, older couples and groups were leaning toward each other half out of their beach chairs in conversation. At one site, three middle-aged women were dancing the Carolina Shag, sliding confidently around in the pine straw to a Temptations favorite. Everyone seemed to be laughing, and almost everyone looking in my direction, whatever his or her age, stopped for a cheery wave as I passed.

For whatever reason, certainly not one I could have articulated at the time or would have approved of back in Maine, I angled over to the right, found an untaken, living-room sized clearing beside the stream, set up my tent, parked my bottom in a comfortable pile of leaves up against a tree, and contentedly ate the last boxed macaroni and cheese that would violate my stomach for at least a decade. It, I must admit, tasted just perfect. And yes, as the heat and light of the Georgia sun dissipated down to twilight, crickets hidden in the bottomland around the stream did start to chirp. Dozens of dark-eyed juncos and several cardinals settled into the trees around me, some staying for a few seconds, some staying as long as I stayed awake. And for all of the time before I went to sleep, the stream continued to make exactly the sad, romantic, and thoughtful music you would expect from the scene. Sitting there, just relaxing and feeling happy, not reading a book after dinner for perhaps the first time of the hike, I sensed that if a sparrow did indeed fall from some nearby tree, someone around me might indeed mark its circumstances and care about its fate. It wasn't, after all, hunting season.

After a bit, dozens and then more kids from the neighboring campsites started wandering over and asking questions, mostly the usual ones. How much did my pack weigh? Had I seen any bears? Where was my family? Was I scared to be alone? Did I want to catch some baseball with them?

After they had moved on to other curiosities, while I was putting my sleeping bag into the tent, one last boy, about twelve, stopped by, one of those kids you could immediately tell was not particularly being made comfortable by his preteen shyness.

"Excuse me, sir."

"Yes?"

"My mom and dad think that you're probably hiking the Appalachian Trail. Are they right?"

I had dodged the question with the earlier visitors. But he asked it directly, and I could tell it had taken some courage on his part to walk over and start the conversation.

"I am."

"Did you start up in Maine?"

"I did. Back in June."

"And you're just about finished, right?"

"Tomorrow morning, if everything goes right."

"Was it hard?"

"Most of the time."

He was having trouble keeping his feet in one place, clearly pretty excited and clearly, I thought, ready with a substantial list of additional questions, probably the ones that I had answered a hundred times by this point. I settled back against the tree for a longer conversation. But he fooled me, astounding me by going right to the heart of all the things that I now knew and probably ever would know.

"Was it fun?"

"Yes."

He didn't seem to expect anything further, satisfied with the answer. But I felt that I needed to say it more clearly, more forcefully, more completely. So I tried again.

"Yes, it was fun. Absolutely."

He nodded and left, headed back to his family. I climbed into the tent and drifted away to the woodsmoke smell of community as old as time and as permanent as anything we have here.

In the morning I finished the walk, sat under the sign marking the southern end of the AT to sew on my pack the "Maine to Georgia" patch I'd now carried for so many months, and headed back down the approach trail, ready to start absorbing everything I had learned over the past 2,000 miles. And as everyone knows, the readiness is all. The second I stuck out my thumb in the parking lot at Amicalola Falls State Park, an older couple in a new white Cadillac pulled over and gave me a ride almost all the way to the Atlanta airport.

The path always leads where the path always leads.

Have at it.

In 2016, the Appalachian Trail Conservancy's official registry added over 1,100 people to the list of hikers who have completed the entire trail, most in one year, some over several decades. The most accepted guestimate is that approximately four out of five people who set out to walk from Maine to Georgia end up leaving the trail before they finish the trek. That means that something like five thousand hikers probably began a thru-hike in 2016. For every one—whether they finished the trek or not—the walk was, I'm sure, just as transformational as it was for me. I did it earlier than most, with considerably less support in place than thru-hikers now enjoy, with considerably more loneliness, and with clumsier and heavier weight on my back. Almost certainly, I started out the trip with more anger in my heart at my elders and at most of my neighbors.

But much more importantly, every one of us, whenever we set out and whenever we completed the walk, all covered almost exactly the same ground, that same long route between Georgia and Maine that someone else first blazed for us all eighty years ago.

My trip taught me to put one foot in front of the other, regardless of how hard it was. I learned to stay on the trail and to finish it. But as I reach retirement age forty-five years after finishing the trail, some of the biggest regrets I carry are the direct result of sticking to somebody else's path for much too long. Following the most hard-earned lessons of the trail, for instance, I trudged along for years doggedly writing away at the expected Chaucer and Dante articles that would earn me a job as a professor of medieval literature—and learned when it was too late that somebody else had written that book on mountaineering writing that I had always really wanted to do. Following the well-tended blazes, I climbed too long on a corporate ladder well after the job became tedious and the money was all the reward that there was.

Thoreau said he would like to have met some of the ancient Egyptians who *didn't* waste all their sad, slavish lives working all night and day to build the pomp of somebody else's pyramid. If we all choose to do our walks on a well-marked trail, none of us are likely to follow Yogi Berra's famous and weighty advice that "when you come to a fork in the road, take it."

Five thousand folks all on the same path heading toward the same ends are a lot of people on the same path to the same glory. And, truth be told, it may not always be all that glorious anymore. I have heard, for instance, that there are now places on the trail in Georgia each spring where your tent peg is almost always going to smush into some other pilgrim's recently buried toilet paper and attendant waste when you try to set up your shelter. At the very least, today's AT is sometimes crowded and noisy. It's a simple fact: the end-to-end hike of the AT has been accomplished many times. Something like 19,000 times, in fact. It's been done. Maybe it's time to move on.

There are other trails. Perhaps when it's your time to choose your own epic adventure, you might want to consider being something more of a pioneer, doing something a little more off the usual paths? You'll feel, I'm pretty sure, much better about it forty-five years from now.

But enough. That last sour paragraph will be, I promise, the very last advice you'll get from this old guy, in this book anyway.

In fact, I don't want to end this book with any sort of easy advice at all. Soiled toilet paper and crowds be damned. As a less preachy alternative conclusion, I offer you a final benediction and one last observation.

Putting away the computer, pushing myself back from the desk, stretching myself upright and tall, I close my tale by enthusiastically saluting those hoards of you who wisely choose to resist the sage wisdom of your elders, those of you with packs at the ready and tickets all bought for your own trip off to Amicalola Falls or Baxter State Park.

Have at it, my friends.

I finished the first draft of this ending appropriately enough on

March 15, the date the hardiest and largest band of thru-hikers traditionally start from Georgia to follow spring north. Over the next five or six months, the trail is going to thoroughly and completely bust your butts, no matter how many hostels you park your weary bottoms at, no matter how many days you slack pack or receive the bounty of local trail angels. Every one of you who keeps to the trail for longer than a week is going to be cold, wet, hungry, hot, thirsty, and exhausted in ways you can't begin to imagine.

The compensation for all that stubborn suffering? I'll let my friend and fellow 1973 alumnus, Richard Judy, step in and offer up the last piece of wisdom from this book of ancient history. At the end of his recent novel, *Thru: An Appalachian Trail Love Story*, Judy sends his characters back to their homes and the rest of their lives sure that, above all the things they have learned on the AT, they will "return to a world that would never again be ordinary."

That's the essence of why the Appalachian Trail has become a beloved rite of passage for so many of us, a cultural icon that promises a path to a richer, more intense life, a life as far as we can possibly get from the scourge of quiet desperation that we, both young and old, see far too much of in the culture around us.

In the past forty-five years, I've often been quiet. It's my nature. But seldom have I felt for long the desperation of heart or soul that outraged Thoreau. I thank the Appalachian Trail for inoculating me from that particular disease of modern life. The trail, in the end, left me with a sense of the sheer delight of walking the earth, a lasting delight that has lightened my own pack for all of the last four decades and five years.

ACKNOWLEDGEMENTS

When I finished my wanderings in 1974, the Ball family welcomed me into their lives and made civilization seem like a worthy thing again. They continue to be some of the most admirable people on the planet. And I cannot thank the Schnabels and the Warkentins enough (all those wonderful grandchildren!) for graciously allowing me to become a part of their delightful and loving families.

Thanks also to John Iler and the late Mike Blue for many more Baby Ruths than I deserved then or deserve now. My sincerest gratitude to Lisa Arney for allowing me to use the late Barry Arney's arch photograph of me on the cover of this book.

Dr. David Allen, Greta Beekhuis, Ronald Jackson, Craig Kayser, and Memsy Price each read *Take The Path of Most Resistance* as it took shape and helped to make it a better book. I owe special thanks to Richard Judy (AT class of 1973) and Laura Waterman for their encouragement at critical times as I struggled with early versions of the manuscript. Any factual errors and all the baroque, unshapely sentences that still remain are due solely to my own stubborn bull-headedness.

Any book about the Appalachian Trail would be ungrateful and rude if it did not end by profusely thanking the thousands of AT volunteers who make sure that—in the wake of floods, hurricanes, fires, the ravages of snow and sleet, and the onslaught of three million hikers each year—the path remains open and the way clearly marked. My most crisp, most grateful salute, however, goes to the generous and wise citizens of the United States, who have insisted for eight decades that this national treasure remain a national priority.

Above all, thanks to Kathleen, who makes any load lighter and all loads worth the carry. She is the blaze that points my way.

ABOUT THE AUTHOR

Since surviving the 1960s, David Hiscoe has been a carpenter, a professor, a communications leader for corporations and universities, a writer, and a collector of vintage guitars and ragged cats. He lives in Chapel Hill, NC, where he often naps and dreams that his grandchildren lived closer to home. He can be reached at: david.hiscoe@gmail.com

Made in the USA
Middletown, DE
01 December 2018